D0929921

Foreigners
in the Homeland

The Bucknell Studies in Latin American Literature and Theory

General Editor: Aníbal González, *Pennsylvania State University*

The literature of Latin America, with its intensely critical, self-questioning, and experimental impulses, is currently one of the most influential in the world. In its earlier phases, this literary tradition produced major writers, such as Bartolomé de las Casas, Bernal Diaz del Castillo, the Inca Garcilaso, Sor Juana Inés de la Cruz, Andrés Bello, Gertrudis Gómez de Avellaneda, Domingo F. Sarmiento, José Marti, and Rubén Dario. More recently, writers from the U.S. to China, from Britain to Africa and India, and of course from the Iberian Peninsula, have felt the impact of the fiction and the poetry of such contemporary Latin American writers as Borges, Cortázar, Garcia Márquez, Guimaraes Rosa, Lezama Lima, Neruda, Vargas Llosa, Paz, Poniatowska, and Lispector, among many others. Dealing with far-reaching questions of history and modernity, language and selfhood, and power and ethics, Latin American literature sheds light on the many-faceted nature of Latin American life, as well as on the human condition as a whole.

The aim of this series of books is to provide a forum for the best criticism on Latin American literature in a wide range of critical approaches, with an emphasis on works that productively combine scholarship with theory. Acknowledging the historical links and cultural affinities between Latin American and Iberian literatures, the series welcomes consideration of Spanish and Portuguese texts and topics, while also providing a space of convergence for scholars working in Romance studies, comparative literature, cultural studies, and literary theory.

Titles in Series

Mario Santana, *Foreigners in the Homeland: The Spanish American New Novel in Spain, 1962–1974*

César Salgado, *From Modernism to Neobaroque: Joyce and Lezama Lima*

http://www.departments.bucknell.edu/univ_press

Foreigners
in the Homeland

The Spanish American
New Novel in Spain,
1962–1974

Mario Santana

Lewisburg
Bucknell University Press
London: Associated University Presses

Associated University Presses
440 Forsgate Drive
Cranbury, NJ 08512

Associated University Presses
16 Barter Street
London WC1A 2AH, England

Associated University Presses
P.O. Box 338, Port Credit
Mississauga, Ontario
Canada L5G 4L8

The paper used in this publication meets the requirements of the American National Standard for Permanence of Paper for Printed Library Materials Z39.48-1984.

Library of Congress Cataloging-in-Publication Data

Santana, Mario, 1960–
    Foreigners in the homeland : the Spanish American new novel in Spain, 1962–1974 / Mario Santana.
        p.   cm.
    Based on the author's thesis (Ph.D.)—Columbia University.
    Includes bibliographical references and index.
    ISBN 0-8387-5450-3 (alk. paper)
    1. Spanish American fiction—20th century—Appreciation—Spain.
2. Spain—Intellectual life—20th century.   I. Title.
PQ7082.N7 S35   2000
863—dc21   99-044108

A mis padres, Encarnación y Manuel

Contents

Figures

Preface

"BETWEEN 1960 AND 1970," MARIO PAOLETTI HAS HYPERBOLICALLY declared, "*everything* happens in Latin America."[1] In literature, the phenomenon known as the *Boom novel* stormed the world at a time when fictional narrative was said to be in the decline and critics throughout the West were once more drafting epitaphs to the genre. Spain was no exception, and there the impact of the Boom was particularly visible: not only were several Latin American authors associated with the new novel published originally in Spain, but some of them also lived there and actively participated in various forms in national literary life. And yet, although the Boom of Spanish American fiction occupied to considerable extent the minds and writing of the majority of critics and readers in Spain during the late 1960s and early 1970s, we still know very little about the phenomenon. Not only do we lack a chronicle of the events, but few attempts have been made to explore the arguments and critical positions taken around them, and to inquire into their meaning and significance for Spanish letters. As David K. Herzberger warned almost two decades ago, "We have also failed for the most part to undertake comparative studies of the contemporary Spanish and Spanish American novel. This kind of approach perhaps risks obscuring the distinctive national identity of many works, but it could also lead to new insights into cultural and literary affinities. Studies in this vein would need to focus on both theoretical and practical elements, and could thereby reveal similarities and differences among novelist on two separate continents who are writing in Spanish."[2]

For the most part, references to Latin American writers are conspicuously absent from the analyses of contemporary Spanish narrative, and Nora Catelli has noted that Latin American letters are presently seen in Spain as a foreign literature, and regarded as nothing more than a peripheral concern to scholars of national literature.[3] And yet, when in 1973 the critic Domingo Pérez Minik published a book entitled *La novela extranjera en España* (a collec-

11

tion of reviews of foreign literature), he did not include any reference to Latin American novels, undoubtedly because they could not
be considered "foreign" to Spanish readers. This absence raises an
interesting question: where should these writers be placed in relation to Spanish literature? Being Latin Americans, they seem to belong properly to the literary systems of their own countries.
However, since they were present both physically and textually in
Spain (and they write in Spanish), there is a presence that has to be
accounted for. Thus, the phenomenon of the Boom novel presents
us with a challenge: the positing of a theoretical framework that
would allow for the integration of Spanish American letters as a
legitimate object of study within Spanish Peninsular literature.
What would happen if we were to make the object of Spanish literary history not simply the literature *of* Spain, but also the literature
in Spain?

Foreigners in the Homeland aims to answer that question by providing a literary history of Spanish fiction during the 1960s and
early 1970s, and a critical analysis of the forces involved in the reception of the Boom novel as the leading model for fictional writing. Needless to say, this is by no means an exhaustive study: not
all the relevant figures and texts of the period receive the attention
they deserve, and the reader will even find that my approach raises
more questions than it answers—but that, perhaps, is no mean ac-
complishment either. Rather than writing *the history* of the Boom
novel in Spain, my aim has been to point to what I believe to be the
main factors involved. I approach this analysis through a reflection
on the methodological and ideological assumptions underlying our
understanding of the relations among different national literatures
written in the same language. Against a nationalistic writing of
Spanish literary history, I argue for the need to emphasize reception
over origin.

Since some Latin American texts, models, and values were appropriated by Spanish readers and incorporated into Spain's literary
system, they had an effect on Spanish literary life, and deserve to
be studied as a legitimate part of the national literature. I do not
mean, of course, that Spanish letters from America should be regarded in any way a sort of subsystem of Peninsular literature; it is
simply a question of recognizing the fact that certain authors, texts,
and models created in Latin America are imported and appropriated
in Spain, and therefore can simultaneously belong to different literatures. Literary geography, therefore, while conditioned by politi-

cal and linguistic borders, is not coextensive with them. I believe such an approach is absolutely necessary to understand the phenomenon of the Boom novel in Spain, and, more generally, the interaction between different literatures in Spanish (and different literary languages within Spain).

A large part of the studies on the topic of literary interrelations between Spain and Latin America have followed Max Henríquez Ureña ("El intercambio de influencias literarias entre España y América," first published in 1926) and concentrated on the tracking of influences. This book takes a different view, as in my opinion the notion of influence—which limits the focus to the exchange among individual writers—cannot solely account for processes that transcend individual biographies and condition the larger system of aesthetic values and the social institutionalization of literature. Systemic approaches, on the other hand, would add very little to our understanding of literature if they were used simply to ornament a series of commentaries on well-known literary works. On the contrary, their full potential can only be reached if applied to literary life in its entirety. Unfortunately, in the case of Spanish literature, we lack studies in several critical areas: the functioning of large-scale literary production (the so-called mass literatures) and its interaction with that of legitimized, "artistic" literature; the economy of publishing (printings, sales, and so on); the presence of translated literature and its interference with, and appropriation by, Spanish literature; the interaction among Spain's four literary languages. My study certainly does not overcome all those deficiencies, and it has to be regarded as a tentative contribution to a larger project still to be undertaken. In this sense, the historical course outlined here is necessarily a partial—although, I hope, convincing—story.

The material in this book first saw the light in the form of a dissertation, and I am grateful to my adviser at Columbia University, Gonzalo Sobejano, and the other members of the dissertation committee, Félix Martínez-Bonati and Alfred Mac Adam, who guided the original project; and to Joan Molitoris, who edited parts of that first text and aided in the translation of Spanish and Catalan passages. The sponsorship of the Chicago Humanities Institute (now the Franke Institute for the Humanities) during the academic year 1996–97 allowed me to devote precious time not only to the research and writing of the text, but also to expose my ideas to the observations of other researchers. The final transformation into a book would not have been possible without the encouragement and friendly criticism of my students and colleagues in the Department of Romance Languages at the University of Chicago, specially René de Costa, George Haley, and Patrick O'Connor. And none of this text would have been written or even envisioned without the personal support and intellectual contribution of Elisa Martí-López.

Some of the arguments I elaborate here were originally presented in a rather primitive form in "El 'boom' en España: una historia necesaria," published in *Letras Peninsulares* (1992), and "La mies y la cizaña: narrativa hispanoamericana y sistema literario en la España de los años 60," included in *Actas del XXIX Congreso del Instituto Internacional de Literatura Iberoamericana* (1994). A slightly different version of the final section of chapter 4 appeared as "Antagonismo y complicidad: parábolas de la comunicación literaria en *Volverás a Región* y *La verdad sobre el caso Savolta*," in *Revista Hispánica Moderna* (1997).

Foreigners in the Homeland

1
On National and Nationalized Literatures

DURING THE 1960S IN SPAIN, THE EMERGENCE OF LATIN AMERICA AS A world literary power sparked a series of developments that questioned the scope and boundaries of the concept of Spanish letters. The phenomenon called attention to the fact that literature in Spain was permeated by foreign elements that seemed to disturb the apparently linear and self-enclosed process of the nation's narrative poetics, making a tremendous impression on the nationalistic consciousness of Spanish writers—who saw the success in their country of those texts coming from the other side of the Atlantic as an intrusion, a direct threat to their position as legitimate inheritors of the legacy of literature written in Spanish. At a time when many authors were getting ready to emerge from the dark years of the Francoist regime, to partake in the artistic developments of the Western world, and to cash in on the new expansion of the literary market, both in Spain and abroad, they found themselves overrun by their Spanish American peers in a competition that seemed to deprive them of their own public and means of communication (publishers, literary prizes, etc.) and, most especially, of their own language. Not since the Golden Age had any literature written in Spanish enjoyed such international recognition and praise—after all, the most canonized texts of Hispanic literature are Cervantes's *Don Quixote* and García Márquez's *One Hundred Years of Solitude*, the only books written in Spanish to have found a companion volume in the MLA series of guides to teaching "World Literature." As it was described in 1970, echoing Emilia Pardo Bazán and her analysis of the turmoil created in nineteenth-century Spain by the introduction of naturalism, the reception of the Latin American novel was the "burning question" (*la cuestión palpitante*) of contemporary Spanish literature.[1]

It is precisely during the 1960s that the national conception of Spanish literature collapsed under the combined pressure of two parallel developments. First, there was the questioning of the category of nation resulting from a reemergent pluricultural conception of the Spanish state as one composed of diverse nationalities and linguistic cultures (with Catalan, Galician, and Basque challenging the centralist hegemony of Castilian). Second, the production associated with the so-called Boom novel proved that literature in the national language was being written, and indeed very successfully, in several countries other than Spain.[2] Thus, by now the expression *Spanish literature* can no longer be used without certain qualifications: either it means *literature of Spain*, in which case it is more than a set of texts written in Spanish and ought to include the production of writers in four different languages; or, it means *literature in Spanish*, and in this case its object of study stretches beyond the limits of one particular nation.

It is surprising that the names of even the most canonized Latin American writers should hardly make an appearance—beyond an occasional footnote—in most studies on Spanish contemporary narrative. We assume that writers "belong" to the literary systems of their own countries, and—unless we are dealing with comparative, that is, supranational, work—it is unwise to mix them with other nationalities. But the realities of Spanish literary life during the 1960s and 1970s tell a different story: not only did many Latin American writers live, write, and publish in Spain, but some of them were even more influential and widely read than several Spanish authors normally included in studies and courses on the period (hence the *burning* quality of their presence). This phenomenon presents us with a challenge for the study of national literatures: where should those writers be placed in relation to the Spanish literary system? More generally, how may we account for the presence of an immense variety of foreign literary texts experienced by the readers of a particular nation when confronting the problems of national literary development? Are they still "foreign" once they are appropriated by the national readership and included in the nation's repertoire of artistic codes and values?

The purpose of this book is to argue in favor of a concept of national literature that is not restricted to the native production of citizens (the literature created by Spaniards) but that also takes into consideration the wider spectrum of literary objects, both autochthonous and imported, available within the national literary market. We will want to analyze the literary world as experienced *within*—and not only imagined *from*—a particular country, a world that would have to include not only native and imported texts written in the national language(s), but also works translated and appropriated as part of the cultural imaginary. I am proposing, then, somewhat paradoxically, that national literatures are both bound and open: limited by the configuration of the nation as a relatively distinct cultural, political, and economic entity, but also permeable, receptive to the appropriation of extrinsic elements. Thus, on the one hand, I will argue against those proponents of a cosmopolitan perspective who would simply like to avoid altogether the concept of national literature—in favor of, say, the broader notion of a literature written in Spanish (or English, French, etc.)—but also, on the other hand, against the nationalist view according to which a national literature is exclusively defined in terms of the production authored by its native-born citizens.

It would perhaps be appropriate to clarify from the outset that I am not directly concerned here with the issue of the nation as object of representation in literary texts, that is, with the question of nation-writing, a topic of extreme and legitimate importance, particularly in recent studies on postcolonialism.[3] My main interest relates to what could very generally be called "literary life"—the social processes of production, processing, and consumption of literature—or what Bakhtin and Medvedev once defined as the literary environment: "the aggregate of all the socially active literary works of a given epoch and social group."[4] What I attempt to do here is to show how such a project must depart from traditional notions of national literature, how nationalism has established itself as a dominant factor in determining our understanding of this problem, and how this factor has restricted the realities of literary life and therefore distorted the object of inquiry. The case presented in this book—the interaction of Spanish and Latin American literatures—deals precisely with the configuration and boundaries of such an "aggregate of socially active literary works" in a world of increasingly international literary languages and of seemingly collapsing national entities.

Mapping the Literary Space: Geography, Language, and Identity

While the issue of time has always received particular attention in literary history, matters of space have recently been foregrounded by a number of critics.[5] The question of how cultural products occupy and operate throughout space has traditionally—for at least two centuries now—been conceived in national terms: following and reflecting the creation of modern states, cultures have been assigned nationalities, and literary histories have been written around the idea that distinct national literatures do exist and deserve independent critical attention. A legacy from romanticism, this notion of national literatures keeps guiding not only scholarly research and academic curricula, but also a variety of public and private programs (writing and publishing grants, national prizes, and the like) that support literary production and consumption in individual countries.

At least three different arguments have been advanced against the conventional study of national literatures: a) literatures are defined by language, not geography; b) literature is universal and therefore transcends national and linguistic boundaries; and c) the identity of literary texts is to be found on more profound grounds than those provided by the nation. The first argument challenges the attempt to circumscribe literatures according to geopolitical boundaries. It contends that the true unifying force of a literature is language, not nationality, and that national literatures artificially divide a production that should be defined by the use of a common language and literary tradition. It prefers to speak of a literature (however complex and diversified it might be) written in Spanish as different, say, from those written in English, French, Creole, etc. It is in this sense that Christopher Clausen has recently argued for the abandonment of the concept of national literature and in favor of a "literature in the English language" that should encompass all literary products written in the many variants of English as it is used around the world: "As a medium that defines the horizon of intelligibility, language is a more principled and useful (though not absolute) basis than nationality for distinguishing one literature from another. To define English literature as 'literature written in the English language, no matter where or by whom written' rejoins conceptually what has been artificially fragmented, makes possible a genuine multiculturalism in English studies, entitles writers who are neither British nor American to more widespread attention, and helps us think more fruitfully about literary relations among authors, literary movements, societies, and periods."[6]

Carlos Fuentes has repeatedly argued that the authentic homeland of the writer in Spanish is the imaginary territory first dreamed by

Cervantes in La Mancha, and which has since then expanded beyond the limits of any particular national geography.[7] Still under the spell of the reception of the Boom novel in Spain, in 1972, publisher Carlos Barral countered the separation of Spanish and Latin American literatures by underlining the linguistic unity of Hispanic letters and advancing the notion of literary dialects: "From a serious perspective of literary history, it seems to me that the various contemporary literatures written in Spanish make up a mosaic of dialectal literatures that are equidistant from one theoretical center—the literary language of the Baroque. . . . In that sense, I think the literature being written in Castile is as dialectal as that from the Yucatan."[8] The history of a language-based definition of the literary realm, however, has been troubled by the uneasy relationships among different national writings in the same language. In terms that could be easily applicable to the condition of the Latin American writer in Spain, Washington Irving once described how former colonial powers do not graciously renounce their claims to exclusive ownership of the mother tongue, and how cultural clashes are likely to happen when societies are confronted with foreign, yet kindred, literary productions: "It has been a matter of marvel, that a man from the wilds of America should express himself in tolerable English. I was looked upon as something new and strange in literature; a kind of demi-savage, with a feather in his hand, instead of on his head; and there was a curiosity to hear what such a being had to say about civilized society."[9]

In what one wishes to regard as outdated and fortunately superseded models of Hispanism, non-Peninsular literatures were akin to appendices, mere transpositions and reflections of a seminal literature; as such, their differences had to be subordinated to the former identity of the original seed. Spanish American literatures were often understood as part of a secondary system that functions merely as a cultural reserve, a depository of Spain's literary past, and judged according to the standards of the original model. Within this paradigm, difference is only legitimized as underdevelopment (which serves to preserve heritage) or localism (which limits miscegenation to acquiring "local color" and the added value of exoticism). This colonial model of interliterary relations—which construes hybridization as mere deviation from the norm of metropolitan art—has been countered by a postcolonial model that, in the case of Hispanic studies, postulates the independence of Latin

American literatures and carefully separates the study of Spanish and Spanish American cultural practices.

The second argument advanced against national literatures claims that the phenomenon of literature, being a truly universal human enterprise, transcends national (and linguistic) boundaries. Thus is made the case in favor of a supranational, comparative study of literature as the artistic expression of a unified humanity—a conception that echoes Goethe's notion of *Weltliteratur*.[10] In this view, strictly linguistic, geographic, or national boundaries should be circumvented in order to honor a higher cultural, political, or ethnological entity. One may notice that, of course, by doing this, we do not deny the validity of those boundaries and criteria for literary mapping—we simply expand them to embrace supranational territories. We are ultimately led to a universalistic conception that finds the essence of art in the timeless—and therefore spaceless—aesthetic unveiling of the human condition. And yet, this is not to deny nationalism, but to posit a more generous, elevated form of the same: its basic assumption is not that great literary authors have no citizenship, but that they are actually citizens of the world, the ultimate representatives of a common (although very often intriguingly Eurocentric) human identity.

The third argument against national literatures addresses the question of identity not by exploding its borders vertically (as in universalism), but by horizontally redrawing its boundaries. As the identity of the nation-state becomes suspect, it would seem that what differentiates a literary product is its relationship to other, presumably more profound defining traits (like gender, class, or ethnicity). Being just a variation of the national model, however, this argument often reproduces its limitations.

What all these proposals and counterproposals for the defining of cultural spaces have in common is a strong reliance on a *genetic* conception of literature: cultural works are associated with the processes of creation and with their origins (by whom are they written? from where?), while the re-creation of texts effected through reading and consumption seems doomed to occupy a secondary position. This genetic identity has played a significant role in defining cultural boundaries, especially when it has been perceived as a matter of fidelity or allegiance. According to such a conception, in order for literary products to belong to a certain group it is not only necessary for their authors to share the community's identifying traits (gender, citizenship, language, and so on), but, at the same time, they also have to represent genuinely the community's *Weltanschauung*. As Julian Hawthorne put it in 1884, "What is an American book? It is a book written by an American, and by one who writes as an American, that is, unaffectedly. . . . What is an American novel except a novel treating of persons, places and ideas from an American point of view?"[11] This nineteenth-century standard of unaffected allegiance continues to be fashionable—and sometimes translates into an uncritical and compulsive quest for identity.

More recently, in an attempt to define the basic characteristics of a national literature, Naftoli Bassel has identified several features concerning ethnic and mythological roots, language identity, systemic stability and dynamism, artistic tradition, and interliterary influences. He finally concludes: "The criteria above exclude from the given national literature works which are thematically linked to the life of its nation yet written by authors belonging to other literary systems; at the same time, they organically include thematically 'alien' works by national writers. . . . Neither the theme nor the nationality of the characters is decisive; rather, the crucial characteristics are the connection with the national literary tradition, or national artistic consciousness, the presence of the 'national point of view,' or national 'way of seeing.' "[12] Such criteria, however, can present serious problems when brought to bear on the peculiarities of certain authors who muddy national and cultural classifications through open disregard for their hypostatized "true" roots. In another example (this time arguing for a decolonization of the literary canon), Georg M. Gugelberger has advanced a definition of a "genuine 'Third World Literature' " that uses similar distinctions to recast the literary census in an ideologically well-intended but, I believe, eventually misguided fashion: "As a kind of preliminary and provocative thought I would like to remind the reader that not all literature coming out of this gigantic geographic area, which embraces almost two thirds of the world, is necessarily 'Third World Literature.' There are writers in Nigeria, for example, who produce 'literature' and there are others who produce 'Third World Literature.' In Latin America one might think about Borges and Neruda. Neruda is obviously a Third World writer, while Borges's writing belongs to the literature we associate with the established canon. The fact that he comes from a Third World nation does not suffice to make him a Third World writer although the precise question as to why he opts to write in a non–Third World tradition is itself fruitful."[13] What Gugelberger chooses to see as this presumed "Third World tradition" is a literature of resistance characterized as "realistic" ("This implies talking about men and women not in the abstract but in the here and now"), "overtly political," and "allegorical and didactic."[14] Those features, however, are not found exclusively in the Third World, and, more to the point, the literary production of those areas—for better or worse—goes well beyond those restrictions. In the case of Borges, for instance, Fernández Retamar has convincingly argued that he is precisely the sort of writer who can only be explained by his eccentricity in relation to the metropolitan model, that is, by his Americanness, since only from the colony it is possible to overcome the provincialism of European canonization.[15] I do not pretend to deny, of course, the validity of certain genetic considerations when analyzing cultural products, or the existence and even the need for the promotion and study of counterhegemonic discourses in contemporary societies, but it is difficult to see how cultural stereotyping can serve as a useful basis for literary study.

Within a conception that grounds the understanding of literature on origin and creation, reception history usually takes a compromised outlook: reception is allowed its due once the filiation of writers is first established by one or another variety of identity searches, and then it is only invoked to review the intercultural projection of the writers' works.[16] The literary space is thus divided into mutually exclusive areas—only texts written in Spanish by Spaniards would properly belong to Spanish literature. Under these conditions, interliterariness is rarely used to contest the national order of things, and literary histories have a tendency to devolve into genealogical enterprises circumscribed to the cataloguing of native populations and the issuing of birth certificates.

However, as we shall see later, a close look at the events involved in the reception of the New Latin American novel in Spain shows that the study of a particular literary system cannot limit itself to the mapping of national origins.[17] The nationalistic concept of literature tends to deemphasize the significance of extrinsic elements by focusing exclusively on the genetic aspect of artistic production, therefore overlooking the wider range of literary objects within a nation's collective experience. By restricting the literary map to a geography of birthplaces, the phenomena of literary life is reduced to only one, and not always necessarily the most significant, of its components: according to that genetic fallacy, it is only by reference to the origin of the work that it is possible to ascertain both its meaning and its value, and therefore only those sharing the conditions of the creative process can fully understand its result. The logical companion of this notion is that only those texts genetically linked to a particular nation can be legitimately considered part of its literature. A nation's literary history, then, would have to be concerned only with the literary production of its citizens.

NATIONAL LITERATURE: GENEALOGY AND NATURALIZATION

For the purposes of literary history the centralizing privilege given to the origin (of author or language) of the literary work represents a limitation similar to what Roland Barthes once identified as the "fundamental vice" of literary history: "the 'centralizing' privilege granted to the author." According to Barthes, "the consequences are grave: by focusing on the author, by making the literary 'genius' the very source of observation, we relegate the properly historical objects to the rank of nebulous, remote zones; we touch on them only by accident."[18] The "properly historical object" of literary research, in Barthes's view, cannot be the creative act of individual authors, but the literary institution. The goal of literary history should then be not simply to catalogue the artistic achievements of the past (a history of works) nor to understand how certain writers ended up writing certain books (a history of creation), but to provide a sort of historical ontology: "What is wanted is nothing more than a historical answer: what was literature . . . what function was entrusted to it, what place in the hierarchy of values, and so on?"[19] While a history of literary creation is inevitably linked to a genetic perspective of art, Barthes's institutional model of literary history takes us beyond the problematic of origins and into the realm of social experience, where the consumption of goods—cultural or otherwise—cannot be restricted (particularly in contemporary economies) to only those autochthonously produced.

Closely related to the primacy of the origin is the primacy of the native language. It has been long established and accepted as one of the building blocks of literary criticism (as it has been conceived under the aegis of linguistics) that the native language is the privileged medium of aesthetic expression. According to Claudio Guillén, "it would be unfortunate to overlook the fact that it is the mother tongue that offers us the most intense access—the most secure and the most intimate—to aesthetic emotion and to the comprehension of what is or what is not poetry."[20] These sorts of judgments about language, however, are significantly often expressed in connection to the value of poetry, and it is precisely the traditional preference in criticism for poetic (as opposed to narrative) texts that has supported a certain sacralization of the relationship between languages and literatures. Moreover, the linguistic delimitation of a national literature (that is, that only works written in a particular national language can be said properly to belong to the literary world of that nation) is conditioned by what André Lefevere—in contrast to a systemic conception—has termed a "corpus conception" of literature: "This conception is based on two essentially Romantic notions: that of genius and that of the sacred character of the literary text. . . . If the original is a work of genius, it is—by definition—unique. If it is unique, it cannot be translated."[21] The reputed untranslatable substance of literary texts (and here again the usual examples relate to the harmony and evocative power of poetry—plots and stories, which seem to adapt more easily to foreign codes, are rarely discussed in this context) has led to a sacralization of origins that is invoked to separate works produced in different languages, even though from the point of view of their reception (in the minds of readers and in bookstores within one particular national system) they might go perfectly together.[22]

It would certainly be naive to diminish the significance autochthonous products have to a particular culture, or the value the members of that culture may assign to what they perceive as their own identity, as opposed to the imported character of foreign products. Spanish readers, for instance, can be certainly prone to give special consideration (and therefore a higher position in the hierarchy of the literary system) to a novel written by a Spaniard—perhaps because the language (identified as an authentically native sociolect), the narrative situation, its characters, or some other features of the text are deemed to be closer to home, to their way of life. Nevertheless, the opposite has been occasionally also true: foreign texts can be valued precisely because they question (or enrich) a collective imaginary or an understanding of life that is perceived as restricted or stagnant.

The impact translated texts may have on the configuration of national literatures is still largely underestimated. The study of literary populations has to take into account the phenomenon of constant migrations and the processes of *naturalization*, in which cultural elements are awarded citizenship in alien configurations. As Even-Zohar has argued, translated works should be considered an integral part of the larger literary system.[23] Literary products—including under this general term not only individual texts but also poetic models, conventions, codes, and values—do travel and function beyond the boundaries of their original birthplaces, and foreign texts often provide the borrowings necessary to satisfy certain needs unfulfilled by the native production.

The centralizing privilege accorded to the national origin of the artistic work underestimates the historical concretizations of literature as objects of experience for a society of readers, as the nation is not simply a monadic sphere, but rather the space from which communication is effected with other geographies. Literary history, according to the program originally described by Felix Vodička in 1942, "must envisage the literature of a given period as a set of existing works but equally as a set of literary values."[24] Here it is crucial to understand the focus on *existing* works and values (reminiscent of Bakhtin and Medvedev's attention to "socially active" texts as the object of sociological poetics), since for Vodička the corpus of a given literature is defined by its living repertoire: "The literary historian's attention focuses on that which constitutes the scope and content of literature at a given moment in literary evolution. We have in mind here living literature, literature that is actively a part of readers' awareness; we are not concerned with historical literary values outside the range of intensive reader interest and, therefore, permanently or temporarily without active aesthetic effect. . . . We investigate which of the works of past and contemporary authors were favored, and we investigate what the relationship to contemporary and past literary trends was."[25]

Such a repertoire of authors, works, and values is never the exclusive result of autochthonous production. The study of bestsellers, too often conspicuously absent from scholarly analysis, provides an excellent example of how literary taste (and marketing) can transcend national, geographic, and—through translation—linguistic barriers. If Vodička's program is to be implemented in our case, it would seem absurd to disregard the literary presence in Spain of Vargas Llosa or García Márquez, among others, simply because they were born abroad. Mario J. Valdés and Linda Hutcheon have recently argued against "any monolithic construction of a national literary history" and in favor of a comparative model, since "people [and texts] can and often do participate in several language communities at once."[26] A simple glimpse at literary journals and debates during the 1960s and early 1970s in Spain will make clear that Vargas Llosa became a prominent presence and a model for young Spanish writers. Shouldn't we study his position in the literary system of the time, not only his influence on particular writers, but also and most importantly his contribution to the creation of a system of values and norms about what literary art was supposed to be at that time in Spain? *This* Vargas Llosa (as distinct from a Peruvian Vargas Llosa, or a French one) as read and actualized by Spain's literary life should indeed be considered as legitimate an object of Spanish literary historiography as native writers Juan Benet or Juan Goytisolo.[27]

Toward a Nationalized Literature

As hermeneutics and reception theory have shown, texts have to be read in order fully to exist, and reading always takes place within a frame of perception. This frame arguably depends on specific national circumstances, as it is determined by a complex set of sociocultural factors (such as conditions of literacy, institutions of transmission and preservation of intellectual capital, the functioning of a market for cultural products, and so on) that varies from one society to another. At the same time, the objects—texts, norms, habits, values—circulating through these channels of cultural communication are not restricted to those nationally produced: they are defined neither by their original center of production (Spaniards read García Márquez, Colombians read Cervantes), nor by their original language (through translation, foreign texts are constantly appropriated by different systems). Thus, a difficulty arises when the study of national literatures confronts the presence of foreign elements, since there is a certain *dislocation* that has to be accounted for: "Special methodological problems arise when we investigate the response to a work in a foreign literary environment. Even translation is, in a certain sense, an actualization [that is, a concretization] which the translator effects. The response to a work by readers and critics in a foreign environment is very often quite dissimilar to response to the same work in its indigenous environment, because the norm, too, is dissimilar."[28] Faced with problems of this sort, a common response is the attempt to relocate a text to its original setting—and analyze foreign reception in terms of the greater or lesser degree of distortion that is effected when reading takes place outside the original, "natural" environment. But my argument is precisely that such a foreign identity often provides privileged insights into both the understanding of cultural works and—more importantly—the functioning of host literatures. Two different literary systems can certainly contain common elements—as in the intersection of two geometric configurations—but the respective positions of these elements in each of the environments will not be necessarily identical, since their final concretizations depend on the specific disposition of the systems.

Still, naming the problem does not solve the issue. If national literatures are expanded to include any text that—either by original creation or by appropriation—happens to be within its boundaries, do we not run the risk of a mapping of the literary space that will eventually be useless and as disorienting as the space itself? (One is reminded here of the cartographical paradox designed by Borges in "Of Exactitude in Science.") David Perkins, for instance, has recently argued against a history of reception that would have to account not only for spatial displacements, but also for temporal transactions of literary values and works (in which case the Spanish literary system of the 1960s should include, say, Benet, Vargas Llosa, and Kafka, but also Cervantes). Such a project, in his opinion, involves a "structural complication": "A reception history of English literature would feature Shakespeare in every period since 1600."[29] But why should the reappearance of Shakespeare throughout English literary history destroy the possibility of describing and explaining the course of that literature? I grant that it does complicate the task, but it would be a mistake to identify that difficulty as resulting from merely a continuous presence of Shakespeare in the English repertory. On the contrary, the reiterative appearance of the expression "Shakespeare" does not imply that the designated object remains unchanged—the signifier may be the same, but the signification is altered by temporal and spatial shifts.[30] As István Sötér has argued for the case of Hungarian literature, these transformations also operate at the interliterary level, and thus—from the standpoint of Hungarian literary life—"Baudelaire or Dostoevsky can be regarded as twentieth-century writers, because it is then that they were appropriated."[31]

It could also be objected that—even if some sort of national delimitation is to be found in the configurations of literary life—it makes little sense to work in that direction at a time when cultural life seems to be leading toward increasing globalization. But, in my opinion, it would unwise to disregard the influence national identities have on the existence of literature as a social institution. Anthony D. Smith, for instance, has recently warned against being too optimistic about the possibilities and virtues of a global culture in the contemporary world. Faced with the increase of international communications, nationalism seems to stand its ground: "Of all collective identities in which human beings share today, national identity is perhaps the most fundamental and inclusive. . . . National identity today is not only global, it is also pervasive. Though there are some situations in which it is felt to be more important than in others, it may also be said to pervade the life of individuals and communities in most spheres of activity."[32] The experience of literature is conditioned not only by the material conditions of the economy (which can be said to become international as, for instance, when the ownership of many Spanish publishers recently passed into the hands of multinational companies), but also by the less tangible, but equally defining, mental components of social life: the common myths, symbols, values, and memories that shape the common heritage of a nation.[33]

Whether we consider the modern nation-state (Spain or France) or some other national entities (Catalonia or the Basque Country, for instance) to be the unit of analysis the fact remains that the cultural life of citizens is fueled by more than the exclusive interplay of native elements. We may ignore or deplore the presence of nonnative values and works, and pretend that they do not exist within the boundaries of the national culture, just as we may want to conceal the fact that any language is full of borrowings from other languages—but that comes closer to wishful thinking than to critical thought. This, of course, does not mean that the critique of cultural imperialism has no place in literary scholarship; only that such a critique, to be effective, needs to be grounded in a more complete understanding of the realities of the cultural world—such cultural borrowings cannot simply be seen as a matter of foreign influence, but also as a question of (real, imaginary, or even imposed) national need and appropriation. Thus, the literary space, I will argue, is better understood not necessarily as national, but as *nationalized* (since belonging is not a matter of essences, but of processes), and this understanding can only be accomplished by departing from traditional conceptions of interliterary relationships. The study of connections among literary systems is usually conceived as belonging to comparative literature, and therefore is seen as somehow "outside" the proper object of "national" scholarship. But this "inside/outside" dichotomy is based on a fiction: the fiction that, somewhere, something like a pure national literature exists.

As I will try to show later in the book, it is in this context that the notion of literary influence must also be superseded, since it tends to emphasize temporal difference (and therefore origin) over spatial simultaneity. Its focus being the creative process, the study of influences is closely tied to literary history understood as genetics (how did the text come into being in the mind of the writer?). Thus, to say that text A influences text B presupposes that in order for B to be created, A had to preexist and determine its production. From the point of view of a literary systemics, the passive character bestowed on reception by the unidirectionality of literary influence—from A to B—must be replaced by a more active interaction. As an alternative, we could consider the notion of literary interference, advanced by Even-Zohar to describe the transferral of poetical items from a source system to a target system. Literary borrowings should not be considered a matter of chance; the condition of a particular system is what creates the necessary context for influence to take place. Interference emphasizes the synchronic axis of literature, the spatial extension of the literary world where heteroglossia takes place. Within a literary system, both A and B are offered to the reader and interact (or interfere) with each other. Temporality (whether, say, text A is originally from the sixteenth century and B from the twentieth) can thus become redefined by spatiality, by a common presence in the paratextual space (a process described by Borges in "Kafka and His Precursors").[34]

We should also object to a certain conception of comparative scholarship that appears to ground the existence of interliterary relationships in the discovery of parallelisms. According to this line of inquiry, in order to substantiate the impact of, say, García Márquez in Spain one would search for a Spanish book comparable to *Cien años de soledad*, and from that point on analyze the differences and similarities between the foreign "original" and the "autochthonous" text. The important question, however, is not: where is the Spanish García Márquez? but rather: how is García Márquez located in the constitution of the literary experience of Spanish readers? We should acknowledge that the Colombian writer is in fact a legitimate, even an integral object in Spain's literary history. Literary works, codes, and values should be considered nationalized as long as they are produced, distributed, and consumed as literary products within a particular national system. National literary histories will have to forgo any exclusive rights over their national heroes: authors will belong to whatever literary community appropriates them through reading and reproduction, which can happen simultaneously at both the synchronic and the diachronic levels.

Let's assume that certain literary borrowings can play a role that goes beyond influencing individual authors; that—as I think is the case with the Latin American Boom novel in Spain during the 1960s and 1970s—such foreign items can have a dominant presence that conditions not only the writing, but also the cultural mediating and consumption of literature; that the formation of literature as an institution of social interaction is not simply a function of genealogy, but rather of experience. Then, we ought to conclude that literatures cannot be defined exclusively in terms of the original space (language, nation, gender, and so on) in which they are written: literatures are also defined by the boundaries of their reading.

2
Book Trade and Literary Production in Spain

Nowhere today is the profile of the Boom as clearly defined as
it is in Spain.
—José Donoso, *Historia personal del boom*

THE USE OF THE WORD *BOOM* TO DESCRIBE A LITERARY PHENOMENON
has often been criticized because it seems to express an abdication
of aesthetic criticism to the language and values of the marketplace.
After all, in the case of the Latin American Boom novel, there is
little poetic foundation to speak of a unified group of writers or
texts, since there are important differences between the narrative
models presented by García Márquez, Vargas Llosa, Fuentes, or
Cortázar—to mention the names most commonly associated with
the Boom. If, as it is still the case for common readers (particularly
in Spain and North America), we also include in the same set the
works of Borges or Asturias—who were writing long before the
new novelists of the sixties, but nonetheless gained worldwide attention with them—the notion of a Boom novel seems even more
deceptive, a materialistic construct foreign to the literary realm.[1]
The label, however, has withstood the passage of time and remained in the vocabulary of contemporary readers, as if it were indeed appropriate to describe its object. After all, it could be argued
that one of the most noticeable features of many of the books associated with the Boom is precisely the fact that they were commercially successful: an unprecedented number of titles (some of them
first published years earlier) acquired wide recognition in the form
of multiple editions and translations, while their authors became famous to the point of being able to turn their writing into a profession and earn a living. I thus propose to focus on the Boom not so
much as a phenomenon of creation, since Latin American fiction
was not born in the sixties, but rather of reception, because it was

33

then that—as had been the case with the "New World" five centuries earlier—the rest of the world "discovered" it.

In Spain and elsewhere, readers turned to Latin American fiction not simply because it was there to be found, but because certain conditions made the finding possible and even necessary. The possibility was given in the form of an increase in the publishing and consumption of books and other publications throughout the Hispanic world, which made accessible to large numbers of readers the production of many authors who had remained until then restricted to their local audiences. The need was created as the crisis of poetic models in Western societies provided an incentive to search for new forms of fiction, and also because the ideological configuration of the postcolonial world demanded attention to other cultures. The object of this chapter will be to analyze the intersection of these developments as they condition the interliterary relations between Spain and Latin America.

THE EXPANSION OF THE SPANISH BOOK INDUSTRY

The understanding of the Boom novel as a material, even a commercial event is essential to grasping its significance in the literary life of the 1960s. According to Ángel Rama, while the production of this literature originated in Mexico and Buenos Aires, it was only when the center of Hispanic book production moved to Barcelona in the sixties that it reached beyond the frontiers of national literatures to become a global Latin American phenomenon. The same idea was advanced by publisher Carlos Barral, who claimed that it was because the Spanish publishing industry secured a central position in the Spanish-speaking world that the Latin American Boom was able to become an international success.[2] This globalization of Latin American literature cannot be disentangled from its roots in the extraordinary development of publishing during the sixties, a phenomenon that is nowhere more visible than in Spain.

In the Spanish case, the transformation of the book industry is closely linked to that of the economic system at large. Thanks in part to a series of structural measures designed in the late fifties to overcome the limitations of the autarkic model that had ruled the economy since the end of the Civil War, Spain enjoyed an unprecedented growth during the following decade—what the propagandists of the dictatorship pompously described as the "Spanish miracle."[3] One of the main pieces of legislation that accompanied that transformation was the decree for a "New Economic Order" (*Nueva Ordenación Económica*), issued by the Spanish government in July 1959, which charted the beginning of a period of economic stabilization through a series of new monetary policies.[4] These measures deregulated foreign investment and offered governmental support for the exportation of national products, and generated the largest expansion of the Spanish economy after the Civil War. Economic development was accompanied by an emerging urban society—the result of a significant internal migration—that created a thriving national market for cultural consumption in Spain. The social structure of the country was throughly transformed as what had been basically a preindustrial society became an industrialized country, complete with the marketing of a mass culture that—flourishing in the interstice left open between the officialist culture of the Franco regime and the culture of political insurgence—became increasingly important for the new economy.[5] This internal market favored the implementation of new strategies for the circulation of cultural goods, such as the creation of book clubs and the popularization of the pocket-book format—the most successful book club, the Círculo de Lectores, was created in September 1962, while the pocket-book revolution took definite hold with the launching of "El libro de bolsillo" series by Alianza Editorial in 1966.

The new legislative setting also provided publishers with the financial basis needed for exploiting the possibilities of the foreign market, both in Europe and across the Atlantic. The concern of Spain's cultural industry for Latin America was certainly nothing new, as the topic has been a central preoccupation in the sector since at least the mid-nineteenth century, for reasons both material and ideological.[6] The presence of the national language throughout the continent seemed to offer a *natural* market for Spanish publications, but the apathy and lack of commercial instinct of Spanish printers had left the field in the hands of their English and French competitors, who became the main providers of books in Spanish in the area. In a parallel move, after the political empire was dismantled by the independence of the colonies in the early nineteenth century, Spanish intellectuals fostered the notion of a pan-Hispanic cultural community, mainly as a reaction to North American pan-Americanism. In its various forms, both liberal and conservative (*panhispanismo, hispanoamericanismo, iberoamericanismo*), and particularly in the twentieth century, the ideal of a Spanish cultural tutelage over its former colonies has remained in theory a constant topic of foreign policy, even though in practice it has often been contradicted by an also persistent lack of action and initiative.[7]

The lackluster performance of Spain's publishing industry in Latin America owed a great deal also to the absence of real interest in the transatlantic cultural production. While English and French publishers were able to profit from the American market by printing in the Spanish original works by American authors, Spain was more concerned with transmitting its own cultural heritage. As Rufino Blanco-Fombona, a Venezuelan publisher established in Spain, warned his audience at a conference organized by the Barcelona Book Chamber in 1922, the Spanish book had in America its vastest audience, but this potential was not being exploited by publishers in the Peninsula because nobody seemed to value what non-European Spanish speakers had to say: "The Spanish book has an audience of nations. . . . [But] no one in Spain realized that they could profit from Spanish American writers . . . at least in Spanish America. They used to think and say—and they still do—that nothing exists there that is worth anything. And I say that Spanish publishers, in general, lack foresight, and sometimes common sense."[8] In fact, Hipólito Escolar has argued that the relative success of Catalan publishers in the American market in this century (in contrast to their competitors in Madrid) is not only due to their proverbial, businesslike "practical sense," but also to their lack of concern for Castilian cultural life: "Catalan publishers had little concern for Spanish contemporary literary movements to which some Madrid minorities clung so closely; their practical sense as well as their detachment from life in the capital, site of administrative centralism, oriented their production toward both nonliterary works and time-honored foreign authors of literature. This lent an international flavor to their catalogues, a flavor that was not bound to Madrid, and favored their entry in Spanish America."[9] While the cultural activity of the Spanish Second Republic enjoyed a high degree of respectability across the Atlantic, in the aftermath of the Civil War Spanish publishers once again lost the Latin American market, as the strict censorship of the dictatorship led to a stagnation of culture and opened the field to Argentinean and Mexican publishing houses—some of them run by Spanish exiles—which became the main sources of literary novelties in the Hispanic world. During the postwar period even translations coming from Spain were regarded as suspicious, burdened by the dullness of Franco's officialist culture, and were left to gather dust.[10]

The sixties witnessed the successful attempts of Spanish publishers to reverse that condition. That they would find official support from a government that maintained a strong censorship to control the production of culture may seem paradoxical. After all, the National Institute of the Spanish Book (Instituto Nacional del Libro Español, or INLE) was created in 1941 not simply to coordinate efforts within the industry, but as an instrument of Francoist cultural politics—as was openly declared in the first issue of its official publication, *Bibliografía Hispánica*, the aim of the Institute was to control the book sector according to the principles of the Spanish Falangist movement.[11] Galán Pérez, however, notes that although even today "the exportation of books is closely linked to the definition of a cultural policy towards Spanish America," the mingling of commercial and ideological interests that is common in programmatic calls of attention within the industry should not lead us to assume a complete harmony between Spanish publishers and the government's foreign policy.[12] The INLE was also a site where the lobbying efforts of publishers could exert some influence over the government. Against the restrictions imposed by religious and political censorship, whose defenders were logically wary of the expansion of cultural production and the ensuing proliferation of potentially destabilizing ideas, the book industry was able to procure through the INLE certain economic concessions (lower postal rates, financial credits) that made it possible for the sector to expand beyond the national boundaries.[13] Those who had declared war against literacy (as in General Millán Astray's famous cry "Death to intelligence!") were convinced, out of concern to secure Spain a dominant position within the geography of the *hispanidad*, to facilitate the expansion of book production—which would eventually contribute to the dismantling of officialist culture.

The analysis of the development of the Spanish book industry during the 1960s must occupy a central position in the study of the production of literature in Spain and its interaction with the Latin American market. While there is a continuous expansion of publishing since the early sixties, as far as the production of literature is concerned the Spanish book industry expands particularly between 1966 and 1973. That these years are also associated with the Boom novel, which is usually dated as beginning around 1963 and ending in 1973, seems to point to a close connection between the two phenomenons.[14] I would thus like to formulate a first observation: the boom of Latin American literature is concurrent with a rise of literary production by Spanish publishers.

The historical development of book production in Spain is visualized in Figure 1, which charts the publication of both total titles and those classified under the category of Literature during the period 1946–82 (see Table 1 for data).[15] The production of books seems more or less stable during the fifties (with a noticeable peak in 1953); it expands at a steady rate during the sixties; in the seventies, it presents a spectacular increase in 1972–73, declines for the following two years, and recovers its growth for the second part of the decade. Spanish publishers go from producing under five thousand titles for most of the 1950s to around thirty thousand in the early 1980s—in other words, an increase of 828 percent between 1946 and 1982. Thanks to this expansion, by the mid-eighties Spain is the seventh largest producer and the fourth largest exporter of books in the world.[16] The production of literary titles also grows in the long term, although not as dramatically—it increases 391 percent in the period 1946–82, with particular peaks in 1966, 1973, and 1981. However, its path is more erratic, with various slumps, the most obvious of them taking place after 1973.

Figure 1

Titles Published in Spain, 1946–1982
(Source: INLE)

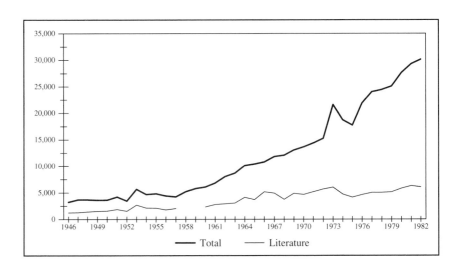

Table 1

Titles Published in Spain, 1946–1982
(Source: Instituto Nacional del Libro Español)

Year	Total Titles	Titles in Literature
1946	3,246	1,237
1947	3,680	1,273
1948	3,692	1,404
1949	3,599	1,513
1950	3,630	1,574
1951	4,208	1,868
1952	3,455	1,547
1953	5,662	2,693
1954	4,678	2,139
1955	4,811	2,126
1956	4,419	1,782
1957	4,243	2,056
1958	5,208	—
1959	5,786	—
1960	6,085	2,342
1961	6,819	2,772
1962	8,045	2,918
1963	8,694	3,073
1964	10,129	4,124
1965	10,425	3,714
1966	10,818	5,164
1967	11,833	4,920
1968	12,085	3,764
1969	13,041	4,870
1970	13,639	4,661
1971	14,378	5,162
1972	15,232	5,681
1973	21,595	6,019
1974	18,720	4,717
1975	17,727	4,129
1976	21,875	4,611
1977	24,034	5,029
1978	24,447	5,045
1979	25,076	5,132
1980	27,629	5,798
1981	29,286	6,285
1982	30,127	6,073

We can confirm this general picture with the data provided by the Instituto Nacional de Estadística (INE). Since my interest here is in framing the phenomenon of the Boom novel, I now concentrate on the period 1960–80. Figure 2 charts the yearly production of both total and literary titles (see Table 2 for data). This chart corroborates two parallel circumstances that were visible in Figure 1. While the publication of total titles seems to thrive more or less continuously after 1962—an upward trend that is only slightly broken in 1970–1971, 1975, and 1978—the publication of literary titles shows important peculiarities. It follows the general trend for most of the period, but it departs from the norm in two significant occasions: first, between 1963 and 1964; then, and more permanently, after 1973. During the years 1966–73, the average annual production of literary titles was 7,604; in the period 1974–79, that average went down to 6,068. The production of literary titles reaches its highest point in 1971: with a total of 8,191 titles published, that year the publication of literature represents the highest percentage of the total of titles produced in Spain (41.45 percent). The significance of the two moments of decline is given by the coincidence with two important poetic phenomenons: the early sixties are asso-

Figure 2

Titles Published in Spain, 1960–1980
(Source: INE)

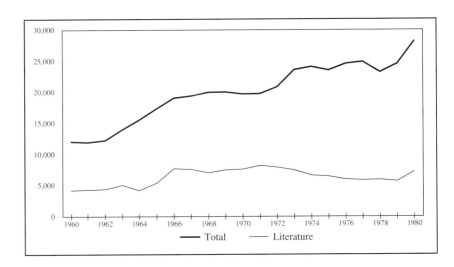

Table 2

Titles Published in Spain, 1960–1980
(Source: Instituto Nacional de Estadística)

Year	Total	Literature	% of Total
1960	12,038	4,205	34.93%
1961	11,950	4,296	35.95%
1962	12,243	4,360	35.61%
1963	13,981	5,052	36.13%
1964	15,540	4,206	27.07%
1965	17,342	5,366	30.94%
1966	19,040	7,672	40.29%
1967	19,380	7,560	39.01%
1968	20,008	7,011	35.04%
1969	20,031	7,463	37.26%
1970	19,717	7,591	38.50%
1971	19,762	8,191	41.45%
1972	20,858	7,883	37.79%
1973	23,608	7,461	31.60%
1974	24,085	6,613	27.46%
1975	23,527	6,439	27.37%
1976	24,584	5,939	24.16%
1977	24,896	5,826	23.40%
1978	23,231	5,916	25.47%
1979	24,569	5,673	23.09%
1980	28,195	7,235	25.66%

ciated in Spain with a crisis of novelistic production, and particularly with the decline of the social novel as the dominant model for writing fiction; by the mid-seventies, it was the Boom novel that lost its aura of canonicity.

One further piece of important evidence is given by the statistics on the printing of copies. A larger number of titles does not necessarily imply a larger distribution of books, or a larger audience; a case in point is the present situation in Spain, where a high number of titles published is accompanied by a decreasing average print run (4,071 copies per title in 1994). Figure 3 charts the printing of copies between 1965 and 1980 (no data is given by the INE for previous years), which follows both the general upward trend observed in the publication of total titles and the decline in literary produc-

Figure 3

Copies Printed in Spain, 1965–1980
(Source: INE)

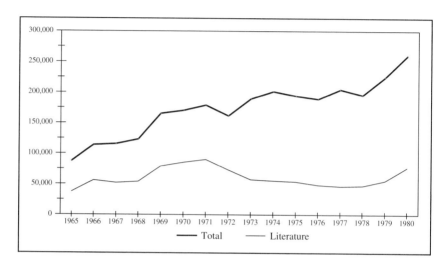

tion in the mid-seventies. The printing of literature peaks notably between 1966 (56 million copies, or 49 percent of copies in all categories) and 1971 (more than 90 million copies, over 50 percent of total copies), drops during the remainder of the seventies, and it does not recover again until the following decade. The highest average print run for literary titles is found in 1970, with 11,252 copies per title, a figure that has not been reached again in Spain since then (the average print run for a title in literature is currently around five or six thousand copies).[17]

It could be argued that the growth of the Spanish publishing industry is just a reflection of a more general trend, as the increase in literacy around the world is accompanied by the implementation of new forms of mass production of books. This is undoubtedly true, and in fact if we compare the case of Spain to those of France and Italy, for instance, we find out that 1966 was also a particularly productive year in those countries. As I indicated before, the introduction of new forms of mass production and distribution of books is responsible for much of the gains in this area, and in this respect the phenomenon is hardly restricted to Spain. There is nonetheless something peculiar about the condition of Spanish publishing,

Table 3

Copies Printed in Spain, 1965–1980
(Source: Instituto Nacional de Estadística)

Year	Total Copies (in thousands)	Literature Copies (in thousands)	% of Total	Average Print Run
1965	87,666	37,403	42.67%	6,970
1966	113,809	55,970	49.18%	7,295
1967	115,485	51.938	44.97%	6,870
1968	123,212	53,984	43.81%	7,700
1969	165,202	79,097	47.88%	10,599
1970	170,226	85,414	50.18%	11,252
1971	178,926	90,222	50.42%	11,015
1972	161,612	73,282	45.34%	9,296
1973	189,665	57,164	30.14%	7,662
1974	201,520	55,502	27.54%	8,393
1975	194,270	54,023	27.81%	8,390
1976	189,153	48,499	25.64%	8,166
1977	204,840	46,286	22.60%	7,945
1978	195,705	47,129	24.08%	7,966
1979	224,958	55,413	24.63%	9,768
1980	260,002	76,871	29.57%	10,625

which sets it apart from the rest of the world and, more particularly, from the Latin American countries. According to the statistics provided by UNESCO, between 1959 and 1976 the total number of titles published in the world increased by 77 percent; the rate was 83 percent in Europe, while Spanish America's biggest publishers, Argentina and Mexico, grew at rates of 82 percent and 94 percent, respectively. During that same period, however, the growth in Spain was four times the world average, an outstanding 327 percent growth.[18]

What I find very telling in the comparison between Spain, Argentina, and Mexico (Figure and Table 4) is the interconnection between literatures and markets across the Hispanic world. It has been argued that the editorial boom in Latin America is not so much a matter of books, but rather of periodicals; the data presented here seem to confirm that idea. In fact, if we concentrate our attention in the publication of literary titles in these three countries (Figure and

Figure 4

Titles Published in Argentina, Mexico, and Spain, 1959–1980
(Source: UNESCO)

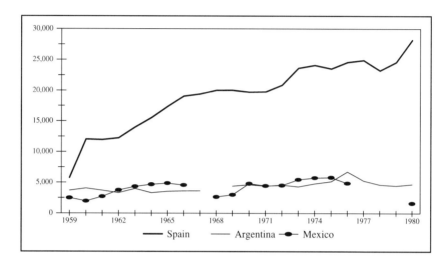

Table 5), it becomes evident that during the years of the Boom the production of literary books and pamphlets in Latin America not only does not increase, but it declines notably. As far as I know, the only exception—significant but less consequential in commercial terms—is Cuba, where the publication of books under the category of literature goes from fifty-seven titles in 1955 to as many as 372 titles in 1977. It is therefore possible to formulate a second observation: within the Hispanic world, the boom of literary production during the 1960s and 1970s is a phenomenon peculiar to Spain's publishing industry.

During the 1960s, Spain becomes the main provider of books in the Hispanic world. This commercial exchange is such that the Latin American market is no longer a last resort in case of economic crisis or the place to send an occasional surplus of production, but a fundamental component of the industry's strategies for production and marketing, as important—and sometimes even more so—than the internal Spanish market.[19] The imbalance in book trade between Spain and Latin America is also evident. According to figures given by Cendán Pazos, during the 1960s publications exported to Latin America represented around 80 percent of

Table 4

Titles Published in Argentina, Mexico, and Spain, 1959–1980
(Source: UNESCO)

Year	Spain	Argentina	Mexico
1959	5,761	3,701	2,500
1960	12,308	4,063	1,964
1961	11,950	3,703	2,679
1962	12,243	3,323	3,760
1963	13,981	3,989	4,326
1964	15,540	3,319	4,661
1965	17,342	3,539	4,851
1966	19,040	3,620	4,558
1967	19,380	3,645	—
1968	20,008	—	2,646
1969	20,031	4,395	2,983
1970	19,717	4,627	4,812
1971	19,762	4,410	4,439
1972	20,858	4,578	4,513
1973	23,608	4,312	5,455
1974	24,085	4,795	5,733
1975	23,527	5,141	5,822
1976	24,584	6,719	4,851
1977	24,896	5,285	—
1978	23,231	4,627	—
1979	24,596	4,451	—
1980	28,195	4,698	1,629

the total Spanish exports for that sector; while that figure goes down to 65 percent in the seventies and to 54 percent in 1985, this is not because of a decrease in trade with Latin America, but rather because the amount of publications exported to other areas of the world (Europe and the United States, in particular) increases dramatically, thus enlarging their share of total Spanish book trade. In contrast, imports from Latin America amounted only to 14 percent during the 1970s, and it goes down to as little as 7 percent in 1984.[20]

Unfortunately, as has been noted, "we know books are exported, but not what kind of books."[21] Not only it is impossible to determine statistically the importance of literary exports in the Spanish

Figure 5

Titles in Literature Published in Argentina, Mexico, and Spain,
1959–1980
(Source: UNESCO)

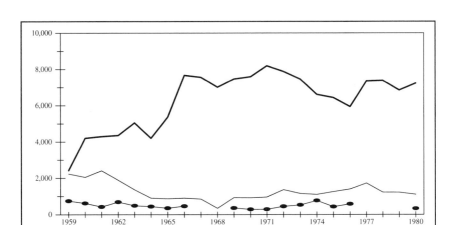

book trade with Latin America, but also the category of Literature—as defined by the Universal Decimal Classification used by UNESCO—encompasses a wide range of production far more unrestricted than the usually associated with canonical understandings of the term. It is coextensive with the complete set of works available within the field of literary production, which includes both commercial and high-brow, texts originally written in the national language(s) and translations. Consequently, we cannot ascertain from these charts the authors or models being promoted.

What we can do, however, is analyze the relative importance of translations in relation to the production of titles originally in Spanish. Foreign literature played an important role in Spanish literary life in the 1940s and 1950s, when, according to Rodrigo Rubio, bookstores "were crammed" with books by international authors—in 1945, as Valeriano Bozal has noted, half of literary titles published in Spain were translations.[22] Novels by Daphne du Maurier, Lajos Zilahy, Maxence van der Meersch, or Vicki Baum were the true bestsellers of the period, far ahead of their Spanish competition, "since the mere fact that a book was written by a foreigner

Table 5

Titles in Literature Published in Argentina, Mexico, and Spain,
1959–1980
(Source: UNESCO)

Year	Spain	Argentina	Mexico
1959	2,429	2,230	750
1960	4,205	2,052	618
1961	4,296	2,410	426
1962	4,360	1,891	690
1963	5,052	1,366	490
1964	4,206	905	444
1965	5,366	869	357
1966	7,672	904	463
1967	7,560	850	—
1968	7,011	347	—
1969	7,463	935	259
1970	7,591	920	286
1971	8,191	960	289
1972	7,883	1,367	452
1973	7,461	1,156	526
1974	6,613	1,105	770
1975	6,439	1,257	431
1976	5,939	1,400	583
1977	7,356	1,727	—
1978	7,384	1,226	—
1979	6,852	1,218	—
1980	7,235	1,104	329

was enough to convince middle-class readers that it was profound."[23] Spanish literature in the 1940s and 1950s is strongly—
and consciously—influenced by models imported from North
America, French, and Italian literatures.

In the 1960s, however, an interesting development takes place.
While the number of titles published in literature increases, the
translation of titles in this category remains rather constant in absolute terms, and consequently its proportional share *decreases*: from
28 percent of all literary titles in 1960 to an all-time low 11 percent
in 1966. Not until 1975 does the number of translations in literature
reach again the level of the 1950s (Figure and Table 6).[24] Thus, ac-

Figure 6

Literary Translation in Spain: Titles in Literature Published, 1959–1980
(Source: UNESCO)

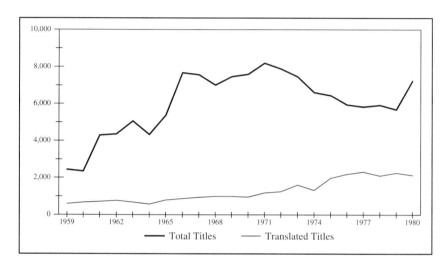

cording to UNESCO data, during the 1960s and early 1970s the publication of literary titles in Spain is concentrated in books originally in the Spanish language. In fact, between 1961 and 1972, the percentage of translated titles in literature is consistently kept under 20 percent, which represents an exceptional circumstance in the history of Spanish publishing.[25] This leads to the formulation of a third observation: the boom of literary production in Spain is a boom of literatures written in the national language(s).

I will make a brief observation at this point concerning the question of national languages in Spain. The increase in the production of nontranslated literary titles should not be read as a phenomenon exclusive of Spanish-language literature, but also in relation to the reemergence of book production in Catalan, Basque, and Galician in the 1960s, after the relaxation of bureaucratic hurdles imposed by Francoist censorship. In 1965, according to INE data, the number of literary titles published in Spain in national languages other than Spanish was 137, with a total of 280,000 copies printed; by 1969, there were 284 titles and 806,000 copies (which represent increases of 107 and 188 percent, respectively). Joan Fuster identified 1962 as the beginning of an "editorial *boom*" in Catalan publish-

Table 6

Literary Translation in Spain: Titles in Literature Published, 1959–1980
(Source: UNESCO)

Year	Total Literature Titles	Translated Literature Titles	% of Total
1959	2,429	589	24.25%
1960	2,342	671	28.65%
1961	4,296	707	16.46%
1962	4,360	767	17.59%
1963	5,052	680	13.46%
1964	4,326	568	13.13%
1965	5,366	783	14.59%
1966	7,672	866	11.29%
1967	7,560	937	12.39%
1968	7,011	987	14.08%
1969	7,463	987	13.23%
1970	7,591	956	12.59%
1971	8,191	1,181	14.42%
1972	7,883	1,248	15.83%
1973	7,461	1,602	21.47%
1974	6,613	1,318	19.93%
1975	6,439	1,974	30.66%
1976	5,939	2,184	36.77%
1977	5,826	2,312	39.68%
1978	5,916	2,098	35.46%
1979	5,673	2,255	39.75%
1980	7,235	2,130	29.44%

ing.[26] Writing in 1969, Fuster's use of the word "boom" to refer to the increase in readers and publications in Catalan is undoubtedly intended to echo in the mind of his readers the Latin American phenomenon. As I will argue later in this book, Spanish literature is challenged during the 1960s and 1970s on two parallel fronts: externally, in the Hispanic world, by the rise of Latin America as the main creative force of literature in the Spanish language; and internally, in the Peninsula, by the evidence of literary production in other national languages.

The analysis of the development of the Spanish publishing industry during the sixties points to certain implications for the understanding of literary trends in Spain as they are determined from both without and within the national system. Once the restricted readership of the autarkical period was replaced by the opening of new cultural markets abroad, the geography of the literary life was likewise expanded toward Latin America, and Spanish publishers were thus required to adapt their merchandise to the newly discovered public and pay attention to Latin American literature—as Carlos Barral declared in 1973, "publishers primarily devoted to literature and the humanities normally sell forty percent of their production to Latin America."[27] At the national level, the social transformations of Spanish society and culture created a demand for new poetic forms (the early sixties, as it is well known, witnessed the crisis of social realism as the canonized narrative model in Spain) and an increasing interest in non-Castilian literatures. Both developments questioned the status of Castilian literature as both the prime representative of Hispanic culture in the world and the only legitimate expression of Spanish creativity. In these two parallel ways, the international boom of Latin American fiction and the nationalist booms of suppressed languages combined to transform the Spanish literary space.

The Globalization of Hispanic Literature

The expansion of the external market helped enterprising publishers like Carlos Barral, who was trying to position himself as a major player in the international cultural landscape. An essential part of this strategy was the organization by the publishing house Seix Barral of a series of annual international meetings of novelists, publishers, and critics that took place in Formentor (Majorca) between 1959 and 1962. These meetings were an excellent opportunity to expose the national literary production to an international audience, and at the same time provided Spanish authors with a much needed and direct contact with other literatures. The first of these encounters took place immediately after the celebration of the "Conversaciones Poéticas de Formentor" (18–25 May 1959), which were inspired by Camilo José Cela and brought together a variegated and multilingual group of poets and critics.[28] That first "Coloquio Internacional de Novela" (26–28 May) was centered around three sessions devoted to the discussion of topics of particular urgency to the then young generation of Spanish novelists— "The Novelist and Reality/The Novelist and Society," "The

Novelist and His Art," and "The Future of the Novel."[29] Reports of
the event underscore the polarization between those who subscribed
to the notion of a socially committed literature and those who gave
priority to the formal aspects of narrative writing—what Michel
Butor, according to Espinás, described then as a conflict between
"thematic" and "technical" concerns. For Fuster, the main interest
of the encounter was the confrontation between French objectivism—Robbe-Grillet and Butor—and Spanish realism.[30] In this
sense, the debates focused on issues that were central to the poetic
definition of social realism, the literary movement promoted finan-
cially by Carlos Barral and critically by Josep Maria Castellet since
the mid-fifties (with Juan Goytisolo—himself one of the writers included in the group—doing his share from his editorial position at
Gallimard). Social realism had been hailed as the artistic expression
of anti-Franco Spain, and it was to one of its representatives (Juan
García Hortelano's *Nuevas amistades*) that the second Biblioteca
Breve Prize was awarded during the meeting.

In contrast, the second meeting, held on 2–5 May 1960, shifted
its attention from writing to publishing, and this time the two topics
presented for discussion were "The Publisher and the Novelist" and
"The Publisher and the Public." If the 1959 meeting could be read
as a showcase for social realism, in 1960 the goal was clearly to
promote the idea of what Ángel Rama has described as the "cultural publisher": publishing houses that invest in new and often demanding literary products and present themselves as devoted more
to artistic than to commercial values.[31] With the participation of
representatives from six prominent publishers—Gallimard
(France), Rowohlt (Germany), Einaudi (Italy), Weidenfeld & Nich-
olson (United Kingdom), Grove Press (USA), and Seix Barral—the
Second International Colloquium on the Novel was not only an occasion for such cultural publishers to discuss their role in establishing literary trade and trends, but also the cornerstone of a larger
cultural operation: it was there that the Formentor Group was officially founded thanks to the initiative of Carlos Barral and Giulio
Einaudi.[32] The original group was eventually joined in their meetings by other publishers—among them: Bonnier (Sweden), Gylen-
dal (Norway and Denmark), Meulenhoff (Holland), Choukorow-
Sha (Japan), and Arcadia (Portugal). It remained active between
1960 and 1968, conceived as an international, large-scale cultural
operation that would serve its members to identify, influence, and
control the production of the contemporary literary avant-garde.

According to Barral's description, Formentor was "the most important and famous literary agora of the 1960s" and comprised a wide spectrum of publishers, writers, and critics: "a group which included not only the thirteen editors of different languages and countries who formed its financial and political leadership, but also the specialists and writers who accompanied them—many well-known people who aspired to represent a lesson in style and succeeded in being taken seriously in that particular respect."[33]

It was an overt attempt to take control of the market of Western high-brow literature, a goal made clear when Barral and Einaudi discussed the bases for the literary prizes to be awarded by the group. The first idea was to create the Prix International des Éditeurs, which would recognize the oeuvre of prestigious authors not widely known beyond their national audiences. Described by Einaudi as the "anti-Nobel," this prize would provide little financial gain to the group, since awards would be given to works already in circulation.[34] And yet, it was essential to the strategic positioning of the publishers involved, Einaudi argued, because it would give them privileged access to valuable information on the condition of contemporary literary creation and criticism: "The publishers would finance the organization, the costly preparation of candidacies, travel for critics and the media. . . . In exchange for what? For priceless information that would place them in the forefront of all narratives. All the Slavists, Hispanists, Orientalists, etc., working with the major European publishers would combine their efforts and establish a virtual monopoly of literary information—with a wealth of criticism that, thanks to debate, would be vastly superior to the sum of the information provided by their separate reading committees."[35] The Prix International was given for the first time in the third Formentor meeting (in May 1961) to Samuel Beckett and Jorge Luis Borges, and it represented the first major international recognition of the Argentinean writer: "As a consequence of that prize, my books mushroomed overnight throughout the western world."[36]

But even cultural publishers have some degree of commercial interest, and to satisfy the economic needs of the group they created another award, the Prix Formentor, which would promote novels that were already in the hands of one of the publishers involved and whose authors would profit from the immediate translation and publication of the book in fourteen countries. The first Formentor Prize, also awarded during the 1961 meeting, was given to Spanish novelist Juan García Hortelano for his novel *Tormenta de verano*, and it was the highest level of international recognition attained until then by the new Spanish narrative. It is thus ironic that the exposure provided by the Formentor Prize would eventually result in a decisive setback for the expectations of social realist writers—in spite of the prestige and backing of the Formentor publishers, and in contrast with the favorable attention previously granted to the movement in European circles, translations of *Tormenta de verano* were poorly received. Antonio Martínez-Menchén has pointed to this failure as marking the end of an era: "The Formentor International Prize was supposed to be the rocket that would put our narrative into the world orbit. Unfortunately for us, it turned out to be a torpedo."[37]

The crisis of social realism has been a common topic of discussion for scholars of Spanish literature, and it helps understand the shift of direction at Seix Barral in the early sixties. I would argue that the original canonization of the movement derives directly from the fact that it performed three basic functions in the Spanish literary field. First, it provided the rebellious intellectual left with an artistic tool with which to confront Franco's officialist culture. The anti-Franco stand gave cohesive force to this new aesthetic movement, and it was strongly supported by the Spanish Communist Party, which since 1953 had made one of its priorities the recruitment of young writers; in the following years, many of them would become party members—among others, Armando López Salinas, José Antonio Ferres, García Hortelano, Gabriel Celaya, and Ángel González—while others would go along as fellow travelers in the cause of bringing down the dictatorship.[38] Secondly, the social novel also intended to serve an informative role in a country where the press was subjected to ferocious state control. One of the main concerns of these novelists was to document social reality, to provide readers with a faithful account of what real life was behind governmental propaganda—"presenting" reality was the most urgent task for writers during the forties and fifties and language was consequently required to be a transparent glass giving direct access to the world of human interaction.[39] Thirdly, social realism provided Spanish publishers with a cultural product that could be attractive to an international audience. Through publishing houses like Seix Barral and Destino, these novelists were presented as the voice of a new Spain on the verge of revolutionary transformation.[40] The international reception the movement enjoyed, particularly in

France, is explained in part by an ideological context prone to find a new historical hero in every Third-World country in turmoil—a role for which Franco's "exotic" Spain easily qualified. The willingness of Parisian intelligentsia to hail young Spanish artists as tokens of a large national liberation front would later be parodied by Juan Goytisolo in *Señas de identidad* (1966). In his autobiography he again describes the reception in 1957 of the French translation of his novel *Juegos de manos*: "The novelty value of a novel from Francoist Spain after fifteen years' opaque silence aroused immediate, disproportionate interest in critics from *L'Humanité* to *Le Figaro*. Left-wing newspapers and weeklies emphasized, logically enough, the novel's rebellious, nonconformist tone, my implicit but undoubted hostility to official values. In spite of its great defects, limitations, and influences, the book fulfilled an expectation and was welcomed with unstinting enthusiasm."[41]

The French translator of *Juegos de manos*, Maurice E. Coindreau, who also wrote the introduction to the novel, offered critical support that would be instrumental in bringing the social realist novel to the European stage; and the publishing house Gallimard— where Juan Goytisolo worked as editorial adviser—announced in 1957 a new collection of Spanish novels in translation that would offer French readers the production of the new generation of writers.[42] Meanwhile, in Spain, the movement found prestigious publishing and critical endorsements in the Biblioteca Breve Prize, which—as critic and novelist Torrente Ballester declared in 1961— quickly became a champion of Social Realism. The prizes awarded between 1958 and 1961 went to three of the representatives of the movement: Luis Goytisolo's *Las afueras* (1958), Juan García Hortelano's *Nuevas amistades* (1959), and Juan Manuel Caballero Bonald's *Dos días de setiembre* (1961; no prize was awarded in 1960). The 1961 Formentor Prize was the logical outcome of the interest at Seix Barral in presenting internationally these writers as the literary avant-garde of anti-Franco Spain.[43]

During the early sixties, however, the conditions of literary production changed significantly. The aesthetic devaluation of the hegemonic poetics of the social novel should not be understood simply as the reflection of the internal exhaustion of a literary model, but as the result of a new process of aesthetic evaluation generated within the context of Spain's social activity during the 1960s—a social process of decanonization in which the grounding force of the dominance of social realism, its alleged harmonization of art and politics, collapsed.[44] By 1963 the informative function of the social novel also became less and less relevant as the Spanish press began to overcome censorship. The successful results of the new economic policies became an important legitimation factor for Franco's regime, as the possibilities for the satisfaction of individual needs displaced the urgency for collective action.[45] The emergence of a mass culture independent of both officialist and leftist intellectual dilemmas left social novelists without a sympathetic audience. Spain, both at the national and the international level, changed its status, from that of a "prerevolutionary" and semideveloped country to that of an assimilated and materialistic society: the romantic search for exoticism that had driven Europeans to Spain since the eighteenth century disappeared, existing only as a trace still able to boost tourism; and most of the political appeal of the Spanish antifascist cause was lost and transferred to the postcolonial world.[46]

It is in this context that the Cuban Revolution played an essential role in promoting Latin American fiction. The appeal the Boom novel exerted in the 1960s throughout the Western world cannot be explained without reference to the political events of the decade. Julio Cortázar was persuaded that the Boom, more than a product of commercial interests of publishing houses, had resulted from the emergence of a new community of readers brought together by a common search for identity.[47] During this period, Cuba became a central element of this Latin American identity, the most visible symbol of cultural and political resistance in the continent. For many Spanish intellectuals it represented the effective realization of what for two decades the Spanish left had been trying to forge against Franco's dictatorship. In Spain, the second half of the 1950s had been politically characterized by the paradigm of the general strike: the definite show of popular strength that would destroy the dictatorship in a mythical moment of truth—and it was mostly to this cause that the testimonial force of the social realist novel was devoted. The increasing awareness of the historical shortsightedness of that expectation was compensated for by refocusing political attention away from the Spanish cause—devaluated by the economic transformation of the country during the following years—and toward the revolutionary causes in countries that, as they were breaking away from colonial control, seemed to be capable of rebuilding a human society.

The intellectual left, which had been instrumental in the production of an alternative literature in Spain during the fifties, refocused its attention upon Cuba in the sixties. Literary critics, writers, and publishers periodically attended conferences and colloquia held at the Casa de las Américas in Havana, which—according to Spanish critic Francisco Fernández Santos—became "a true *home*" for Spanish-speaking writers, something no other contemporary institution in the Hispanic cultural world could claim to be.[48] Castellet, also a regular visitor at the Casa, explained in a 1968 lecture in Havana how the connection between Latin American narratives and politics was perceived in Spain:

> Through Cuba we began to understand better the Latin American phenomenon and Latin American literature because, in the first place, we began to understand what we could call the dynamic and militant unity of Latin America, and therefore, this dynamic and militant unit called Latin American literature. . . . And Latin American literature is revitalizing because, for all its achievement as a purely literary creation, it provides something of a guide that links a series of men who write and produce very different literatures but who have definitively sketched out a line along which their works coincide. They are absolutely distinct from one another but coincide in many things. And this common line, I believe, is Cuba's meridian.[49]

Two important issues are raised by Castellet in this lecture. The first is the recognition of the influence of Latin American fiction on Spanish writers, and particularly on the social realist generation, which had previously followed French and Italian models. This influence is not characterized in terms of form, but around the notion of committed literature (*unidad dinámica y militante*), which had been the building block of the literary practice of social realism. As we shall see in the next chapter, Castellet's characterization points to a feature essential to the reception of Latin American fiction in Spain, namely the fact that it could replace social realism at the center of literary life precisely because it was perceived as carrying on, in an updated and revitalized form, the same central concern for social transformation. The second element is the image of Cuba as the "meridian" of the Hispanic world, which is a direct reference to the various polemics that date back at least to the 1920s, when Guillermo de Torre's editorial in *La Gaceta Literaria*—"Madrid, meridiano intelectual de Hispanoamérica" (15 April 1927)— provoked a heated debate about the interaction between Spanish and Latin American cultures.[50] That the Cuban Revolution was instrumental in the reception of the Latin American Boom novel throughout the world is clearly manifested in the crisis created by the Padilla affair in 1971, an event that can arguably be used to indicate the moment when the cohesive forces that supported the international interest in that narrative came apart. The indictment of the Cuban poet Heberto Padilla and the ensuing sense of political repression clashed with the expectations of many intellectuals and opened an insurmountable chasm among the writers directly connected to the Boom. Juan Goytisolo has described the dissolution of the Hispanic literary community resulting from this event, as individuals previously united in the defense of the Revolution emerged at opposite ends of the affair and "feelings of doubt, mistrust, and even outright hostility replaced the old warmth and camaraderie."[51] From an ideological standpoint, that rupture not only eroded to some extent the prestige and legitimacy of the revolutionary process in Latin America, but also did away with the belief in the historically effective powers of literature—an imaginative potential that, as seen from Spain, the Boom novel had inherited from the hegemonic literary model it came to replace.

Castellet's declaration thus openly acknowledged that, for Spanish leftist intellectuals, the center of Hispanic culture was no longer in Spain, but had moved across the Atlantic. It was to this new center that publishers like Carlos Barral shifted their attention. Barral was the first Spanish publisher of the postwar period to answer Blanco-Fombona's challenge and look at Latin America not simply as a market, but also as a source for his publications. His efforts to become a player in the international arena, a move facilitated by the economic transformation of the country and the expansion of the book industry under the "new economic order" of the 1960s, were a further incentive to promote Latin American fiction.

The shift in publishing practices and interests was made clear in 1969, when in his contribution to a special issue of *Cuadernos para el Diálogo* (devoted to postwar Spanish literature) Carlos Barral himself offered a rather bleak perspective on the stylistic fruits of postwar literature, including neorealism: "it seems to me that, as far as the history of style is concerned, its most outstanding characteristic is its extreme poverty, its quasi-destitution. . . . [We] all know that, from all viewpoints, the history of the postwar Spanish novel should be written around a few exceptions dotting a terrible general norm: the equilibrium of mediocrities. In any event, talking about the stylistic evolution of Spanish postwar poetry and novel is like meditating on the decline of grand families."[52] Barral was of course careful not to put the blame over such a condition on the writers themselves, but rather presented it as the consequence of the cultural impoverishment of Franco's Spain. It was immediately noted, however, that the aesthetic proposals of neorealism were being declared officially dead by its foremost representative within the publishing industry.[53] In his essay, Barral used the adjective *indigenista*—indigenous as both native and, perhaps more to the point, primitive—to negatively describe the traditional literary landscape of the generation of 1898, and a few months later he described again the work of neorealist writers as an "indigenous experiment," thus portraying the movement as an aesthetically unaccomplished enterprise: "In Spain there has not been anything remotely equivalent to Joyce, Kafka, Musil, Proust, Svevo, or Babel. The Spanish novelistic tradition of the 20th century is virtually destitute, and the Spanish novel of the 1940s and 1950s is practically reduced to a voluntarist exercise I would like to name indigenous Spanish experiment [*experimento indigenista español*]. Novelists of my generation, with Sánchez Ferlosio and Martín Santos as almost the only exceptions, attempted an experience—which I supported, as is well-known—grounded on social criticism. That experience, set in motion with limited aesthetic resources, seems today exhausted."[54]

It should not be forgotten that the disengagement of the publishing industry from the literary model of neorealism runs parallel to a process of critical self-reflection on the part of social novelists and critics themselves.[55] In "Examen de conciencia" (1963), Juan Goytisolo—who significantly did not publish any work of fiction between 1962 and 1966—had already denounced his own generation as blinded by ideological manicheanism and advocated a new realism and a new language for the transformed social reality of contemporary Spain: "Spain is fattening up, but remains mute." His "Literatura y eutanasia," published in 1966, furthered the analysis of the limitations of Spanish neorealism and explained them as resulting from two main factors: a paralyzing respect for the language and forms of Spanish literary tradition, and a misguided identification of literary and political commitment. It was in this context that Goytisolo presented the work of Latin American writers as an example of the necessary refurbishing of literary language.[56]

Goytisolo's indictment of social realism was followed by that of

Castellet, who had provided the movement with most of its theoretical grounding in the 1950s. In "Tiempo de destrucción para la literatura española" (1968), Castellet traced the intellectual evolution of the *generación del medio siglo* in an attempt to account for the cul-de-sac it had encountered, and explained neorealism as resulting from the historical conditions of postwar literary life. The ideological circumstances of Francoism accounted for the aesthetic creed of realism as an instrument of political resistance against the regime's cultural myths, while the intellectual isolation of the period—marked by censorship and the exile of most of the cultural figures of the previous generation—made autodidactic training the only choice for writers.[57] Insisting on Goytisolo's ideas, Castellet outlined a threefold program for the new Spanish novel: the renewal of literary language as Barthesian *écriture* ("an effort to destroy contemporary linguistic structures"), the critical demythologizing of Spanish cultural tradition ("the History of Spain, which is a history of differences rather than *unity*, of indigence rather than *greatness*, of oppression rather than *liberty*"), and the objective, nondogmatic analysis of social reality.[58]

The cultural situation of the Franco era is also an important factor to keep in mind when considering the generational differences exposed by the reception of the Boom novel. While many of the older writers questioned the novelty of the Boom as a mere recycling of forms already existing and emphasized its borrowings from other Western literatures, there is no question that the younger generation raised during the dictatorship saw the achievement of Latin American writers as an original and renovating force for the novel. Thus, for instance, Torrente Ballester denies the supposedly renovating influence of Latin American writers on their Spanish counterparts: "we had no need for Spanish American writers to write in a particular way, because we were already familiar with the more or less innovative or revolutionary authors [in reference to Joyce, Kafka, and Faulkner] from whom that way originates." Andrés Amorós, however, correctly notes that knowledge and circulation of works by such authors was hindered after the Civil War and Torrente's assertion does not apply to the writers of the following generation, an observation supported by Juan Goytisolo's discussion of the shortcomings of university education during the 1940s and 1950s.[59]

While fustigated from within by their own mentors, social novelists were also discredited by both conservative critics and younger writers. On the one hand, neorealism was criticized on ideological grounds for being a politicized art, and it is from this position that the proposal of an alleged new novel—with metaphysical, antidocumentary intent—emerged as an alternative in Manuel García Viñó's "Última hora de la novela española" (1965) and *Novela española actual* (1967). On the other hand, emerging young novelists began questioning the literary prestige and authority of the previous generation, a revolt that simultaneously crystallized in 1968 in some of the first critical texts by writers like José María Guelbenzu and Manuel Vázquez Montalbán.[60] In "Literatura, una insoportable soledad" (1968), Guelbenzu criticized social realism for its lack of linguistic imagination, and tried to reclaim the work of Martín-Santos against what he deemed to be the outdated model of Sánchez Ferlosio's *El Jarama*. In the meantime, Vázquez Montalbán undermined the aesthetic positions of the Spanish political left, which seemed unable to come to terms with any sort of cultural production offered outside the constraints of traditional revolutionary ideology: "There is a problem in Spain for a cultural producer who does not renounce the idea of nationalizing the means of production but who flatly refuses to believe that art or literature owe more to Gorky, Visconti, Orozco, or the builder of the Moscow subway, than to Mallarmé, Losey, Miró, or Charles Eames (American armchair designer): that of convincing himself that the two feet of his cultural consciousness do not belong to two separate entities, but to a single one that lends coherence to art and literature's internal logic and to the internal logic of historical dialectics. . . . The cultural avant-garde is being lined up against the avant-garde's political establishment. This divorce could have grave consequences."[61]

The aesthetics of neorealism was again furiously criticized by the most prestigious representative of experimentalism, Juan Benet. His famous debate with the novelist Isaac Montero in 1970 emerged around his notion of a literary art completely independent of social conditions and needs. In "Una época troyana" (1975), Benet concluded that the poetics of neorealism could not be conceived as belonging to the literary realm, thus completing the exorcism of the social novel: "With regard to narrative, if one considers somewhat impartially Spanish literary production from the Civil War up to the present day, it must be recognized that novelists, with very few exceptions, did not attempt to write exclusively literary works. . . . In all of them there was a hidden meaning that, whatever it may have been, had nothing to do with literature. . . . After the Civil War, almost all Spanish novels were Trojan horses."[62]

This indictment of social realism took place within a more comprehensive reevaluation of postwar Spanish literature as a whole that concentrated the critical attention during the late 1960s, as can be seen in the feverish publication of books and journals devoted to the last three decades of cultural life, and it undoubtedly marks a turning point in Spain's literary consciousness.[63] Emerging from the long and disgraceful years of the postwar period, Spain was regaining contact with the modern world, and the general tendency was to break away from any manifestations of that previous era. In this context, it is not surprising that in August 1968, at a conference on the Spanish and Spanish American contemporary novel at the Universidad Menéndez Pelayo, the neorealist writer Daniel Sueiro pronounced an elegy for the Spanish novel as he addressed the relationship between Hispanic letters. Sueiro ended up describing with somber words the condition of both Spanish and European letters ("We can no longer stand this boredom, the boredom of this country, the boredom in all of us"), in striking contrast to his view of Spanish American writing:

> There is something in this torrential phenomenon of the new Latin American novel that makes a particular impression on us Spaniards, and especially on Spanish novelists, by shaking us up and undoubtedly making us think—this powerful and lively new novel, so overwhelming and free, is written using our own means of expression, it is written in our own language. . . . When we read Vargas Llosa, García Márquez, Cortázar, Carlos Fuentes, Cabrera Infante, Rulfo, etc., we simply realize one thing: they are alive, and they write freely about live things. You can see they write without fear, they are not tied; they use a living language, and anything they touch with their words, pen, or voice, throbs with movement and is—I say it once and a thousand times—simply alive.[64]

Barral Editores, founded by Carlos Barral in 1970 after his departure from Seix Barral, was another example of the same displacement of interests. Its first publication was *Un mundo para Julius*, by Peruvian Alfredo Bryce Echenique, and the newly created Barral Prize was awarded for the first time in 1971 to Argentinean Haroldo Conti's *En vida*. Interestingly, the six members who had made up the jury for the Biblioteca Breve 1970 prize (Félix de Azúa, Barral, José María Castellet, Salvador Clotas, Juan García Hortelano, Gabriel García Márquez, and Mario Vargas Llosa) reemerged a year later to decide the newly created Barral Prize.[65] The change, however, did not affect the Latin American connection to the Biblioteca Breve: Guillermo Cabrera Infante and Juan Rulfo were jurors in 1971, together with Juan Ferraté, Pere Gimferrer, Luis Goytisolo, and Jorge Semprún.

Besides the Biblioteca Breve and the Barral, other important literary prizes were awarded to writers from countries other than Spain. The prestigious Critics' Prize (Premio de la Crítica) was twice awarded to Vargas Llosa, in 1964 and 1967, and he was a finalist in 1970. In 1969 there was a heated debate motivated by an unsuccessful attempt to change the regulations for the award—which was expressly intended for texts originally published in Spain—in order to give the prize to García Márquez's *Cien años de soledad*. The Planeta Prize, commercially the most famous in Spain, had two winners from Latin America (Marcos Aguinis for *La cruz invertida* in 1970, and Jesús Zárate in 1972 for *La cárcel*) and two others were considered in the final rounds (Manuel Scorza in 1969, and Hilda Perera in 1972). Sponsored by the publishing house Destino, the Nadal Prize was given to Manuel Mejía Vallejo in 1963 (*El día señalado*), to Eduardo Caballero Calderón in 1965 (*El buen salvaje*) and to Luis Gasulla in 1974 (*Culminación de Montoya*), with Guillermo A. R. Carrizo as the runner-up that same year. The list also includes the Alfaguara Prize given to Carlos Droguett's *Todas esas muertes*, and the Gabriel Miró to José Baidal's *El país del largo viaje*, both in 1971. The presence of Latin American literary figures in Spain's literary system was further extended by a surge of introductory publications devoted to the different Hispanic literatures of America.[66]

The promotion of the Boom Novel in Spain during the 1960s was facilitated by the weakness resulting from the decanonization of the Social Novel—a circumstance that, according to Even-Zohar, is the "main condition for a literature to become dependent."[67] Other poetic models were presented in an open struggle to occupy the central position left vacant by the crisis of social realism—among others, Spanish versions of the French *nouveau roman*, and the self-labeled "Spanish New Novel." In the end, however, the Latin American novel filled that gap. It was fit to take over the cultural space left by the declining social novel as it was the only narrative production that could fulfill the functions of the previous model: it was critically and commercially supported by the same critics and publishers that had been behind the previous model; it became ideologically identified with Cuba, the new revolutionary hero of the decade; and it revitalized the ideal of a commited literature as it

seemed that—aesthetically furnished with an elaborate combination of the heavy weaponry of modernist writing and a playbook
full of popular-culture narrative games—it could go beyond simply
documenting reality and transform our imaginary constructions of
the world. With these credentials, it came to occupy in a few years
a dominant position within Spanish literary life.

3
The Search for Poetic Realism

THE ABUNDANCE OF DEBATES, REVIEWS, DOSSIERS, LITERARY awards, citations, and interviews Latin American novelists elicited in Spain during the Boom years (it is almost impossible to browse the literary pages of a Spanish newspaper or magazine without finding such references) clearly indicates that their works were more than simply available to readers—they were not only readable but also highly *visible*. In this chapter, I will argue that the visibility of Boom novelists and their consequent naturalization took place thanks to an extensive process of evaluation that presented their production as a challenge and alternative to autochthonous forms of fiction. The analysis in the previous chapter of the conditions that made possible the circulation of Latin American literary works in the Spanish market has provided a quantification of the degree of interaction between Hispanic literatures. Literary consumption, however, is not only a matter of quantity, but also—and more importantly—a question of values. Thus, in order to understand how Latin American narratives became an integral element in the transformation of Spanish fiction during the 1960s we need also to analyze the presence they acquired in entering the national literary life.

Literary works are never born or received in an immaculate condition, on the contrary, they are defined by the times and spaces in which they happen to come into open existence. Thus, the public meaning of a literary work does not originate from the text alone, but from "the process of circulation and consumption" in which it becomes implicated.[1] How texts acquire a visible status in any particular environment is a complex process. To date, perhaps the most important study in this area has been Gérard Genette's *Paratexts*, which focuses on the issue of presentation and analyzes the strategies and instruments used by authors and publishers to ensure a certain image to their productions. Since we are concerned here with how Latin American texts and novelists gained visibility for Spanish readers, Genette's notion of paratext has a direct bearing on our project and requires some consideration. Either directly accompanying the text (what Genette defines as the *peritext*: prologues, illustrations) or surrounding it at a distance (the *epitext*: advertising messages, interviews with the author), the paratext (thus, peritext plus epitext) encompasses the means by which a work is publicly presented and constitutes the site where the terms of the contract between work and reader are established:

> a text is rarely presented in an unadorned state, unreinforced and unaccompanied by a certain number of verbal or other productions [that] surround it and extend it, precisely in order to *present* it, in the usual sense of this verb but also in the strongest sense: to *make present*, to ensure the text's presence in the world, its "reception" and consumption in the form (nowadays, at least) of a book. . . . This fringe, always the conveyor of a commentary that is authorial or more or less legitimated by the author, constitutes a zone between the text and the off-text, a zone not only of transition but also of *transaction*: a privileged place of a pragmatics and a strategy, of an influence on the public . . . at the service of a better reception for the text and a more pertinent reading of it.[2]

From the outset, as is clear in this definition, paratextual study is concerned with two closely related but distinct aims, which point respectively to broader and more restricted conceptions of the paratext. The first goal of paratextual study is to analyze how a book is introduced to readers, and emphasis is accordingly placed on the *presence* a text obtains by being exposed and thrust into the world. This presentation, however, is the result of a process that involves a universe of means of acquaintance so variegated that its study risks extending the notion of paratext to cover an almost limitless universe of cultural practices—Genette, for instance, mentions reviews and recommendations as elements that could be conceived of as paratextual in a broader sense. Since such an extended notion of paratext would eventually, according to Genette, render it useless for practical purposes—what he identifies as one of the "methodological hazards" in this area—he resorts to restricting the object of analysis. Thus, the second goal focuses on the study of the reception of a text insofar as this process is designed by the author. Here, emphasis is directed toward *authorial intention* and, consequently,

the paratextual space is limited to those elements that are con-
trolled—or controllable—by the legitimate authorities (in the case
of a book, the author and the publisher). Over the first, presentational function of the paratextual message, a second, strategical one
is imposed to ensure that the text reaches "a destiny consistent with
the author's purpose."[3]

Genette's critical stand could be understood as designed to differentiate between forms of presentation and forms of interpretation—
which in *Palimpsests* were respectively linked to paratextuality and
metatextuality.[4] Metatexts offer commentaries that are by definition
beyond the text, separated from it by virtue of their physical and
ontological character: they not only exist away from the text, but
also aim to establish for it an identity that is independent of authorial and editorial intent—according to certain criteria that are either
personal (the critic's) or collective (agreed upon by the literary establishment or the academia) and, as such, independent in principle
from those proposed by the creator of the text. Paratexts, on the
other hand, necessarily condition the identity bestowed upon the
work before it reaches the reader, and—being normally attached directly to the text (in the same volume)—they cannot be ignored.[5]

In my opinion, Genette's restricted notion of paratext eventually
diverts our attention from the relation between a text and its readers
to that between the text and its author. This shift is made very clear
when Genette confronts the issue of the physical limits of the potential epitext—paratextual elements that are not included in the
same volume as the text. Here, authorial productions (interviews,
diaries) are included in the paratext of a particular work by the mere
fact of originating from its author, even if they might not be directly
related to the text in question: "Everything a writer says or writes
about his life, about the world around him, about the works of others, may have paratextual relevance. . . . The epitext, a fringe of the
fringe, gradually disappears into, among other things, the totality of
authorial discourse."[6] This inclination toward privileging the author
over the text (which we have noted before in reference to literary
historiography) risks distorting the potential of paratextual analysis
for the study of literary pragmatics, as critical attention is centered
on creation (what the author wanted to do) rather than reception
(what the text actually does). Thus, for instance, what Genette calls
factual paratext—"the paratext that consists not of an explicit message (verbal or other) but of a fact whose commentary alone,
known to the public, provides some commentary on the text and

influences how the text is received"—is initially acknowledged but later disregarded on account of its independence from authorial control. Since it would include facts like "the age and sex of the author," the "historical awareness of the period in which a work was written," or "receipt of a literary prize," all of them clearly beyond the domain of the individual author, the factual paratext is eventually left by Genette outside the limits of his book.[7] Seen from the standpoint of creation, as Genette does, any authorial production becomes potentially paratextual, since it might offer valuable insight into the image the author wants to project onto his or her work. Accordingly, most nonauthorial comments on the text have to become by definition metatextual, since they are not direct expressions of the author's intended interpretation of his or her own text (the exception is here the case of commentaries encouraged and approved by the author or the editor of a work). From the standpoint of reception, however, the differentiation between paratext and metatext requires some reconsideration.

Since I am concerned with the task of reconstructing the image of Latin American texts as they were made available to readers in 1960s Spain, I would argue that such a *presence* can only be accounted for by paying attention to two parallel sets of productions: on the one hand, the properly—that is, "official"—paratextual productions that originate from the author and the publisher; on the other, the critical commentaries and reviews imposed upon those novels by Spanish critics. The role of the review as a component in literary reception constitutes an area of study largely ignored by literary criticism, but it would seem logical to agree that it cannot be minimal. After all, most readers first become acquainted with a work not by direct and immediate reading, but through a more or less disparate set of messages (advertisements, reviews, recommendations) that often reach them even before they can actually hold the book itself in their hands. Not all these messages are sanctioned by the author's or the publisher's authority, yet they fulfill a presentational function equivalent to the one attained by the official paratexts, and they may even clash with the authorized image intended by those responsible for circulating the text. To classify—and thus disregard—those introductory messages as metatexts ignores their contribution in articulating a presence for the text. While the function of the metatext is to interpret a work, and as such it assumes the *previous* existence of the text of which it is a commentary, critical reviews do not always fall into that category, since they—as is the case with properly paratextual productions—do not merely point to the existence of the text, but usher it into the world and therefore exist *simultaneously* with their object. Anteriority and simultaneity, it should be noted, are understood here as indicating the connection that can be established between a text and its paratext according to the temporality of reception (when they reach a certain audience), and not in reference to that of original publication—which is the guide used by Genette as he ascertains the various temporal situations available for the authorial paratext (prior, original, later, and delayed paratexts).[8]

The ambiguous status of the review, which occupies a boundary between the introductory paratext and the interpreting metatext, leads us to postulate the existence of what, for lack of a better term, could be called a "critical paratext"—sometimes in agreement, sometimes at odds with the authorial and editorial intentions—which furnishes readers with additional prejudices and provides the necessary conditions for the apperception of the work.[9] The critical paratext creates for the text a presence in the literary world by informing readers about its existence and framing its identity, imposing upon the work the values and norms of the contemporary literary community. Like the (authorized) paratextual prefaces studied by Genette, critical paratexts perform important functions characteristic of other presentational practices: they are intended as a recommendation to read—or a warning not to read—a text, since they are normally addressed to those who have *not read* the text yet. While there are, of course, various kinds of reviews—which may range from a basic presentation (properly paratextual) to more elaborate forms of interpretation (properly metatextual)[10]—I believe they represent an invaluable source for the analysis of the reception, and they are a necessary element to consider in the study of the presentation of Latin American narratives in Spanish literature. Labeling a text a literary masterpiece—awarding it a prize, making it required reading for students—might be as decisive for its reception and presence in the world as having a catchy title or being published in a prestigious series.

The critical paratext will serve as a guide to chart the process of reception of the Latin American Boom in Spain. As a first case study, I will concentrate on the reception of Mario Vargas Llosa's *La ciudad y los perros*, arguably the first Latin American novel to create a major impact in Spain in the 1960s.

Mario Vargas Llosa's *La ciudad y los perros*: The Spanish Paratext

The case of Mario Vargas Llosa and *La ciudad y los perros* is of particular significance for more than one reason: first, the novel was the first Latin American text to captivate a sizable number of critics and readers and become a bestseller in Spain after the Civil War; second, it appeared at a moment of transition in the literary system when the crisis of the dominant model of the 1950s, the social novel, opened the way to a reshuffling of values and codes; and, finally, the author became a central figure in the literary debates of the decade, not only as a prominent novelist, but also as a critic of contemporary fiction. The history of its reception is truly exemplary: on the one hand, it serves to illustrate the process of naturalization of Latin American literature that took place during the Boom in Spain; on the other, it can be seen as a prototype of that same process, since the paratextual activity it generated became a model that would be repeatedly imitated. In what follows I will first trace the history of Vargas Llosa's text in Spain in order to map the different coordinates of its impact on the contemporary literary field.

The publication of *La ciudad y los perros*, following the award of the 1962 Biblioteca Breve Prize, is traditionally considered the moment of introduction of Mario Vargas Llosa to the Spanish public. The prize, however, was not the first recognition the Peruvian writer would receive in Spain, since a few years earlier, in 1959, he had obtained the Leopoldo Alas Prize for his collection of short stories *Los jefes*.[11] This earlier award went largely unnoticed, a fact possibly due to the combination of several factors: the brief history of the prize itself, which was created in 1956; a traditionally lower status of the short story within the hierarchy of genres, as opposed to the novel; the limited distribution of the volume by a minor publisher (Editorial Rocas, of Barcelona); and the overall condition of the literary market, which had not yet seen the expansion of the early sixties. In fact, the first edition of *Los jefes* (published in July 1959) was practically unavailable in Spain and became something of a bibliographical rarity until 1971, when a second Spanish edition was issued by Barral Editores.[12] Vargas Llosa was the first non-Spanish writer to win the Leopoldo Alas prize, a fact that was emphasized by Juan Planas Cerdá in his prologue to the first edition of

Los jefes: "The book awarded the prize by the 'Leopoldo Alas' jury
. . . has the fundamental and, among the literary prizes awarded in
our nation, unheard of characteristic of being a book arriving from
the Other World. But there is more: it is not simply a book coming
from South America, but a book made, lived, and clearly inscribed
in that unique and unfamiliar world that is Spanish America."[13]

Los jefes, contrary to Planas's claim, was not the first literary
work from Spanish America ever to be awarded a literary prize in
Spain—Rómulo Gallegos's *Doña Bárbara*, for instance, had been
declared best novel of the year in 1929[14]—but it certainly was, at
least to my knowledge, the first one to do so after the Civil War.
For Planas, the book was important not only in itself, but also as
representative of a world hitherto unexplored that could offer new
blood to the exhausted culture of the Western world (*la antigua y
cansada cultura occidental*)—and particularly to Spanish literature.[15] Given these credentials, and notwithstanding the circumstances outlined above, it may still seem surprising that *Los jefes*
did not elicit much response when first published—specially if we
consider that, as we shall see, four years later *La ciudad y los perros*
would be introduced by similar arguments about the exhaustion of
contemporary Spanish letters. The answer lies, I believe, in the dramatic changes that overturned the condition of Spanish letters between the late 1950s and the early 1960s: if Planas's warning about
the debilitation of national fiction and the renovating contribution
of Latin American narrative did not find an audience in 1959, a few
years later it was already a commonplace of contemporary criticism.

There is an enormous disparity between the fate of *Los jefes* and
that of *La ciudad y los perros*. The outcome of the 1962 Biblioteca
Breve Prize was doubly original: it was the first time that the
prize—arguably the decade's most influential literary award as far
as aesthetic prestige is concerned—was awarded to a non-Spaniard,
and—as was swiftly announced in the press—it was also the first
time that the jury had voted unanimously. After that, the prize
clearly tilted toward the promotion of Latin American narrative,
with which it became openly associated.[16] Vargas Llosa's novel became the wedge that opened the new Latin American literary world
for readers in Spain, and its impact on Spanish narrative can be
gauged by the exceptional recognition it received by the literary establishment. *La ciudad y los perros* also received the Critics' Prize
in 1964, an award which, since it was presumably decided aside

from the commercial interests of publishing houses and had no monetary value, was generally considered to offer an independent and impartial judgment on contemporary fiction. Vargas Llosa's second novel, *La casa verde*, won the prize in 1967; his third, *Conversación en la Catedral*, was a finalist in 1970.[17] The novelist also played a very important role as a critic: in 1965 he became a permanent member of the jury for the Biblioteca Breve Prize, a position he occupied until 1970, when the breakup of Carlos Barral with the publishing house led to the creation of the Barral Prize (1971–1974), for which he also served as juror.[18]

In the case of *La ciudad y los perros*, the editorial paratext of the first edition provides a privileged insight into the reception the publishers wanted to secure for the work. One of the first public editorial communications about the novel appears to have been cunningly intended to whet the literary appetite of readers: "Carta de Seix Barral a los lectores de *Destino*" appeared in the weekly *Destino* on 6 April 1963 as an advertisement of the publisher's most recent books. As if responding to the reader's curiosity about Vargas Llosa's novel, which remained unpublished, the note proclaimed that as winner of the Biblioteca Breve *La ciudad y los perros* (here still referred to as *Los impostores*) would be submitted to the Prix Formentor, which required that the publication of the novel be delayed until the verdict.[19]

When it was finally published in October 1963, after some skirmishing with Spanish censorship, the novel was escorted by an editorial insert, included in at least the first two printings issued in 1963 and discarded in later editions (it has not been reprinted since). It consists of two parts. The first offers a brief biographical note about Vargas Llosa, along with information about the award of the 1962 Biblioteca Breve Prize—some statistical data about the manuscripts submitted for consideration (eighty-one in total, thirty from Latin America), noting particularly the unanimous vote of the jury—and the submission to the Prix Formentor. The second and more interesting element is what ought to be considered the very first critical commentary on the novel (fulfilling the functions of an original preface), written by one of the members of the jury.[20] "Juicio del Dr. José María Valverde" draws the lines of contemporary literary expectations as Valverde carefully threads his argument through the assumptions of two distinct and even opposite audiences: the conservative censors of the Francoist state, whose job was to prevent the printing of "subversive" literature, and the leftish readers of Seix Barral, who had been educated by the publisher to appreciate engagé literature of the social realist mold.[21]

The first and obvious function of Valverde's preface—as Valverde himself noted years later—was to provide the novel with a sort of endorsement by a "respectable" university professor.[22] Given the novel's ferocious criticism of a military institution—the Leoncio Prado school—the publishers feared that it could be perceived as too scandalous and controversial in Franco's Spain, and it was therefore necessary to justify its value in order to shield it from censorship. Consequently, "Juicio del Dr. José María Valverde" opens with tactful or, as Valverde put it, "diplomatic" considerations on the meaning of the novel, which is presented—detached from any political or social contention—as a "moral unveiling" of adolescence. The message of *La ciudad y los perros* would thus seem to be the ahistorical manifestation of an anthropological truth: "its essential theme is the critique of mankind, individual by individual, in most cases considered as it exists underneath society's own institutions." A difference is also posited between the fictive and the real in order to disarm any significant connection between the two orders: "one would have to guard against the mistake of judging fictitious characters as real ones, whether or not they are representative of their social groups" (vi–vii). If the novel was to pass censorship, it had to be set apart from the kind of testimonial literature that was rightly seen as an attack against Franco's regime and was expected to objectively portray historical instances of human interaction. Thus, it is no coincidence that Valverde's thematic characterization of *La ciudad y los perros* is almost the negative image of the model of committed literature: instead of a concretely historical and political message, it was said to contain an abstract morality play. It was clearly a camouflaging maneuver aimed at facilitating the publication in Spain of a text that Spanish censors would have not accepted coming from a native author—as Juan Goytisolo stated a few years later, "had Vargas Llosa been a Spaniard, *La ciudad y los perros* would have had to be published in Lima."[23]

This strategy may have been successful with Francoist censors, but it seems to have failed to convince Valverde's own camp. The insert of the first edition also includes a photograph of the military school in Lima—with the following caption: "Entry to the Leoncio Prado Military School, where the action of the novel takes place"— and in the second printing, apparently replacing the photograph, there is a map of Lima that highlights the location of the school.

This paratextual disparity between the words in the preface and the images of the school and Lima printed in the original insert shows that the publishers were playing two cards at the same time: while verbally denying the connection between the content of the novel and the reality depicted and emphasizing the moral quality of the text to placate censors, they were at the same time iconically encouraging other readers to establish that same connection—thus guiding the understanding of the text in reference to the parameters of social realism.

The second function of the "Juicio" is no longer aimed to contain ideological suspicions, but rather to instruct the Spanish reader not to confuse Vargas Llosa's novel with current, national forms of writing. *La ciudad y los perros*, Valverde argues, is indeed a *different* kind of fiction. At a time of generalized skepticism in Spain toward the possibilities of the novelistic genre—which, according to Valverde, was "deceased" (*difunto*)—and with its most prominent paradigm being in critical condition, Valverde claims that *La ciudad y los perros* offers signs of a new literary practice characterized by two essential features: narrative power and linguistic lyricism. Technique and intrigue are skillfully combined to provide a "classical" literary experience: "Vargas Llosa [is] capable of incorporating every experience of the 'vanguard' novel into a 'classical' sense of the tale—'classical' in the two basic points of the art of fiction: 1) it must recount a profound experience that will move us when we imaginatively experience it; and 2) it must recount it artfully, . . . skillfully, in order to daze and sweep the reader along towards the denouement" (vii).

But the use of language in the novel, argues Valverde, manages to generate as well a lyrical sense: "it is a 'poetic' novel, where the understanding of narrative prose now common among Spanish Americans—fortunately for them—reaches its high point. Every word, every sentence, is pronounced and heard as in a poem" (vii). Genre characterization, as Genette has noted, is one common function of original prefaces as they aim to guide the reading and interpretation of a new text, and it is bound to appear in periods of transition and friction between canonized and innovative literary norms.[24] Valverde's concern with describing *La ciudad y los perros* as both a "poetic novel" (as opposed, we are led to assume, to other somehow antipoetic forms of fiction) *and* a representative of a Latin American conception of narrative (for which, we are told, they— that is, Latin American readers—are fortunate) appears clearly informed by dissatisfaction with Spanish narrative.[25] Valverde's words openly exposed this void in the national literary offer and—as Planas Cerdá had done four years earlier—instructed Spanish readers to find the answer to their aesthetic dissatisfaction in Latin America. He was bold enough to risk his judgment and reputation as a critic by comparing *La ciudad y los perros* to Joyce's *Ulysses* in the concluding remarks of his "Juicio": "When it was awarded—by rare unanimous vote—the 1962 Biblioteca Breve Prize, I told a journalist, 'This is the best novel written in Spanish since *Don Segundo Sombra*.' . . . I repeat it now, with a cool head, saying—as J. Middleton Murry did when he recognized a masterpiece in Joyce's *Ulysses*—: 'Let's say it clearly, so we can have our piece of contempt or glory in a hundred years' " (viii).

Valverde was not the only one to invest literary capital and prestige in backing Vargas Llosa's novel. In fact, the increasing significance the publication of the novel was to gain over the years has opened the ground to a debate around its "discovery" at the publishing house. In a 1970 interview, Carlos Barral claimed to have discovered the novel when his curiosity was piqued by a favorable "but unenthusiastic" report presented by one of the members of the reading committee at Seix Barral (he does not reveal the reader's name). Barral decided to read the manuscript himself, which provoked in him "an unbridled enthusiasm" as it was, he then declared, "the most important manuscript I had ever seen."[26] Curiously enough, the same interviewers got a second version from writer Luis Goytisolo—one of the readers in charge of selecting original manuscripts for Seix Barral in the early 1960s—who credited himself with championing Vargas Llosa's novel in the first place: "I know that more than one person claims credit for discovering *La ciudad y los perros*, but the truth is that the discovery is mine, or rather, my wife's. I was a reader for Seix Barral at that time, receiving loads of manuscripts that I would as a matter of course pass on to my wife. . . . Well, the book immediately caught her attention, she handed it to me, and I liked it, and I told Barral that we could propose that it be presented for the Biblioteca Breve Prize because it was of high quality."[27] There is even a third version advanced by J. J. Armas Marcelo—allegedly supported with direct testimonies from both Carlos Barral and Vargas Llosa—who claims that it was Barral who discovered the manuscript in the basement of the publishing house, "buried" there along with all those dismissed by unfavorable reports of the readers. The reader responsible for the temporary rejection would have been none other than Luis Goytisolo himself.[28] Whether we should subscribe to one version or the other is not important here, particularly because they remain unsubstantiated beyond their own advocates' word. Yet the most revealing aspect of this debate is the fact that there is one in the first place, and that it creates a pattern. As we shall see, the discovery of Latin American narrative became a hot topic in the following years, as various Spanish writers and critics claimed to have been familiar with Latin American writing and its authors well before the Boom. The important thing here is not, then, who read them first, but who had the ability to understand its consequences for Spanish fiction—a distinction between those who were devoted to traditional and outdated forms of fiction (the *exhausted* literature noted by Planas Cerdá and Valverde) and those who were looking into the future of literature.

It has been argued that Vargas Llosa's novel owed its success to its load of "sex and violence" or its "exotic ingredients."[29] Certainly—as Valverde pointed out—there were no military schools like the Leoncio Prado in Spain. However, although some of the elements in the text like the portrayal of race relationships in Lima or the use of *americanismos* could indeed present a novelty to the Spanish reader, the main thematic focus of the novel—the degraded culture of a military school and the subordination of truth to order—was far from being something exotic in Franco's Spain (which is precisely why the original preface had to play down the similarities between fiction and reality). In fact, reading Valverde's preface, one has to suspect some degree of irony is contained behind his characterization of the school as "an unusual environment . . . organized by the military and under military discipline" (vi).

I would contend that the success of *La ciudad y los perros* in 1960s Spain rests not in its exoticism but rather in both its similarity and its difference with the then still dominant but crumbling model of the social novel, what could perhaps be expressed by describing the text as a *poetic social novel*. On the one hand, the content of criticism and denunciation—much more relevant to the text than Valverde's diplomacy revealed—put it in close relation to the attempts of contemporary social realist writers in Spain. But, on the other, the careful attention it devoted to language and form—evident in the shifting focalization and voices, the contrapuntal interweaving of temporal and spatial perspectives—posed a new challenge and expanded the boundaries of the genre as it was then

practiced. Such was the effect the novel had on the younger generation of writers, according to fellow member Javier Alfaya: "*La ciudad y los perros* had, among others, the tremendous merit of acting
as the first revulsive on the frail scene of our fictional literature. We
discovered that good writing was not an aristocratic luxury, that one
could stir up the anger of the 'establishment' without having to
write in a flat and underdeveloped style."[30] Thus, the editorial paratext of *La ciudad y los perros* marks a transitional moment in the
development of Spanish narrative and accurately defines the two essential coordinates for the triumph of Latin American novels in
Spain—imaginative storytelling and creative language—that were
to break with the stagnant and familiarized conventions of social
realism. But, as the paratextual disparity indicated above clearly
shows, the novel succeeded not by displacing the dominant model
of social realism, but rather by opening a way to improve it. It was
because readers of *La ciudad y los perros* could approach the text
as if it were a social novel that it lent itself to appropriation within
a field still defined by the values of that canon. At the same time, it
was because the novel departed from some of those dominant conventions that it could be perceived as something *original*.

If we turn our attention to the critical paratext of *La ciudad y los
perros* we find confirmation that Valverde had wagered in the right
direction. Early reviews of the novel pointed to the realist content
of the story—often noting the harshness of the depicted events—
but they were also careful to point to the distinguishing quality of
its representation. Following Valverde, reviewers consistently described that quality as poetic, and they did so explicitly in order to
warn against confusing Vargas Llosa's style with the *normal* (supposedly "nonpoetic") variety of realism:

> Everything happens in a private school, what here we would call a
> boarding-school. . . . Readers who are warned about these things as-
> sume, to begin with, that the subject lies somewhere in between a realist
> view and the putting down on paper of a personal experience. They are
> not exactly mistaken, but they run the risk of accepting a very limited
> reading. There is indeed realism in the novel, even the sort of realism
> that has nothing to hide and is not concerned with risqué language,
> slang, or the difficult coexistence with the obscene or the scatological.
> There is something, and it is necessary to make it clear from the begin-
> ning, that even in this elementary consideration demonstrates the quality
> of the novel: *something mitigates, surrounds, sublimates this realism,*

the coarse dialogue, the dirty or taboo quality of some scenes. We shall need to speak of poetry.[31]

What a nonpoetic realism looks like is not always explicitly stated, but it should not have been difficult for contemporary readers to identify the target of criticism (in fact, it did not take too long for some critics to discredit Spanish social realist novelists as "the cabbage generation"). The norm successfully transcended by Vargas Llosa is the poetics of social realism, in which narrative and language were restricted to mere functionality in order to accommodate a documentary goal according to which it was considered enough simply to *name* reality—since, according to Fernando Morán's rendering of the referential principle of neorealist poetics, "reality was not elusive; it was perhaps covered."[32] While *La ciudad y los perros* contains both "testimony and denunciation," Campos significantly notes, they do not constitute simply a "report," because Vargas Llosa is not interested in presenting "facts seen from the outside with documentary objectivity." Language is used not simply as a mechanical tool to transfer reality from the outside world to the printed page, but rather as a way of conferring meaning beyond the particularity of the depicted events; thus, Vargas Llosa achieves what another critic called a "perfect realism of language" that "deepens" reality without reproducing it.[33] It is precisely because of this transcendent value that the autobiographical content of the story becomes secondary to these critics: "I don't know what there is of direct experience—if there is any—in each of these two novels," argues another reviewer, "but the observation of life, people and environments, of their intrinsic relationships, their analyses and the power of purely novelistic elements, they are all indeed direct and authentic."[34] Perhaps the clearest reading of *La ciudad y los perros* as a rebuttal of social realism is found in José Batlló's assessment of the novel:

We are not concerned here with the author's position, which is never given an overwhelming presence . . . but rather with a transfigured reality endowed with a basic primitive power, which is gained by having total control over the word. This, then, is not an objective novel, as someone has suggested; on the contrary. . . . It goes well beyond the realm of aseptic and dry critical realism, which usually leads only to a dead end and—although it might have seemed useful and advisable at one time—which has been completely superseded and should be avoided. Vargas Llosa bursts onto the scene with a vitality, youth, and vigor rarely seen in the area of narrative, which thanks to this rejuvenating blood denies its supposedly decaying and impoverished condition.[35]

The notion that Spanish fiction was in crisis was anything but new in 1963, as we have seen in Planas Cerdá's prologue to *Los jefes*. In fact, there was a generalized conviction that the novel itself was a form on the verge of extinction, not only in Spain but also all over the Western world, where the focus of criticism was the practices of a waning modernism. The never-ending debate about "the death of the novel" was being carried with special virulence, and symptoms of discontent could be detected everywhere: conferences and monographic issues in specialized journals were full of essays and manifestos declaring the demise of Western literature.[36] In Spain, however, the debate took a peculiar form, since the dichotomy was not conceived in terms of high and low art, but as a rupture between art and politics. It had been precisely the pairing of politics and aesthetics that provided writers of the so-called Generation of 1950 with the cultural and ideological capital necessary to dominate Spanish cultural life since the mid-1950s until 1962. The production of social realist novelists has been extensively documented in various studies.[37] What has remained less explored are the parallels between the concerns of those novelists, particularly as they tried to develop their literary practice and overcome its limitations, and those of the new generation of Latin American writers, some of whom also came from a strong tradition of realistic writing. In the case of Spain, we need to trace how the social novel became one of the dominant models in the Spanish literary system, in order to better understand how its eventual displacement from that privileged position paved the way for the success of the new Latin American fictions.

FROM SOCIAL TO POETIC REALISM

The social novel made its formal official appearance as a literary movement in the mid-fifties, heralded by two manifestos: Juan Goytisolo's "Problemas de la novela" (1956) and Castellet's *La hora del lector* (1957). Goytisolo's essay—later included in a 1959 volume with that same title—argued against contemporary criticisms of three of the most influential novels of the decade: Camilo José Cela's *La colmena* (1951), Jesús Fernández Santos's *Los bra-*

vos (1954), and Rafael Sánchez Ferlosio's *El Jarama* (1956). What had been perceived as two shortcomings of those texts—scarcity of ideas and absence of psychological analysis—were for Goytisolo the characteristics of a new form of narrating where the direct presentation of life's material conditions and of human behavior substituted for narratorial digression and mental introspection. Psychological analysis is portrayed here as the epitome of bourgeois leisure, a reflection of a well-to-do social class with enough time to worry about "delicate problems of the soul."[38] In a clear attack to Ortega y Gasset's understanding of the novelistic genre, Goytisolo declares that it is in the realm of objective—that is, external—human interaction, not in the production of "imaginary psychologies" (as Ortega had proposed in "Ideas sobre la novela"), that the true material of the novel is to be found. According to Goytisolo, Ortega's ideas would be responsible for the literary divorce of writer and public in the contemporary Spanish novel.[39] Choice of novelistic technique is closely associated with social positionings: "The use of the psychological or analytical method implies . . . the requirement to deal with characters who, due to their privileged cultural and economic condition, have the ability, time, and material means to observe themselves. Because of this, virtually all of the novels published in Spain during the last thirty years are concerned with only a select minority—upper and middle class—and disregard because of technical weaknesses those other, less favored sectors of society, the discovery of which constitutes the fundamental merit of works like *El Jarama*, *Los bravos*, or *La colmena*."[40] The models for this new Spanish novel were to be found in the behaviorism of the North American novel (Dos Passos) and in the Spanish tradition of the picaresque novel, which provided postwar novelists with a model of realism fit to comply with the demands of social criticism. In "La Picaresca, ejemplo nacional" and "La herencia de la Picaresca"—both from 1957—Goytisolo defined the essence of that genre as the perfect alliance of observation and denunciation.[41]

Similar ideas were presented in a more elaborate manner by Josep Maria Castellet in *La hora del lector*. Castellet's book focused on the two main topics that would frame the literary debate in Spain for almost a decade: the social and ethical responsibility of the author and the question of the artistic technique appropriate for a critical portrait of human reality. The social commitment of artists was required as the only way to regain the critical position lost to the "social betrayal" of nineteenth-century novelists:

> The nineteenth century was, for the writer, the era of individual triumph—but also of social betrayal. And, sooner or later, all treason has to be paid for. If nineteenth-century novelists had bothered to heed the meaning of some prophetic voices rising around them, they could have at least contributed to the progress of ideas that were eventually going to prevail. . . . It would have been enough for them to give a certain content to their works and to make public their separation from the dominant bourgeoisie, and thus join the ranks of those banned from society (where they belonged firstly and in their own right), of the oppressed (workers, women, blacks, etc.), and finally of all those who would have supported them in building a more just world. Nineteenth-century novelists leaned toward the bourgeoisie, toward order and injustice—and in doing so, their days were numbered.[42]

The most striking feature of Castellet's statement is perhaps the crusading tone social realism was to adopt thereafter. The contemporary culture of insurgence against Franco's dictatorship was permeated by a similar sense of historical justice—the imminence of a radical reversal of the political situation was signaled by the myth of the ultimate General Strike. For Castellet, the time had come for those on the co-opted side of literature to pay for the outcome of the Civil War. This was the wishful thinking that sustained most of the literary production of the social realists, a "performative illusion" that would finally crash against the cultural transformations of Spanish society.[43]

The artistic counterpart of that social engagement was described as a new objectivity in which the textually personalized authority of the writer—the omniscient narrator, perceived as a remnant of the nineteenth-century realist commitment to the bourgeois social order—would be replaced by an anonymous cinematographic camera: "The new way of fictionalizing consists of narrating stories with the same objectivity that a cinematographic camera would, that is to say, *by faithfully reproducing*—without adding the least bit of commentary or attempting any analysis that might show the presence of a subjectivity separated from the world in which the story develops—*that which is pure exteriorization of a human behavior in a given situation.*"[44] The authorial voice was then to disappear, its subjective presence displaced by the solidity of objectified reality. Narrators would be given the task of reproducing material images and presenting the reader with the textual correlate of cinematographic representation. The inspiration for this sort of objectivism was provided by the *nouveau roman*, but the potential association of the social novel with the French movement—which was viewed as the representative of the contemporary avant-garde in European letters—was rapidly denied by their profound philosophical differences.

Those differences were openly exposed in an international conference on "Realism and Reality in Contemporary Literature," which took place in Madrid in October 1963—at exactly the same time as *La ciudad y los perros* was first published in Spain. The event, sponsored by UNESCO and the French Institute, assembled a large group of writers and critics to debate what was then the most important topic concerning the practice of novelistic writing in Spain, and—in the opinion of Castellet—it marked the end of social realism as the hegemonic aesthetic model in Spain.[45] According to several reports, the discussions among the participants clearly showed deep differences of opinion between Spanish and Western European writers: on the one hand, those who defended a socially committed literary realism and, on the other, supporters of a literary practice unrestricted by political considerations.[46]

Martín-Santos, who was present at the debates, identified the basis for the disagreement between European and Spanish writers as a matter of disparate social environments: while the former enjoyed political and intellectual freedom that allowed for "ideological nihilism" and "formal refinement," the latter had to deal with the oppressive conditions of Franco's dictatorship:

Spanish writers find it difficult to understand that Chiaromonte is a leftist. When Chiaromonte says the novel has finished its legitimate cycle and that it is no longer possible to write novels except with a certain degree of intellectual hypocrisy, Spanish writers hear something akin to blasphemy. Because the fact is that nowadays the only weapon Spanish writers can count on to modify an unbearable reality is precisely that of writing novels that are sufficiently adept to pass through the censors, or sufficiently real to engage the reader politically. . . . When Mme. Sarraute speaks of the invisible reality writers should bring to light with their creative effort, many Spanish novelists think the reality they need to change is visible, very visible. Under such conditions, dialogue had to be difficult. Not only are previous suppositions and tacitly accepted intentions completely different, but so is the situation in which such positions arise.[47]

The conflict, then, was not between aesthetic freedom and ideological dogmatism, but "between free people and those desperately seeking freedom."[48] What is highly significant in Martín-Santos's account is that instead of writing an arraignment of social realism—which could be reasonably expected from the author considered to have put an end to the movement—he set out to defend it, albeit critically. He explicitly mentioned the dogmatism and naiveté of national novelists, but presented it as a necessary evil, not so much the result of some sort of literary immaturity, but rather the product of national sociopolitical deficiencies. Between the outdated realism of Spanish writing and the antinovelistic proposals of Chiaromonte and Sarraute, Martín-Santos envisioned a third way, defined by both the internal requirements of literary art and the external demands of Spain's historical situation: "One should assume that the Madrid meeting won't be useless. The impact on young Spanish novelists will be indicative of a change, not as its sole cause but correlated with those accelerated social and economic transformations in progress, and with the progressive maturing of the Iberian intelligentsia. This change will come about through the effective arrival of a new generation of writers whose technical and aesthetic ability begins to rise to the level of their European counterparts, though in the foreseeable future their intentional direction will continue to be different."[49]

This third way is that of a literature that still attempts a transformation of the social order, but does so with the technical tools of a new dialectical writing. As Martín-Santos declared to Castellet, literature has a double functionality: description of a social reality and creation of new social mythologies.[50] Such an artistic program for a new realism—what has been termed "dialectical realism"—demanded a literary practice technically and aesthetically comparable to that of modern European models but intentionally different from them, and has certain parallels to the program for the Latin American new novel as outlined in 1969 by Carlos Fuentes in *La nueva novela hispanoamericana*: a new literature built on the language of myth and the structural refurbishment of traditional narratives. In fact, we could argue, while Fuentes was right to include Spaniard Juan Goytisolo together with the group of Spanish American writers representing a "new novel," one of the most surprising aspects of his study is precisely the absence of Martín-Santos in the roll call of new Hispanic writing.[51] This was the poetic model that, participating in both the testimonial and the poematic trends, occupied a central—although unstable—position in Spain's literary field during the 1960s.[52] It is important to note here that criticism of the *nouveau roman* and its objectivism was not exclusive of the aesthetic creed of Spanish social realism, but is also present in the writings of Latin American writers. Vargas Llosa, Ernesto Sábato, and Mario Benedetti, for instance, were simultaneously questioning the French poetic model in 1963.[53] (We will return later to the reception of the French new novel in Spain.)

It is revealing in this context to consider the parallels betwen *La ciudad y los perros* and Luis Martín-Santos's *Tiempo de silencio* (1962), which is probably the most canonized Spanish text of the decade. It is commonly accepted that the two building blocks of social realism (a quasi-naturalistic mimesis in danger of anachronization and a language loyal to the real but lacking imaginative power) would receive a ferocious and definite blow with Martín-Santos's novel. As we have seen, the early reception of *La ciudad y los perros* shows that Vargas Llosa entered the Spanish literary field on similar terms. Both novels were perceived as exhibiting the shortcomings of the social novel without surrendering the artistic scrutiny of society. Regardless of important differences in their respective poetic models, Martín-Santos and Vargas Llosa can both be seen as designating and standing at the threshold of that change of perspective, setting the structural requirements for the future paradigm while at the same time honoring the thematic demands of the former one. On the one hand, they problematize the direct representation of their object, so that the discontinuity of the historical world is conveyed through the discontinuity of the narrating itself: as indicated by Sobejano's analysis, testimonial objectivism gives way here to creative subjectivism. On the other hand, they do so without failing to account for a world of social conflict systematically denied by ideological powers: in the Leoncio Prado school, crime goes unpunished in order to preserve the appearance of social harmony supported by the military structure; in the Madrid of Martín-Santos, medical research and philosophical discourse go undisturbed by the social inequities of the shantytown, whose existence they refuse to admit but nevertheless require for their scientific progress and economic privileges. Ultimately, both writers showed the possibility of creating a political novel that was, at the same time, a work of art; they proved, as Spanish writer Caballero Bonald declared in 1971 in reference to Vargas Llosa's *Con-*

versación en la Catedral, that "the social effectiveness of literature depends on its artistic effectiveness."[54]

It is somewhat surprising that, given the similarities between those two authors and their novels, the paratextual evidence we can gather would point in different directions. Compared to the editorial support granted to Vargas Llosa in 1963, *Tiempo de silencio* was left to fend for itself. Martín-Santos's novel was published in 1962 by the same press, Seix Barral, but it does not appear to have elicited the same degree of editorial apparatus even though, according to Carlos Barral himself, its weight and literary ambition were unsurpassed by any other Spanish novel of the postwar period.[55] The difference of treatment did not go unnoticed to Mario Benedetti, who in 1964 expressed surprise at the fact that Valverde's eulogy of *La ciudad y los perros* as poetic novel had not been also used to describe *Tiempo de silencio*: "the Spanish critic had in his very own country a novelist like Luis Martín-Santos, who was able to understand narrative prose in the same way [as Vargas Llosa]."[56]

The issue here is not whether *La ciudad y los perros* was more successful or influential than *Tiempo de silencio*, but why the presentation of the novels was so different. In the absence of a better answer, I would like to suggest three possible explanations. The first takes us back to the economy of publishing and has to do with the previously discussed growth of literary production in Spain and expansion of the Latin American market. While the reading of novels, as attested by various protagonists of the period, was in the decline in the Iberian peninsula, Spanish publishers—and particularly Seix Barral—turned their attention and investments to products oriented to the newly discovered transatlantic readership. It seemed appropriate that any attempt to establish a stronghold in Latin American market had to give prominence to Latin American writing. A second explanation, which is obviously concurrent with the first, lies in the specific condition of Spanish cultural life: the Latin American origin of the novel and its author provided an added value also within the national sphere, since the culture and ideological climate of the period would confer on the southern continent an aura of excitement; being Latin American, as we will see later, was an asset at a time when being Spanish was synonymous of aesthetic impoverishment and political stagnation. The third is biographical: the sudden disappearance of Martín-Santos, who died in a car accident in January 1964, precluded his direct participation in the debate about the renewal of social realism as it was carried out in the literary environment (journals, newspapers, conferences) after his novel began to be critically acclaimed. As Carlos Barral noted in comparing the condition of the Spanish novel and the Boom novel in 1971, "the truth is that, apart from mistakes in their poetics, none of the Spanish writers of the same generation has the stature, for now, of the four or five leaders of the Latin American generation, with the exception perhaps of the late Martín-Santos—who, *since he is dead, doesn't count.*"[57] In this context, I would like to advance the hypothesis that the death of Martín-Santos created a void that was partly filled by Vargas Llosa, who would thus become a central figure in the movement to attempt a balance between social and artistic commitment. In fact, as José María Guelbenzu argued in 1968, it was the Latin American Boom that prompted his own generation of young novelists to see in Martín-Santos a "launchpad" for their program of literary renovation.[58]

The impact of Vargas Llosa's writing in Spain, I would argue, hinges on its ability to offer to Spanish readers the possibility of a new reconciliation of social and aesthetic interests. Such a double concern for social criticism *and* aesthetic awareness marks a middle point in the gradual transformation from the 1950s model of social realism into the 1960s surge of experimental writing. During this period, Vargas Llosa emerged as a model for those who wished to keep the faith of a literature committed to social reality while finding new ways of artistically expressing its complexities. As a critic put it in 1966, the only novels to escape from the "depressive" condition of the Spanish novel were those that were able to offer a "lofty and dignified narrative" together with "sociological and political interest." It was still realism, but it was presented and welcomed as a new form of realism, or—as the title of a published dialogue with Vargas Llosa emphatically proclaimed—a "realism without limits."[59]

The singularity of the presence granted to Vargas Llosa's novel can perhaps be best grasped when put into contrast to other Latin American novels that followed a similar path into Spanish literature but did not get quite the same reception. I will consider here *El día señalado*, by Colombian writer Manuel Mejía Vallejo, which won the prestigious Nadal Prize in 1964. As had been the case with Vargas Llosa and the Biblioteca Breve a year earlier, Mejía Vallejo was the first Latin American writer to win the Nadal.[60] There is no question that *El día señalado* became another important step in the emergence of Latin American writing in Spain. In fact, the critical and editorial paratexts of both *La ciudad y los perros* and *El día señalado* were similarly mapping the literary field in order to create a space for the new Latin American narratives. In the public introduction of Mejía Vallejo's novel we find at work the same strategy Seix Barral used for the presentation of *La ciudad y los perros*: the association and contrast with the dominant mode of realistic writing. Both *La ciudad y los perros* and *El día señalado* were jointly reviewed as examples of the "hard lesson" Spanish novelists had to learn from their Latin American colleagues.[61] Another review showed its satisfaction with the "growing permeability between the literary *Españas*" across the Atlantic.[62] And it was even claimed that the meaning of the concept "Spanish novel," for which the Nadal Prize was supposed to provide a representative sample, could no longer be restricted to the national production: "instead of 'Spanish novel,' we should begin to speak of 'novel in the Spanish language.' "[63]

The paratextual evidence concerning *El día señalado*, however, shows a divided opinion on the novel. Novels awarded with the Nadal Prize, published by Ediciones Destino, used to be printed with very limited editorial paratexts: they did not include a prologue and were usually restricted to a brief informative note on the author and the text, a list of previous winners of the prize (both printed in the inside of the jacket), and the indication of the series (Áncora y Delfín). That seems to have been the case with Mejía Vallejo's novel, although I have been unable to find a copy of the original jacket. Yet the lack of much editorial commentary on the novel is only illusory. In contrast with other publishing houses, Ediciones Destino had its own weekly magazine (*Destino*), which would publicize the yearly deliberations of the jury and the ceremony of the prize; it was in its pages that novelists were interviewed and introduced to the public, and the novels were extensively reviewed—in other words, we should regard *Destino* as the proper editorial paratext for all the Nadal novels.[64] Moreover, in the particular case of *El día señalado*, there were members of the jury—Juan Ramón Masoliver and Antonio Vilanova—who also penned reviews of the novel in the Spanish press which can legitimately be read as expressions of a public positioning of the jury of the Nadal Prize and, by extension, as part of the editorial paratext. Masoliver's "Y ahora, el público" was, as its title explicitly indicated, intended to raise the readers' interest in the novel, and it appeared as the first edition of the novel (published in February 1964) hit the bookstores.[65] The review represents a clear effort to frame and ensure a proper reception for the text, and the main lines of this presentation of the novel are already familiar to us: *El día señalado*, according to Masoliver, represented a breath of "fresh air for our [that is, Spanish] novel" because of skillful combination of realism and poetry. Realism in this novel is, as we can expect, of a special sort, which Masoliver very tellingly described as "realism without tricks" (*realismo sin trampa*)—"avoiding both affected *costumbrismo* and discourses of protest or moralizing allegories." At the same time, the critic also mentioned the "linguistic consciousness" and the "poetic aura" of the novel, which according to him were features inescapable to all readers at the Nadal Prize: "everyone insisted on the poetic, merciful aura that envelops the story, and on the poetic mode threading together these pages: the memories and iridescence of the characters; the nature, assembly and counterpoint of episodes; and the disposition of paragraphs, words and sentences, which is far from a simple or sickening musicality."

Masoliver, however, was also careful to note another important development which clearly points to the increasingly conscious displacement taking place in Spanish letters: as the Spanish social novel was in decline, its central position in the literary field was being taken over by the new (or, at least, what from Spain's point of view was perceived as such) Latin American narrative.[66] What Masoliver saw in this case, however, was that the issue was not simply a matter of dealing with a foreign influence—after all, as he pointed out, it had been normal for Spanish postwar novelists to look for models elsewhere—but with a literature that made use of the same language:

> A cold wind also blows on our literary republic. . . . There isn't anyone who cannot, in a survey of contemporary novel, rattle off the names of half a dozen authors from the United States, as well as from France, Italy, etc. I wonder who in this neck of the woods could line up half a dozen novelists from Argentina or Chile, never mind those of the nineteen countries that speak and write our language? . . . If that's the case, it shouldn't surprise anyone that people throw up their hands in horror when the Nadal crosses the ocean and there's such a big scandal when one of the judges extols the winning work as a lesson in language from someone who, without resorting to colorful dialecticisms, shows a very correct and intimate knowledge of our common language.[67]

We will return to this conflict, what Masoliver described as the "frustration" of Spanish novelists as they were confronted with the competion of their transatlantic colleagues, which became much more dramatic later in the decade. What is important now is to note the disparity between the open acceptance of Vargas Llosa and the resistance to do the same with Mejía Vallejo, even though they were both introduced in the same terms.

How was it that Vargas Llosa could claim a central position in the Spanish literary field, while the impression left by Mejía Vallejo was quickly forgotten? We could argue that it can be explained, first, in terms of biography and geography: Mejía Vallejo briefly visited Spain in spring 1964 to collect the prize and tour the country, but he continued living and publishing in Latin America. Apart from *El día señalado*, only his 1958 novel *Al pie de la ciudad* was printed in Spain during the years of the Boom (in 1972 by Destino). Vargas Llosa, on the contrary, established himself in Europe (in Paris, London, and finally in Barcelona in 1970) and was in close contact with the literary circles in Spain, including, of course, his association with Seix Barral, where he would publish all of his work. As Carlos Barral argued in reference to the importance of Spanish publishers in the circulation of Latin American literature, it was easier for Vargas Llosa to reach Argentinean readers from Barcelona than from Lima.[68] It is also probably safe to affirm that, of the novelists associated with the Boom, Vargas Llosa was the one with whom Spaniards felt closer to home. As was proclaimed in 1974, when he ended his residence of four years: "The four years he has spent with us . . . have made Vargas the Latin American *boom* writer most closely linked to Barcelona. Unlike García Márquez, Vargas Llosa cultivated a life of social and intellectual relationships, and it was likely that you would see him at the Barral Prize ceremony or arranging his farewells around a drink with friends."[69]

Perhaps, and more importantly, it was also a matter of poetics. The critical paratext of *El día señalado* shows that the novel did not get the same unanimous acclaim as *La ciudad y los perros*. Rafael Conte, for instance, spoke of the Nadal Prize as an attempt to grant "official recognition" to the Latin American new novel and warned that *El día señalado* could not legitimately be considered a representative of *new* Latin American writing: "The young Spanish-American novel is searching for new paths. That is not the case in Mejía Vallejo's work, which belongs in style and form to narrative models that have already expired."[70] This interpretation, of course, plays down the lyric aspects of the narrative, and therefore calls attention to the fact that Mejía Vallejo's novel was closer to the model and goal of social realism (testimony and denunciation of instances of social injustice) than the editorial paratext was willing to acknowledge. While *La ciudad y los perros* indulged itself in the discontinuities of the narrative (with dramatic shifts of characters, perspectives, and spatial and temporal locations), *El día señalado*, like most of Spanish social realistic fiction, keeps its storytelling within a rather restricted chronology and geography—except for the "Prólogo" to the first section of the novel, the action takes place within a few days in the small village of Tambo—and features a comparatively simple alternation of first- and third-person narration that does not preclude a certain objectivism for the reader, who is not placed by the narrative in a position to question the reality of the narrated events. *La ciudad y los perros*, on the contrary, challenges the reader to unveil the limitations and prejudices of each narrative voice, and requires an active role in the reconstruction of a diegetic content that is perceived as opaque as a result of the fragmentation it is subjected to by the discontinuities of discourse. These features would become almost the norm in the experimental fiction of the late sixties in Spain, but it is also the trademark of novelists like Juan Goytisolo or Juan Marsé, who are commonly regarded as working to expand the boundaries of social realism.[71]

Gonzalo Sobejano has characterized the process of the Spanish novel during the 1960s as a paradigmatic shift from the mostly testimonial narratives of the 1950s to the preeminently poemlike forms of the 1970s. I would argue that, after the crisis of the social novel, two parallel trends opened in Spanish narrative poetics. On the one hand, as Sobejano has shown, the predominant testimonial poetics of the 1940s and 1950s gave way to a more "poematic" aesthetics—in the next chapter I will show how the Latin American production participated in the constitution and sustenance of predominantly lyric models. But the poematic novel did not clearly succeed in Spain until the end of the decade, when Juan Benet's work began to gain full recognition after winning the Biblioteca Breve Prize in 1969 with *Una meditación*. Testimonialism, on the other hand, did not disappear: the search for poetry in fiction ran parallel and concurrently with the rehabilitation of testimonial features that later in the process—beyond the simplifications of both the social novel and experimentalism—would prove essential to the functioning of the novelistic genre itself. Displaced by the rebuttal of a limited understanding of literary engagement, the testimonial novel had to be reconsidered, but it could not be completely rejected; if the cameralike objectivism and linguistic directness of the previous decade had to go, the same did not necessarily apply to the need for what Sobejano has identified as the ideal of a public knowledge—"a common knowledge [*consaber*] (between author, actor and reader) about the represented world."[72] This attention to the constitution and disclosure between writer and reader of a collective world of experience in its conflictive discontinuity, characteristic of testimonialism, would later reappear as an essential component of new varieties of narrative storytelling.

Perhaps the most overlooked effect the variety of Latin American writing represented by Vargas Llosa had on Spanish literature was this rehabilitation of the idea of a socially committed literature. As I have argued here, the Boom novel could replace the social novel as the object of attention of critics and readers not only because it provided an *alternative* (as was the case, for instance, of the French new novel), but because it was presented as a fortunate *supplement* that—following the logic described by Jacques Derrida—both added to and replaced the dominant model of writing. During the 1960s, after the demise of social realism, there are rare occasions when the idea itself of social and political engagement is not the object of suspicion or negative criticism. However, it is significant that it appears to be only in reference to Latin American writers that support for the notion of a socially committed narrative could be legitimately expressed. It was particularly in the works of Vargas Llosa that the pairing of poetry and realism seemed once again possible.

4

Experimentalism and Narrativity

PAUL VALÉRY ONCE NOTED THAT IN ORDER TO STUDY THE CULTURAL milieu that surrounds the production and reception of literature, a distinction can be made between works that are created by their public—that is, determined by the expectations and knowledge of the intended readers—and those that seek to create their own audience.[1] Testimonial writing usually follows the first path, as it draws on collective imaginary structures either to endorse them by conservatively conforming to accepted ideological or generic codes, or to expose them by critically unveiling the misrepresentations such codes promote. Broadly understood, the mundanity of novelistic prose necessarily embeds a vision of the social and—since it mirrors a world intended to be recognized by its readers—it is opposed to the personal lyricism of poetry. This is why it needs to make use of intersubjective notions about temporal and spatial coordinates or psychological traits: as readers, we are expected to identify and understand the narrated events as possible within our own realm of experience. Poematic writing, on the other hand, flourishes along the second route, attempting not so much to expose the collective world but to impose an individual *Weltanschauung*: its ultimate goal is not the recognition of mundanity but the unveiling of an intimate perspective or truth. Hence the often cryptographic text it generates, since the social language of the testimonial writer is substituted by a lyric voice in self-contemplation.

Spanish social realist novelists had tried to build upon the social language of everyday speech and provide a better, clearer picture of reality. In the 1960s, however, and nurtured under the presence of the French *nouveau roman*, the next generation of writers was generally more interested in exploring linguistic and imaginary realms than in illustrating the processes of social history. The criti-

91

cal representation of the human world was then replaced by the display of antihumanitarianism, the monadic examination of inner psychological realities, the exploration of the possibilities of literary language, or even the questioning of representation itself. Working against the grain of the previous model, experimental novelists searched for the second reality Nathalie Sarraute had advocated in the 1963 Madrid conference on "Realism and Reality in Contemporary Literature." The French writer, to the dismay of Spanish realists, had proposed a novel of the unknown: instead of documenting the world we already perceive as existing, writers should explore what is yet to be discovered:

> There are . . . two forms of reality. A reality that each one sees around himself, that each one can capture when facing it, a reality that is familiar or capable of being so, and has been researched, studied for a long while, expressed in familiar forms, reproduced a thousandfold and a thousandfold imitated. This is not the reality writers address. This type of reality means nothing more than appearances to men of letters. Reality for the writer is the invisible, the unknown. It is that which seems fundamental, what does not allow itself to be expressed by forms that are already known and used. . . . It is evident that no sincere realist tendency can consist of an effort to investigate banal reality and re-create it in traditional forms—this effort belongs to the document, to journalism. To overcome this and arrive at literature, writers should look beyond appearances.[2]

As we saw in the previous chapter, some writers answered this challenge by following Vargas Llosa's example and expanding testimonialism beyond the limits of reportage. Others, however, decided to do away with documentary intent and follow the exploratory model presented by the *nouveau roman*.[3]

The first Spanish translations of texts representative of the French movement appeared in 1956 in the "Biblioteca Breve" series published by Seix Barral: Robbe-Grillet's *La doble muerte del profesor Dupont* (translation of *Les gommes*, 1953) and *El mirón* (*Le voyeur*, 1955). In 1957, the first critical commentaries on the poetics of objectivism were penned by Jaime Gil de Biedma, Castellet, and Juan Goytisolo, all names associated with the same publishing house. In 1958 Jorge Cela Trulock published *Las horas*, perhaps the first Spanish novel to incorporate the punctilious descriptions advocated by the *nouveau roman*. Very soon, writers linked to the French new novel were present in almost all the literary debates taking place in those years in Spain, where their artistic vision often clashed with that of the social novelists, who deplored the lack of social concern and dehumanization of their narratives.[4] It was not until the sixties, however, that the full impact of this new writing was explicit in Spain (clearly visible in the texts usually analyzed under the label of "experimental novel" and flourishing between 1966 and 1972), and it is with the publication of Juan Benet's *Volverás a Región* in 1967 that several critics have dated the introduction in Spanish letters of the *nouveau roman*.[5] José Corrales Egea criticized this appropriation of French techniques as a mimetic move contrary to the authentic tradition of Spanish narrative: "realism, of whatever kind, is nevertheless what all in all adapts best to our narrative tradition and . . . to attempt to replace it with such a radically opposite experience . . . seems to be at odds with the very structure of our thinking and expression, which is little given to circumlocution."[6]

Although both the French and the Latin American *new novels* show some formal and evolutionary parallelisms, these movements enter Spain's literary landscape in quite distinct ways.[7] As we have seen in the previous chapter, the Latin American novel was received in Spain as engaged literature, committed to the transformation of historical realities in such a way that—aesthetic and linguistic differences notwithstanding—initially kept it close to the political assumptions of the Spanish social novel and its audience, and was thus appropriated as a fortunate supplement to it. The *nouveau roman*, on the contrary, was largely presented not as a supplement but as an alternative to the political writing of Spanish neorealism, and it was viewed as directly opposed to it. Antonio Vilanova in 1967 pointed to the reception of the *nouveau roman* as one of the main causes behind the demise of social realism: "Nathalie Sarraute's subjectivist reaction not only represents a sure attack on the myth of objectivity, but also a sharp negation of the social and realist novel as an instrument of revolutionary and political action."[8] The *nouveau roman* appeared not as another way of doing the same, but as a new way of doing something else: instead of enhancing the critical representation of the common social world it aimed at unveiling another, non-ordinary reality.

At the paratextual level, perhaps the most important influence French novelists had on Spanish literary life is to be found in the emerging self-consciousness of the writing act. Their tendency to make explicit the theoretical grounding of their practices helped bring to the surface the aesthetic principles behind fictional forms, and thus open the genre to a fruitful debate. This is particularly relevant, since with the *nouveau roman*—as happened later with the Boom novel—came along a new interest in most of modernist art that had until then remained sidetracked by either Francoist censorship or leftist aesthetic orthodoxy. The updating of the Spanish literary landscape during the 1960s was facilitated in no small degree by the publication of works previously banned in Spain and by the proliferation of pocket book collections that made accessible texts whose circulation had until then been limited within circuits of restricted readership.[9] In fact, the experimentalism typical of this period results not only from an anxious attempt to get rid of the decanonized forms of neorealism, but also from a delayed, simultaneous and overwhelming reception of narrative modes present in Western literatures—including, of course, that of Spain—since the 1920s, but that had been forced out of view in the aftermath of the Civil War by the cultural agenda of the Falange. Most of the narrative production characteristic of the late 1960s presented many similarities with that of the 1920s, since—parallel to the recovery of the literary production of the exile—there was a reconnection with prewar fictional forms and techniques. Amid this context, the *nouveau roman* was perceived as one of the leading forms of contemporary literature, and it became widely recognized as a contestant in the Spanish literary field during the 1960s, even though—as Leo Pollmann has noted—it was already losing ground after its peak in the previous decade.[10] With the *nouveau roman*, young Spanish novelists began to see the novel not as a mirror of reality, but—as described by Michel Butor—a "laboratory of narrative."[11] Thus, considering novelistic production itself, what the French new novel brought to Spain was a poetics modeled after this notion of the text as a laboratory for the artistic invention of reality.

German Sánchez Espeso's *Experimento en Génesis* (1967) is a representative of this sort of experimental writing flourishing in Spain after the crisis of the social novel. In fact, the plot itself could be understood as a parable illustrating the trials of the testimonial writer in a world deprived of clear-cut moral verities. The unnamed protagonist is a journalist who embarks upon an eremitic experiment in the mountains, where he enters in relationship with a woman. The quiescence of this affair—we are only allowed to overhear a few conversations between the lovers—is disturbed by the arrival of another man who, escaping from the police after killing his own brother, is given refuge by the protagonist. The fratricide will eventually flee again, this time with the woman, while the protagonist returns to his previous life. The journalist's experience will produce just one boring article on the local cathedral (a long and detailed description that occupies several pages in the novel), but when asked if the country life (an exemplary topic for a social novelist) has given him any material for a novel he rebukes the idea: "Do you think this sort of life provides stuff to make a novel interesting? Nothing exciting happens here" [¿Crees que este género de vida da materia para hacer una novela interesante? Aquí no pasa nada que apasione a cualquiera].[12]

Experimento en Génesis departs from the conventions and ideological prescriptions of social—and dialectical—realism. The analysis of collective realities is absent from the minimal story: the few instances in which social conflicts are addressed—the comments on the nature of the prosecution against the fratricide—lack any sociohistorical character and seem to pertain more to the realm of a moral debate on the nature of punishment. As an intertext for the novel, constant references and retellings of the Book of Genesis provide insight into the two moral topics concerned: the relation of man and woman (Adam and Eve), and the breach of fraternal bonds (the story of Joseph). These intertextual connections seem to favor the ahistorical portrayal of human interaction. Beyond this humanistic front, however, the bulk of the text is devoted to an abundance of reifying descriptions à la Robbe-Grillet that render all sorts of beings into aggregates of surfaces: people, animals, and spaces are presented in a geometrized language that takes special care not to include any humanizing metaphors. The first pages of the novel are devoted to a meticulous view of an aquarium, where all creatures—both marine and human—are portrayed in the same aseptic language:

seres con lentes engarzados en armazones plásticos y metálicos articulados con bisagras a presillas que se afianzan detrás de las orejas, vidrios circulares limitados por superficies esféricas cóncavas y convexas, sujetos a los pabellones cartilaginosos que sobresalen a ambos lados de la cabeza detrás de la articulación maxilar cuya porción posterior bordean, comprendidos entre las líneas horizontales que pasan, la superior por la extremidad de las cejas y la inferior por debajo del subtabique nasal.

[beings with lenses set in plastic and metallic frames joined with loop hinges secured behind their ears, circular pieces of glass bound by concave and convex spherical surfaces, fastened to cartilaginous auricles sticking out on both sides of the head behind the maxillary joint whose back part they border, contained between crossing horizontal lines, the upper along the edge of the eyebrows and the lower beneath the nasal septum.][13]

Sánchez Espeso's depiction of the world is built around the absence of any humanistic analogies, since reality is not understood as a function of a social or personal existence—and, following Robbe-Grillet, the intrusion of humanism in literature had to be repudiated as pure metaphysics.[14]

The narrative in Sánchez Espeso's novel destroys the temporal sequence by decomposing it into discrete instants. Every time a functional unit is about to be constituted in the text—that is, every time something is going to "happen" in the plot—it is dissolved by the accumulation of what (borrowing from Barthes) could be described as "spatial informants," pieces of information intended to extend the representation of space at the level of discourse without advancing any signification at the level of the story.[15] They disjoint the metonymic search for the narrative of events and overwhelm the reader with extensive blocks of unmitigated, objectified reality. In the novel, the first indication of someone fleeing from the police—"Creo que me persiguen, dijo. No sé" [I think they're following me, he said. I don't know][16]—awakens our interest only to disappear immediately under three full pages devoted to a description of the cabin where he arrives. The mere sequence of events is obscured by the discontinuity of narrative, and it should not surprise us that commentators have differed in their understanding of the details of the plot.[17]

Sánchez Espeso's *Experimento en Génesis* represents one of the earliest attempts by the young generation of writers to break away from the fictional mode of social neorealism. Their endeavor was displaced, however, by the success of the new Latin American novel and its own literary innovations.[18] Pollmann differentiates between the variety of experimentalism implemented in the *nouveau roman* and the forms it adopted in the Latin American new novel, according to the prominence they grant to either phenomenal or ontological orientation: the French variety would be characterized by its attention to the purely phenomenal world that conditions all stylistic, thematic, and formal considerations, while its Latin American counterpart attempts a synthesis of formal, ontological, and practical concerns.[19] *Experimento en Génesis* is a clear representa-

tive of the first trend: its cameralike narrative is presented by means
of an aseptic language totally devoid of humanistic interest. This is
at odds with the jocular usage of language so often found in some
of the most popular authors of the Boom novel: humor—as noted
by Donald L. Shaw—is one of the most important resources of authors like Julio Cortázar or Cabrera Infante, both of whom were
instrumental in changing the prospects of Spanish narrative poetics.[20]

THE TEXT AS GAME BOARD: EXPERIMENTALISM AND BOOM NOVEL

If Vargas Llosa, as I have argued, was appropriated mainly by
those who—working closely within the testimonial tradition of the
social novel—saw the need to renovate or *poeticize* realistic writing, those who aspired to a completely different trajectory of poematic writing found inspiration in the work of other Boom novelists
like Julio Cortázar and Guillermo Cabrera Infante, whose work
opened the way for a conception of the novel as a playfully linguistic, self-referential work. In the case of the Argentinean writer, his
introduction to Spanish literary life took place fairly late: imported
copies of *Rayuela* did not find their way into the bookstores until
1967 (the novel was by then already in its fourth edition in Argentina), and the first Cortázar book published in Spain was *Ceremonias* in 1968, by Seix Barral—a volume that combined the stories
originally published in Latin America in *Final del juego* (1956) and
Las armas secretas (1959).[21] It was also in 1967 that Cabrera Infante's work became widely available to Spanish readers: although
his novel *Vista del amanecer desde el trópico* had won the Biblioteca Breve Prize in 1964, it could not be published until three years
later because of a ban from Spanish censors—which gave the author the opportunity to rewrite most of the text and change its title
to *Tres tristes tigres*.[22]

The first critical notice about Cortázar in Spain was Pere Gimferrer's early "Notas sobre Julio Cortázar," published in October
1965. As Valverde had done before with his own presentation of
Vargas Llosa, Gimferrer sees in Cortázar's writing a sort of antidote
against the contemporary decay of narrative fiction: "at this moment in which critics and novelists seem to celebrate Black Mass in
the funeral chapel of narrative . . . Cortázar's internal confidence
returns things to their rightful place and proves to be tremendously

comforting." And the consolation he finds in Cortázar is, once again, of a poetic quality: "Cortázar's is an intellectual world, a meditation on narrative rather than on life, open to the trembling waters of the poetic, an image of a skepticism that constantly inquires beyond its limits; and it nevertheless possesses—excuse this personal confession from a Spanish reader—the magical dimension of exoticism. . . . Cortázar is not, however, a moralist (he is, of course, in the sense that writing is always a moral act), because his poetic, conceptual and closed universe constitutes more an adventure in style—what Salinas would call an adventure toward the absolute—than an enterprise of inquiry into the ultimate meaning of human relationships."[23]

While in the various Spanish readings of Vargas Llosa's *La ciudad y los perros* previously analyzed poetry had been linked as a potential supplement to testimonial mimesis (under the notion of a "poetic" social novel), here it is being used in a markedly different direction. In Cortázar's literary project, according to Gimferrer, the emphasis is on *narrative* and *style* rather than *life*. It is therefore not inconsequential that Gimferrer would compare *Rayuela* to Joyce's *Finnegans Wake* rather than to *Ulysses* (which had been the literary icon evoked by Valverde in relation to *La ciudad y los perros*), given the even more experimental quality associated with the former text: "*Rayuela* is also an experiment. But here the dog is chasing its tail: the work turns against itself, refutes, reaffirms, insults, creates, and uncovers itself on every page. . . . Despite its extreme ambition—or perhaps because of it—I don't think that this intelligent, bold, and passionate book should be considered the author's most successful work. For the same reasons we don't hold *Finnegans Wake* to be so, for instance. . . . There is no doubt that *Rayuela* is . . . a unique enterprise in the history of narrative in Spanish, one of those extreme books [*libros-límite*] that have to turn out to be bad in order to be good, one of the explorations we so desperately need."[24] The exploration suggested by Gimferrer here is clearly intended as a necessary antidote against mimetic discourse—a message that threads through all Spanish readings of Cortázar. The endorsement of experimentation is not meant to *enhance* testimonialism (à la Vargas Llosa), but rather to *revoke* it. *Rayuela* was epitomized as the guidebook in the crusade to liberate Spanish narrative from the grip of realist poetics, being its perfect negative: "Nothing could be further away from the chronological and linear architecture of the old realist novel than that 'Table of Instructions,' in which the reading of the book is offered to the reader as a game," declared the first reviewer of the novel when it finally arrived in Spain.[25]

A further step in this same direction was given by Valeriano Bozal, who contrasted the new Latin American narrative with the traditional novel—the latter being identified with naturalism and, more particularly, with Galdós. A heavy accent is put on the negative aspects of naturalism—formal linearity, fossilized and uncritical representation of reality, metaphysical concept of being and truth—which, Bozal argues, have managed to disguise and impose as a "natural" way of seeing what is no more than a technical artifice. On the other hand, Latin American novelists are presented as a liberating force against the traps of such an outdated mode of representation: "This way of narrating was ruined by Marcel Proust and James Joyce. At the heart of the Spanish language it is now being ruined by the new South American novel, and especially by Julio Cortázar, José Lezama Lima, Mario Vargas Llosa, and Gabriel García Márquez. . . . What these novelists have come to tell us is that the world is much richer, that it cannot be simplified as it was being done, and that we must disentangle its vast complexity with every resource and freedom at our disposal."[26]

Bozal's focus on Galdós as the epitome of Spanish naturalist writing echoes the comments on the nineteenth-century novelist made by Horacio Oliveira, the main character in *Rayuela*, in chapter 34 of the novel—the now-famous interlinear weaving of a fragment of Galdós's *Lo prohibido* and Oliveira's thoughts while reading that text (Oliveira also makes a brief and derisive reference to Pardo Bazán in chapter 13). The chapter was soon interpreted as an attack not only on Galdós but also on Spanish realism in general. "Cortázar has unjustly attacked Galdós," declared Dámaso Alonso in a 1968 interview—with those same words repeated and highlighted in a blowup on the same page—where he otherwise expressed his admiration for the Latin American new novel.[27] Amorós, however, argued that, since the derogatory comments on Galdós are articulated by Oliveira the character and not by Cortázar the author, no disrespect for the Spanish writer should be inferred. Galdós was what Bernstein called the "sacrificial victim" in the indictment of the realist tradition in general, and this larger criticism—present both in Oliveira's comments and throughout the text of *Rayuela* in general—was clear to most readers.[28] But in Spain chapter 34 was most particularly read as an attack against *national* and *contemporary* forms of realism. And that reading was further fueled by Cortázar himself when he showed his disaffection toward Spanish novelists in a 1969 interview, where—after listing twenty-two authors he deemed influential on his literary formation, among them two Spanish poets (Garcilaso and Pedro Salinas)—he underlined the absence of narrators from Spain: "you'll notice that I don't name Spanish prose writers, whom I only use in cases of insomnia, with the exception of *La Celestina* and *La Dorotea*." Spanish novelist Alfonso Grosso reacted immediately: "I'm fed up. Don't you see that Cortázar holds Spanish writers in colossal contempt? Haven't you noticed his disdain for Galdós?"[29]

If Cortázar became the patron saint of the young generation of experimentalists, his brand name was also brandished by others who had remained marginalized by the hegemony of neorealism, namely the so-called Spanish "New Novel." Eagerly promoted by the critic and novelist Manuel García Viñó in *Novela española actual* (1967) and *Papeles sobre la "Nueva Novela" española* (1975), the label referred to a variegated selection of writers whose literary proposals he attempted to formulate and legitimize under the umbrella of the successful French and Latin American movements. García Viñó, himself a novelist, openly rejected the direction signaled by Martín-Santos in *Tiempo de silencio*, a work he criticized for its pessimistic depiction of humanity. The authentic new Spanish novel, represented for him in the novels by Antonio Prieto, Manuel San Martín, José Tomás Cabot, José Vidal Cadellans and, especially, Andrés Bosch and Carlos Rojas, is characterized by ontological thrust and aesthetic intellectualism.[30] In a roundtable originally broadcast on Spanish television in 1967, the "metaphysical novelists" (as they became known) attempted to appropriate the prestige awarded to the new Latin American novel in their rebellion against what Carlos Rojas called a "dictatorship of the realist novel": "Unfortunately for us, we lack here works of the caliber of *Rayuela*, by Argentinean writer Julio Cortázar, or *El tambor de hojalata* [*The Tin Drum*], by Günther Grass, where the writer is tested by his imagination, fantasy, and his desire to create and reveal vis-à-vis a world to which he refuses to resign himself. . . . What I regret is that we are—*with regard to literature*—living under a *dictatorship of the realist novel* and there is no way of creating a novel that transcends those limitations."[31] Interestingly, the participants in the roundtable (Bosch, García-Viñó, and Rojas, together with Romanian writer Vintila Horia and journalist Manuel

Calvo Hernando) claimed to have found in Cortázar the example of a "total realism"—as it has been already mentioned here, a month earlier the same publication that printed the transcript of the round-table published a discussion of Vargas Llosa's work under the banner of a "limitless realism." This new Spanish novel, however, did not succeed in obtaining the favor of critics or the public in general, as it was regarded by many as a conservative attempt to mitigate the political implications of novelistic writing in Spain. The emphasis on universal conceptualizations and the retreat from any sort of historical conditioning of human experience had strong ideological overtones that not only positioned these writers in a different orbit than that of the Latin American novelists they claimed as peers, but rapidly disqualified them in a country where revolutionary practices—either political or aesthetic—still had an important currency in the cultural market.

In the experimentalist camp, on the other hand, perhaps the first outstanding example of the trend imposed by Cortázar is José María Guelbenzu's *El mercurio* (1968), finalist of the 1967 Biblioteca Breve Prize. As David K. Herzberger has described it, *El mercurio* "consists of a potpourri of innovative techniques and stylistic complications derived in large part from Joyce, Beckett, and Cortázar, and modified to fit the peculiar requisites of Guelbenzu." The author openly positions himself against the neorealism of the previous decade, and his work was widely hailed as one of highest achievements of the renewal of Spanish narrative at the end of the 1960s.[32] Interestingly, as we saw in Sánchez Espeso's *Experimento en Génesis*, Guelbenzu opens the novel with a geometrical imagery reminiscent of the *nouveau roman* school:

> Superficie de circunferencias incontables, estrechamente relacionadamente incontables. Veo el juego de surcos pasar y pasar. Veo circularmente el tintineo de una franja de luz como doble triángulo horizontal unido por el vértice: curvas simétricas las bases, estriados los catetos.

> [Surface of innumerable circumferences, closely and relatedly innumerable. I see the play of the grooves go by, pass by. I circularly see the jingling of a strip of light as a double horizontal triangle connected at its vertex: the bases symmetrical curves, the legs striated.][33]

Soon, however, the reader is introduced to a scene that could have been taken directly out of *Rayuela*: Jorge Basco, the protagonist, is

among his group of intellectual friends and listening to jazz record-
ings by Billie Holiday while they discuss their diverging preferences for Coltrane, Hodges, Fats Waller, or Stan Getz. Jorge Basco
is an aspiring novelist, and *El mercurio* is largely devoted to the
trials of the writing process of a novel that, in the end, seems to be
the same text we read—it is thus a perfect example of what could
be considered a metafictional chronotope typical of contemporary
writing: both the temporal and spatial structures of the text are conditioned by the adventure of writing.[34] As such, the text presents
itself completely self-conscious of the literary tradition, and in this
sense it is strikingly evident the absence of any mention to Spanish
authors, while the names of Cortázar, Joyce, Bellow, Kafka, and
others constantly pop up—interestingly enough (perhaps a sign of
the declining importance of the *nouveau roman* as aesthetic model),
and despite the opening lines quoted above, Guelbenzu does not
mention either Robbe-Grillet or Butor.

The renewal of literary language is the outstanding concern of
Guelbenzu's literary generation. In his essay "Literatura, una insoportable soledad" (1968) he established a contrast between the two
most prestigious novels of the previous generation, *Tiempo de silencio* and *El Jarama*, and vindicated the legacy of Martín-Santos
against what he considered the erroneous canonization of Sánchez
Ferlosio's objectivism. Echoing Juan Goytisolo's argument against
the language of recent Spanish literary tradition, Guelbenzu issued
what is perhaps the harshest criticism of Ferlosio's novel—which
had remained exempt from the general disqualification of the neorealist movement—and could be considered one foundational motif
of the generational shift implemented with the experimental novel:

> in the last thirty years, with regard to narrative, the Spanish language
> has become a plate so polished that it ends up being *inexpressive*, which
> is like saying there can be no narrative; which is like saying as well that
> Sánchez Ferlosio (a linguist and not a narrator, as he himself declares)
> does nothing but mark and summarize the limits of this metal plate,
> which is identical to itself. A whole series of reasons—keeping in mind
> that in my opinion it is better to say our narrative is dead than to say it
> does not exist—explains how it is that a mythical pedestal that should
> belong to Martín-Santos is instead occupied by Sánchez Ferlosio; and
> how what with Martín-Santos would amount to a search for the new
> novel, with Ferlosio means the continuance of today's suffocatingly
> poor narrative.[35]

Guelbenzu argues that the acceptance of the new literary language proposed by Latin American authors is essential to the proper estimation of Martín-Santos as a leading force behind Spanish experimentalism.[36] Accordingly, *El mercurio* attempts to follow this path: in the novel, language is twisted not only to open it to a depiction of interior monologues (a technical tool typical of poematic subjectivism, and dominantly present in *Tiempo de silencio*), but also—and here Cortázar's influence becomes clear—to play with its transposition at the graphic level:

> renacimiento arcón el, cortina la de definitiva asunción la a
> me- la observen) arcón el y silencio el demoliendo carcoma la,
> rereco- paso a paso mismo sí de trayectoria una Pero. (táfora
> cár- apoplético mísero inmenso pausado vertiginoso rriendo
> adya- mundo el, adyacentes callejuelas las sentimental deno
> mismo sí de adyacente muerte la, adyacente reclusión la, cente
> primera vez por apaleado Miguel llegar a va dónde porque

> [chest Renaisance the, assumption definitive curtain's the on
> me- the observe) chest the and silence the demolishing anxiety the,
> retraver- step by step himself of trajectory a But. (taphor
> li- apoplectic miserable immense unhurried dizzy sing
> world adjacent the, alleys adjacent the sentimental vid
> himself to adjacent death the, seclusion adjacent the,
> time first the for up beaten go to going Miguel is where because][37]

This fragment has been presented as an example of excessive experimentalism, in which the interior monologue would end up as mere chaotic and meaningless expression. The text, however, is simply to be read backwards, from right to left, a trick that immediately calls to mind the textual intertwining of Galdós's *Lo prohibido* with Oliveira's reading in chapter 34 of *Rayuela*. In general, the novel is equally and entirely built upon a foregrounding of language—humorous wordplay, phonetic alterations of traditional writing, unconventional syntax, attention to sound and rhythm over meaning and communication—that takes aim at the programmatic core of neorealist aesthetics of the previous decades.[38]

El mercurio testifies to a Spanish novel that, according to Juan Goytisolo (and borrowing from Benveniste), has shifted from the poetics of "history" represented in texts like *El Jarama* to a poetics of "discourse" implemented in *Tiempo de silencio*.[39] The experimental writing of Cortázar, Sánchez Espeso, Guelbenzu, and Goytisolo himself—starting with *Señas de identidad* (1966) and, more dramatically, in *Reivindicación del conde don Julián* (1970)—together with Juan Benet's *Volverás a Región* (1967) and *Una meditación* (1970), can be seen as some of the earliest representatives of the experimental trend emerging from the crisis of social realism and supported by the simultaneous reception of the new novel from France and Latin America—a trend that was rapidly joined by authors of the older generation, such as Miguel Delibes and Camilo José Cela, with *Parábola del náufrago* and *San Camilo, 1936* respectively, both published in 1969.[40]

While the narrative of the 1940s and 1950s in Spain was mostly written following the picaresque model, after the sixties it is Cervantes who—recuperated as an antidote against the restricted vision of social realism—becomes "the patron saint" of the renewal of the Hispanic novel.[41] Critics have seen the use of Cervantine strategies in Marsé's *Últimas tardes con Teresa* (winner of the 1965 Biblioteca Breve Prize), Goytisolo's *Revindicación del conde don Julián* (1970), or Torrente Ballester's *La saga/fuga de J.B.* (1972). At the same time, several Hispanic writers turned their attention to Cervantes also to support theoretical observations on the nature of the novel—Torrente Ballester in *El Quijote como juego* (1975), Carlos Fuentes in *Cervantes o la crítica de la lectura* (1976), and Juan Goytisolo in several essays. In these fictional and critical works, Cervantes is reappropriated to legitimize the notion of writing as critical reading (Fuentes) and the idea of literature as playful game (Torrente).

In 1976, Juan Goytisolo discussed the return to Cervantes apropos of Cuban writer Guillermo Cabrera Infante in "Lectura cervantina de *Tres tristes tigres*." I would like to concentrate on Goytisolo's essay, in order to understand not only the impact of the novel in Spain, but also the larger influence of Latin American fiction in the recanonization of a poetics of discourse. According to Goytisolo, the trend toward a Cervantine model of writing is heavily supported in the 1960s by the Boom novelists, and it is not by chance that Goytisolo—himself being close to the Boom in terms of aesthetic intention and paratextual prestige—should define the model according to its discursive power: "Cervantes's novel is purely about different stories, discourse about earlier literary discourses which at no time conceals the process of enunciation; on the contrary, it makes it clearly evident. . . . Cervantes has touched all the keys and played all the registers of the game. For this reason, when today's avant-garde novelists, abandoning the restricting 're-alism' predominant in these last centuries, try to return to the genre its possibilities of expression that have been lost or left fallow, they are following, deliberately or not, the path traced by Cervantes."[42] The parallels with Cabrera Infante's novel are evident. *Tres tristes tigres* is a discourse generated by means of self-reference and pun, whose meaning is conveyed through the constant interlacing of texts—as it is the case, for instance, in the parodic collage that con-stitutes the section "La muerte de Trotsky referida por varios escri-tores cubanos, años después—o antes" [The Death of Trotsky as Described by Various Cuban Writers, Several Years After the Event—or Before], where Cabrera Infante (as Cervantes had done with the various narrative modes of his contemporaries) playfully imitates José Martí, Lezama Lima, Virgilio Piñera, Lydia Cabrera, Lino Novás, Alejo Carpentier, and Nicolás Guillén.[43]

Goytisolo highlights the entangled construction of the novel, which requires an active reading to re-create the work.[44] *Tres tristes tigres* presents an itinerant plot whose diffused connections along its numerous pages are left undecided, and it is up to the reader to put them in order. Fragments of dialogues, psychoanalytical ses-sions, iterative or parallel stories (such as "La historia de un bas-tón" [The Story of a Stick], whose plot seems to disintegrate as the reader confronts several differing versions, or the aforementioned "Death of Trotsky"), all combine to create a textual kaleidoscope. In Goytisolo's reading, a parallel is established between *Tres tristes tigres* and *Don Quijote* in terms of the essential position dialogue occupies in both texts.[45] The itinerant conversations along Havana's streets mirror the Quijote/Sancho exchanges. First, we have the dia-logue of the characters, which in the "Bachata" section occupies some 150 pages with the loquacious exchange between Silvestre and Cué, as well as with others. This, in turn, exposes at a second level a dialogue of languages: that of the Emsí at the Tropicana and his continuous leaping from Spanish to English in the opening sec-tion of the novel, the translation games in "The Story of a Stick," or the polyglot speech of Silvestre and Cué. The text, furthermore, reveals itself as a dialogue of literary traditions, in this case the con-versation between the past and present of Cuban literature. Even the physical reality of the city is built upon the personal views of its inhabitants, the streets covered with commercial signs and bill-boards about which the characters always have something to say. The deceiving exception, the apparently monological voice articulated from a psychoanalytical couch, takes in turn the reader as its intended interlocutor.

Cabrera Infante's writing is not an exception, since fragmentation and multiplicity are both technical features employed by most of the new Latin American novelists.[46] And it is in the understanding of fictional writing as self-referential intertextuality that Goytisolo locates the essence of the new novel: "*Don Julián* is the most Spanish work I've written, and for a very simple reason: because its very material, at a purely verbal level, is the Spanish literary discourse, from its origin up to the present day. . . . My focus allows me to strike up an intertextual dialogue with authors I admire, or to parody and pervert the style of those I do not respect very much. . . . This intellectual or migrating nomadism of ideas undoubtedly links me to the new Spanish-American narrative, much freer than the Spanish in its relationship with the past—not only with Spain's past but also with that of other cultures and languages."[47]

Goytisolo sees the value of this sort of experimentation not in the creation of new forms and yet undiscovered realities (as is the case in French experimentalism), but rather—paradoxically—in its own conventional foundation, that is, in the strong and overt relationship it establishes with the literary ancestry. It is not, however, a question of respectfully preserving the past—Goytisolo harshly criticizes most of Spain's literary tradition. The goal is critical transposition: to invert the received generic order (as Borges does when playing with the boundaries between fiction and encyclopedia, or Manuel Puig in confusing disparate narrative modes) and, at the same time, to invest productively the cultural capital accumulated by that same tradition. Thus, the aforementioned discursive character is manifested in a nomadic dialogue with the totality of literature. Likewise, Goytisolo deplored that Spanish writers had lost sight of the satirical tradition and its "ability to smile."[48] Irony and parody, two traits that established the connection between Cabrera Infante and Cervantes, were to become again fashionable.

GARCÍA MÁRQUEZ: THE NOVEL AS STORYTELLING

At a time when novelistic writing in Spain seemed to have available only two routes—the refurbished realism à la Martín-Santos or Vargas Llosa, and the varieties of experimentalism described above—the ability of a text like *Cien años de soledad* to appeal to and surprise its readers with a good story was perhaps the most striking feature of García Márquez's model. Regardless of his self-proclaimed realism, it is not hard to detect in García Márquez's work the preeminent value of narration over the verisimilitude of the depicted world. In his novels the alleged transcription of American reality is subjected to a hyperbolic process that responds to the mesmerizing requirement of narration: the novelist resorts to the artifices of traditional storytelling—the magical effect of disproportionate but precise numbers, the iteration of names, the mythical framing, and also the use of a narrative voice able to relate the most extraordinary events without astonishment—in order to captivate and seduce his readers.

As in most of the rest of the world, García Márquez did not rise to fame in Spain until the publication of *Cien años de soledad* in 1967, even though he had been included in 1961 in Gastón Baquero's *Escritores hispanoamericanos de hoy*, a brief volume intended to introduce Spanish readers—particularly students and the larger, nonacademic public—to major authors of Spanish American literature.[49] And despite the fact that the first edition of his novel *La mala hora* (winner of the Esso Literary Prize in Colombia) was printed in Spain in 1962—although in a poorly circulated edition that the author would later repudiate because the text had been "corrected" to conform to Spanish Peninsular usage.[50] But after 1967 his name appears regularly in Spanish literary supplements and magazines, as a result both of the success of his first bestselling novel and his residency in Barcelona. Pere Gimferrer seems to have been, once again, the first Spanish reviewer of the novel, and the first to coin there a formula that would be repeated over and over to explain the novel's major contribution to Spanish poetics: the notion of a "return to imaginative narrative."[51]

The potential for an elemental, almost puerile pleasure of reading is what generally impressed Spanish critics. And it was clearly the feature that presented the most dramatic contrast with the national supply of contemporary letters:

Cien años de soledad is not just a great novel, but one that is totally different from what is common today. Why this singularity? Simply put, because García Márquez *narrates*: he recounts things that happen, new, marvelous, moving events . . . but above all, an enormous amount of events. In contrast to so much quintessential psychologizing, so much photographic description of objects or mathematical reproduction of languages, García Márquez returns to the old eternal tradition of the narrator (an experienced man, according to all classical norms) who tells us an interesting story with such wit that all of us—listeners and readers alike—hang like children on the spell cast by each one of his words. . . . García Márquez shows in practice the possibilities of a way of narrating that is almost forgotten nowadays.[52]

The publication of *Cien años de soledad* opened a breach and forced a reexamination of the tools and goals of narrative. Félix Grande, for instance, confessed to have abandoned the writing of a novel after the impact of García Márquez.[53] The key word here is, of course, the adjective "forgotten," which, interestingly enough, also appears a year later in Ricardo Gullón's essay *García Márquez o el olvidado arte de contar* (1970). It calls to mind two complementary notions—suppression and tradition—that are central to the understanding of the paradigmatic shift from experimentalism to narrativity. First, it indicates a sense of yearning for a kind of narration that had been not only disregarded, but even overtly demoted by previously dominant models—as Castellet had declared in 1957, "nothing justifies any longer the gratuitous creation of imaginary worlds; on the contrary, writers will necessarily have to try to represent their own world as they know it."[54] In a sort of return of the repressed, the aesthetic crisis in the 1960s generated a receptive climate that favored the recovery of storytelling at a time when the novel was focused on the laboratory workings of textual experimentation. Jacques Joset has explained the success of *Cien años de soledad* in Latin America in socio-ideological terms as a reinterpretation of the myth of paradise lost. Perhaps in the case of Spain such an explanation should be traced back to the narrative loss resulting from the excesses of both documentary and experimental poetics.[55] If in the previous models, as Francisco Ynduráin has noted apropos of the *nouveau roman*, the imperfect tense—the central domain of traditional narration—was replaced by the present (whether in the objectivist, cameralike form of the social novel or in the subjective consciousness of experimentalism), the recovery of narrative marks a return to the preterite tense and the fictional force of the imaginary has-been. Authors like Torrente Ballester or Alvaro Cunqueiro undoubtedly benefitted from this trend, and their work, which had remained for a long time at the periphery of the literary canon, became rapidly popularized.[56]

But the forgotten mode of imaginative narrative was also *tradi-*

tional in the best sense of the word: it was a practice anchored in what was perceived to be the genuine roots of Hispanic literary heritage.[57] On the one hand, both Vargas Llosa and García Márquez legitimized the chivalric romance as a model for their writing. In a public debate that took place in Lima in September 1967, they both discussed this topic and declared their admiration for *Amadís de Gaula* and what they considered to be its most outstanding feature, narrative freedom (we shall return later to the case of *Tirant lo Blanc*, vindicated by Vargas Llosa as the greatest ancestor of a "total realism"). According to García Márquez: "in chivalric literature, as we have already said, the knight gets his head cut off as many times as is necessary for the story. In Chapter III [of *Amadís de Gaula*], there's a great battle and it is necessary to have the knight's head chopped off, so it gets chopped off. And in Chapter IV, the knight appears with his head, and if necessary, it gets chopped off again in another battle. All this narrative freedom disappeared together with the chivalric novel, where you would find things as extraordinary as those we find now, every day, in Latin America."[58]

On the other hand, the reception of *Cien años de soledad* should be inserted in the process of Cervantinization of Spanish letters noted in the previous section, and the assessment of this traditionalism plays an important role as the antithesis to the criticism of the Boom novel as mere imitation of foreign—that is, non-Hispanic— modes of writing (which will be commented on in more detail in the following chapter). Thus, Latin American novelists would be praised for their profound knowledge of Spanish literary past: "It is not gratuitous to add that these writers took also the *trouble* to get to know our Golden Age writers, a trouble that few Spaniards of the last generations—I am referring to major novelists—have taken."[59] Because in Spain the tradition recovered by García Márquez and others is strongly perceived as *national*, the appropriation of imaginative writing is felt not only as necessary, but also as legitimate.

Within the field of Spanish fiction, a large part of the production of the postmodern era—which in the case of Spain has to be dated as beginning sometime during the mid-1970s—is characterized by the tendency to write eventful narratives, that is, to call the reader's attention through the interest in the plot. This is, however, a new kind of plot, whose power does not necessarily rest on the unveiling of the discontinuities of the social world (as it was the case in the neorealist mode of documentary writing) or on the epiphany of subjectivity (through poematic varieties of fiction), but on the seduction of openly imaginary constructions. Eventually, this movement attempts to overcome the document/poem dichotomy and reestablish the legitimacy of romance.[60] This narrative turn triggered by the reception of *Cien años de soledad* was by no means universally endorsed, but its power can be followed across the whole spectrum of the literary system. Perhaps the greatest evidence of this is the ability of the novel to function as an hypotext for contemporary fiction. I would like to show this condition by turning to the contrast between two Spanish novels among the most highly regarded texts published in the early seventies: *Una meditación* (1970), by Juan Benet, and *La saga/fuga de J.B.* (1972), by Gonzalo Torrente Ballester. Both became models of writing for the decade: Benet as the most prestigious writer of experimental fiction, Torrente as the main renovator of narrative storytelling among the already established writers of the period.[61]

Juan Benet, one of the most outspoken opponents of the rising popularity of the Boom, won the Biblioteca Breve Prize in 1969—that is, at the height of the canonization of the Latin American new novel in Spain—with his second novel, *Una meditación*.[62] The novel, perhaps even more than the previous *Volverás a Región*, constitutes an excellent embodiment of Benet's highly difficult reading: loaded with the usual marks of experimentalism (scientific vocabulary, complex syntactical constructions, absence of traditional plot, stylized characters, preeminence of wandering introspection over straightforward narrating) the reader is left alone before a single, unbroken paragraph that extends for 329 pages in the Spanish original. The narration—hardly an appropriate term to characterize Benet's writing—is set in motion by the enigmatic interests and workings of the narrator's memory. The inchoate story is soon confronted with digressions that deviate the attention from the diegetic world toward the realm of philosophical and moral discourse and end up dominating the course of writing. Thus, we are presented with a variety of thoughts on the mimetic tendencies of the bourgeoisie, the trials of memory, the passage of childhood, the destructive force of time, the moral evaluation of war, copulation, and so on. And yet, I would like to argue that, in negating the ideal of narrativity, *Una meditación* shows in fact the dominant position bestowed on the new poetics of narration within the Spanish literary system, as the novel takes special care in explicitly reversing and destroying that model.

The stagnant atmosphere of the novel and its carefully orchestrated depiction of decadence have been profusely analyzed by Benetian scholars. Contrary to the historical detachment of other post-neorealist texts, however, behind the experimental texture of Benet's novel there remains a central concern for the Spanish Civil War and its consequences. The narrator devotes several pages to judge the event, and the novel contains such a severe criticism of Franco's victory that it is indeed surprising that such a text could be published. Not only it is an indictment of the moral flaws of those who won the war, but (in lines that perhaps escaped the censors' attention) it also directly addresses the intellectual deficiencies of their leadership:

> Nunca habían dejado de saber (o temer) que un juicio muy distinto se les había adelantado y seguía impertérrito, aparejado a una edad moral muy distinta a las suyas, observando con una óptica inalterable los frutos del triunfo, cualquiera que fuese el progreso del país. Dicho progreso no sería capaz nunca . . . de superar su retraso moral; y el gobernador tenía que demostrar unas cualidades, hasta entonces no vistas, para borrar el carácter de la usurpación. Y así como un pueblo delega su soberanía y a veces gusta de ser gobernado, incluso con beneplácito, por una persona que no encarna ninguna idea ni promete grandes innovaciones pero personifica las virtudes de la recta administración, así ha de estar muy agotado para dejarse arrebatar todo su poder por aquel que ha hecho una profesión de la falta de ideas.

> [They have never ceased knowing (or fearing) that quite a different judgment had brought them forward and continued on intrepidly, teamed up with a moral age quite different from theirs, observing with an unalterable optic the fruits of victory, no matter what the progress of the country might have been. Said progress would never be capable . . . of overcoming its moral backwardness; and the one who ruled had to show qualities, not seen until then, that would erase the sense of usurpation. And just as a people will delegate its sovereignty and sometimes likes to be governed, even with consent, by a person who doesn't embody any idea or promise great innovations but personifies the virtues of upright administration, so it has to be quite exhausted for it to let itself be bereft of all its power by one who has made a profession of his lack of ideas.][63]

Ken Benson has seen in this novel an attempt by Benet to transform the narrative conventions of neorealism. The novel opens with what seems the beginning of a family story in an almost traditional fashion: the grandfather's house is described and given a precise geographical location within Región, the time is clearly indicated for the purchase of the land (the end of the nineteenth century), and it proceeds to introduce its characters (the grandfather, his daughters, the neighboring Ruan family). According to Benson, "in this work the author elaborates a polished remodeling of the prevailing literary sensibility of the time, by transforming the narrative contract shaped by realist poetics into a new fictional pact that will mold a new hermeneutic attitude on the part of the reader. In this way, although the beginning of the novel complies with the canon of realist referentiality, Benet will slowly introduce the reader into more complex passages, in which the rules of realist literature are abandoned or ridiculed to establish a metaphorical conception of literature which refers to an internal experience of possible worlds created through imagination."[64]

Without denying this indictment of the referential poetics of neorealism, I would like to explore the possibility that the text also—perhaps reluctantly—pays tribute, although a negative one, to the new narrativity. A novel that begins by describing the founder of a family saga and ends in destruction (a fire) has to bring to mind García Márquez's *Cien años de soledad*, which does seem to work as a hypotext for Benet's novel. According to Genette's analysis of hypertextuality, *Una meditación* could be viewed as functioning according to a semantic transformation that affects the signification of the hypotext—*Cien años de soledad*—by changing its diegesis (that is, the course of events and the fictional world in which these take place) and by overturning its axiology.[65]

Una meditación begins by charting the narrative world of Región, the fictional geography first created in *Volverás a Región*. Almost as if to prevent the reader from comparing Región to García Márquez's Macondo, some of the fictional similarities between these two worlds are soon degraded by an ironic voice that from time to time provides some surprisingly humorous tones to the meditation. The patriarch is, like the first José Arcadio Buendía, a visionary entrepreneur who aims to lead the transformation of the land he and his family come to inhabit by bringing in electricity; the stature of his vision, however, is devalued by showing his own ignorance of the "power" (that is, electrical energy):

Todavía cuando yo era niño nadie sabía demasiado bien (ni siquiera el abuelo) lo que era la fuerza ni para qué servía y por eso se la tenía en

mucho e incluso se la temía. . . . En el espíritu de todos estaba que el
único que de verdad sabía lo que era la fuerza era el señor Hocher . . .
pero nadie se lo quería preguntar. Y el que menos mi abuelo porque ni
siquiera podía imaginar (y eso era lo que más le aterraba) a qué clase
de cosas quedaría obligado a cambio de la información.

[When I was still a child nobody knew too well (not even grandfather)
what power was or what it was good for and that was why it was held
in high regard and even fear. . . . It was on everybody's mind that the
only person who really knew what power was was Mr. Hocher . . . but
nobody wanted to ask him, least of all my grandfather, because he
couldn't even imagine (and that was what frightened him most) what
sort of things he would be obligated to exchange for the information.][66]

In a similar fashion, and reminiscent of the Buendía's fate, all the
women in the family are solemnly declared to be affected by a flaw,
which in the case of Aunt Isabel manifests in a "passion" for reading every night a Parnassian poet (José María de Heredia), a practice that will eventually render her sterile, although the narrator
indicates somewhere else that "it seemed" that what she actually
used to read was Dumas's *The Count of Monte Cristo*.[67] The passage is thus doubly ironic: it exposes the pretentiousness of Aunt
Isabel, who is so dominated by her own self-image as reader of
high-brow poetry that she ends up declaiming Heredia's French
verses at her deathbed, but it also makes mockery of the same family flaw motive the narrator was supposedly presenting to build up
the story, thus canceling the inchoate storytelling of the narrative.

In a 1970 interview, right after the publication on *Una meditación*, Benet praised García Márquez, even comparing *Cien años de
soledad* to Velázquez's *Las Meninas*.[68] This remark, however, has
to be read keeping in mind the sort of doublespeak Benet was so
fond of delivering, and that is present as well in "De Canudos a
Macondo" (1969), Benet's review of *Cien años de soledad*. Although this text presents itself as a positive appraisal of García Márquez (whom Benet describes—together with Carpentier, Rulfo, and
Vargas Llosa—as representative of an outstanding epic writing in
the tradition of Euclides da Cunha), the reading is not completely
univocal. Part of the review is devoted to narrating the numerous
obstacles Benet found in reading the novel, which are attributed to a
ludicrously defective copy—"transposed paragraphs, lines printed
backwards, a few semitransparent pages that made it impossible to
read any of their sides."[69] Benet proceeds to narrate the story of his

relationship with a genie he blames for such contingencies: working as an unsolicited mentoring figure, its interventions would have served to conduct Benet's literary tastes in the right direction (exemplified by Kafka and Faulkner) and away from the wrong one (represented here by Spanish writers Pérez Galdós and Pérez de Ayala). However, since in the case at hand the genie seems to be disapproving rather than facilitating the reading of *Cien años de soledad*, such a tale would actually place García Márquez on the same position as the authors of *Torquemada* and *A.M.D.G.*, that is, belonging to the sort of literature to be avoided. It could be argued that Benet is using here the same ironic reversal at work in the opening pages of *Una meditación*. This duplicity was cleared up in 1975, when—once again discussing his ideas on the Latin American new novel—Benet declared: "I like García Márquez, but he doesn't interest me at all—neither his themes nor his way of writing. Pleasure is something that, occasionally, suspends morality and can become corrupted, while interest is purer and immutable, a permanent vector. Pleasure, to a certain extent, is so capricious that one day it can be satisfied with García Márquez's pages."[70]

Una meditación, however, does more than simply play ironic games on García Márquez. It takes many of the essential elements of its hypotext and transforms them, resemanticizes them in a different order of fictionality. Both authors, for instance, share a common preoccupation with the passage of time. At the end of Benet's novel, where the slow-paced meditation is set in motion by the sudden movement of Cayetano Corral's clock, the text regains a certain familiarity with the roaring ending of Macondo. The figure of Cayetano Corral, who is said to hold the key to the end of the narration,[71] plays a structural role similar to that of the last Aureliano Buendía: both are self-incarcerated characters who devote themselves to analyze the fabric of a mechanism (a clock in Benet, a text in García Márquez) in a process that will eventually lead to destruction. In *Una meditación*, the throbbing sound of Cayetano's clock echoes across the physical and psychological geography of Región, which until then—and after the terrors of the Civil War—has been dominated by the silent, dark mass of Mantua:

> Toda esa masa de monte negro y bajo, apelotonado al otro lado del río, de horizontes superpuestos en los que asoman escondidos en la maleza tramos de veredas que aún producen escalofríos, no es en sustancia más que la masa de silencio precipitado en miedo con que el país aceptó y disfrazó su renuncia a la violencia.

[That whole mass of squat, low mountain, piled up on the other side of the river, with horizons superimposed on those that appear hidden in the underbrush, stretches of trails that still bring on shivers, is not, in substance, anything but the mass of silence precipitated in fear with which the country accepted and disguised its renunciation of violence.][72]

The order of things, however, has been reversed: in *Cien años de soledad* the final apocalypse marks the end of events, the closure of history; in *Una meditación*, on the contrary, the fire signals an end to an era of silence and stagnation and the reintroduction of Región into history—a movement that should not be understood as uplifting, since in Benet's cosmology ruin and decay prevail and history remains unstable.[73]

I will not attempt to press any further the similarities between the two texts. My objective is not to postulate García Márquez's text as a necessary instrument in reading Benet's, but to show how they can be related at certain junctures and to suggest that such similarities are not the result of a chance parallelism of heterogenous inceptions. That is the reason why, following Genette, a case should be made here for a hypertextual—rather than intertextual—relation.[74] What those texts have in common points to the active presence of Latin American writing as a model to be reckoned with when defining the course of Spanish fiction, even when this was done through fictional forms that distanced themselves from the patronage of such model.

Torrente Ballester's *La saga/fuga de J.B.*, on the other hand, advocates a model of fictionality completely different from that of Benet's. The monotonous meditative narrator of the latter is replaced here by a tongue-in-cheek polymorphous voice that, instead of working through the remains of memory, plays with openly fictitious stories. If Región and its misfortune have been properly understood as a metaphor of Spain, Castroforte del Baralla (Torrente's imaginary territory) is more of a playground where wit roams unleashed. The fantastic tale of the city crosses over several centuries and is full of stories that overlap—and often contradict—each other; sometimes the same event is narrated several times, not in order to offer different perspectives and thus to honor or question a search for the truth, but simply to play out its possibilities and entertain the audience. The central core of the novel shows a fundamental debt to Cervantes's *Don Quijote*: the text is constantly insisting on the interplay between imagination and reality, and the ironic narrative ambiguously supports both the wisdom and the foolishness of the hero, José Bastida.[75]

The issue of the comparison between the novels by Torrente and García Márquez seems to have been a permanent theme in Spanish scholarship at the time of the publication of *La saga/fuga de J.B.* Dionisio Ridruejo established that connection in 1972: "[*Cien años de soledad* is a] book that we should never completely lose sight of when reading *La Saga*, which in a way rebels against it."[76] In fact, many similarities can be listed, although they do not necessarily provide evidence of direct influence. Castroforte del Baralla is created as the setting for the story of a family saga that is full of fantastic anecdotes and has its own share of incestuous couplings. The story is constantly intertwined with mythical references, although—contrary to García Márquez—they tend to be drawn more from pagan than from biblical sources. The narrative also makes constant use of prolepses and analepses that disrupt the traditional linearity a genealogical tree would seem to suggest, and this is further complicated by the repetition of names (in this case, initials: J.B.). Furthermore, while it was the Buendía's destiny to live for a hundred years, the lineage of J.B. is summoned to be defeated and disappear after exactly one thousand years.[77] Important differences, however, exist between the novels: whereas García Márquez is more interested in the interaction between myth, history, and fiction (the three being put together by the driving force of storytelling), Torrente delights in playing out intellectual games with culture—a good example is the story of Pedro Abelardo and Heloísa being narrated against the figures of Jean-Paul Sartre and Simone de Beauvoir.[78] Such is the presence of metafictional interplay between different diegetic levels, such is the overwhelming weight of ironic discrediting of the narrating voices, that the story seems on the verge of self-destruction. In *La saga/fuga de J.B.* the reader is rarely allowed that suspension of disbelief that makes a narration credible and therefore effective as fiction. The pleasure the reader takes in reading this novel is not to be found in the fictional display of imagination, but in the metafictional laying bare of the formal and conceptual components of the text.

What the analysis of the reception of *La saga/fuga de J.B.* does prove, however, is how the model of narrativity popularized and legitimized by García Márquez was instrumental in framing the reading of Torrente's text. Many reviewers saw the novel not only as a much needed response to the narrative shortage of the 1960s, but also and especially as the first to be autochthonously produced by Spanish—as opposed to Latin American—writers. After years of simultaneously analyzing the success of *Cien años de soledad* and deploring the absence of stories in Spanish fiction, many critics quickly seized Torrente's novel as evidence of a turning point. *La saga/fuga de J.B.* was thus seen as a sort of Spanish reaction to the invasion of Latin American narrative. This is clearly seen by Martín Vilumara (pseudonym of the publisher José Batlló) in his review of the novel (1973):

> At least, Torrente's work shows us that the alleged inferiority of Spanish literature in comparison to that of countries linked to it by a common language is not due to any biological and congenital (some might say racial) incapacity on our part. And it also shows that despite the "hindrance" of the all-too-frequently reviled Academy . . . on this side of the Atlantic there also exist people who are capable of using the "stagnant Peninsular Spanish" as a living language, powerful and apt for expressing the subtlest ideas or nuances that the human mind can imagine. In case that's not enough . . . even if there were no other examples to offer, which is not the case, . . . [*La saga/fuga de J.B.*] destroys by itself that cliché about the lack of imagination suffered by the Spanish novel, and it does so not theoretically but by practicing what it preaches.[79]

The early reception of the novel seemed to have blurred the differences between *Cien años de soledad* and *La saga/fuga de J.B.* to such an extent that Torrente once admitted that questions about possible relationships between those texts were so common that he had become used to expecting them. Interestingly, however, he complained that such a connection was a distinct Spanish phenomenon: "Not one single foreigner has ever questioned me about my possible relationship to García Márquez. . . . Since they do not share in our inferiority complex, they admit that a Spaniard can create something decent without copying it from anyone. But we have lost faith in ourselves to such an extent that we doubt it and are unable to explain it."[80] It is here that Latin American fiction, and especially García Márquez, can be seen as playing an important paratextual role in Spanish literary life. Whether influenced or not at the production stage, at the time of processing and consumption Spanish texts were interpreted taking into consideration the codes set forth by the dominant Latin American models. For it is indeed a measure of such dominance by a certain poetics that other fictional products should be judged and appreciated according to the parameters it introduces within the system.

THE ROLE OF THE READER: ANTAGONISM AND COMPLICITY

In a 1969 essay, published at the height of García Márquez's success, the critic and poet Félix Grande described how the reception of the Latin American novel in Spain had functioned as a reminder to both writers and readers that literature could be a vivacious and even entertaining activity: "it has recalled that the practice of literature . . . can be a Faustian, ludic—however we want to call it—act. And this serves . . . to realize the possibility that the presumed reader of novels will not get bored to death. . . . This, in itself, seems too modest a goal; but when you nearly get flattened by one of those weighty representatives of the Spanish severe style in its purest form, you understand that the enjoyable quality [of Latin American fiction] almost deserves that we grovel on the floor howling with gratitude."[81]

As we have seen, the praise for such an ideal of *charm* and *amenity* in writing, that is, the canonization of the entertaining function of literature, is perhaps the innovation of greatest consequence during this period. The recovery of fictional narrativity was one central concern for those who considered that the Spanish novel was losing ground by denying its readers anything that could be regarded as a compromise of high-brow aesthetic principles, that is, a concession to a storytelling that had been associated with traditional and outdated novelistic forms. A tension between two understandings of literary communication, either as instruction or delectation, permeates the production of the period. Until the arrival of the Boom novel, most Spanish writers had been more interested in documenting reality and, later on, in experimenting with form, than in providing good stories to read. The militant attitude social novelists had instilled in literary practice as exhortative discourse had not disappeared, but merely displaced itself from political to aesthetic principles: in both cases it was the author—not the reader—who knew what was to be done with literature. I would like in this context to compare two paradigmatic novels of the period, Juan Benet's *Volverás a Región* (1967) and Eduardo Mendoza's *La verdad sobre el caso Savolta* (1975). While the first has been considered one of the peaks of Spanish experimentalism, the popular and critical recognition awarded to the second signaled the revival of the narrative of adventure.

There is little doubt that Juan Benet has been one of the most aggressive opponents of an abdication of high-brow literary principles in contemporary Spanish letters. In 1974, Benet wrote a brief note recounting the history of the writing and publication of his first novel *Volverás a Región*. The text of this note had for a while a double existence: it was published as "Breve historia de *Volverás a Región*" in *Revista de Occidente* and, simultaneously, it appeared as a preface—under the title "Prólogo a la segunda edición"—to an ephemeral printing of the novel in Alianza Editorial's paperback series "El libro de bolsillo."[82] Critics have rightly read it as a more or less faithful account of the novel's creative process, and as such those pages have become a required point of reference to those interested in reconstructing the history of the writing of the novel, or the origin and inspiration of its constituent elements.[83] The specifically prefacial function of the note, on the other hand, seems to have suffered the same destiny as the edition it introduced, and has been relegated to an anecdotal status. But it is precisely because it functioned as a prologue that the text acquires a special significance: it transcends the chronicle to become a prescription, an *exemplary* history.

The exemplary will of the preface is manifested in two complementary aspects: first, Benet gives examples of the original reception of his manuscript and comments on them; second, and since those comments directly give an evaluation, Benet also sets an example for future readers about how to read—and, equally important, how not to read—his novel. In reviewing the various comments elicited by his manuscript, Benet remembers with particular emphasis the following: "The best I got were a couple of letters . . . signed by young ladies who, not content with declaring the impossibility of publication, took pleasure in pointing out to me the vices into which I had fallen as a storyteller. 'Your novel,' one said, 'lacks dialogue. Don't forget that almost all the public reads is dialogue, which is also the best exponent of a novelist's skill.' I think that around the beginning of 1965 I sent the original to two friends, Dionisio Ridruejo and José Suárez Carreño, who, startled by several of its pages, insistently urged me to correct and unburden them."[84] Benet appears to relish pointing out a particular feature of his novel: the text sets up for the reader a position of inescapable and deliberate strangeness. *Volverás a Región* has produced admiration, but also uncertainty: in one of the first reviews, Guelbenzu declared that the novel "plunges the reader in a profound puzzlement"; its argument, according to Gimferrer, "is virtually inextricable."[85] It is not my concern here to enumerate or decipher the various forms that strangeness adopts in the novel, but rather to verify that Benet knew about the distinctive effect his work was going to have on the reading public of the 1960s in Spain and that he was consciously writing against their expectations.

But the reactions listed by Benet as examples serve also to set up important distinctions between them. Describing the changes he introduced in the last revision of the manuscript, Benet returns to his readers: "In that last transcription the modifications were minimal; I eliminated one whole dubious passage . . . , I divided the whole into four chapters and—unable to forget the censure of that secretary who knew the duties of a writer so well—I eliminated all dialogues except one."[86] Of all these changes, the first ones are clearly intended to accommodate the suggestions made by those readers who deserve Benet's respect, that is, Ridruejo and Suárez Carreño; the last one, however, is explicitly conceived to contradict or even to incommode the *young ladies*. Years later, in an interview published in 1991, as Benet remembered again the vicissitudes of his manuscript, the same female figure would pop up once more in the same disgusted light: "She gave me a lesson, because I then opened my draft, which had only three pieces of dialogue in three hundred pages, and crossed two out. I did not think her reasons were sufficient to stop me from doing what I wanted."[87]

It is not difficult to share with the writer an ironic and offended gaze upon the meddling lesson of the publishing secretary. Our profession, after all, demands the defense of creative independence and the custody of those difficult texts that provoke the creaking of the often indulgent mechanisms of culture. But the anonymous figure of that early reader of the first Benet novel also deserves consideration, as it can be taken as an index of a period in which profound transformations are taking place in the relationships between creation and reception. Because, ironically, those pages by Benet exist in the paratextual frame of the second edition of the novel—and it is here that the prefatory nature of the text becomes relevant: while the series "El libro de bolsillo" has had from the very beginning an openly popularizing intent, Benet's novel—as the preface clearly indicates—is not, and does not wish to be, *pocket-book literature*.[88]

The implacable Benetian defense of the freedom of the author

and the creative work before all kinds of external pressures is sufficiently known: "I can't think about the audience when I sit down
to write. No one thinks about the audience, save for the professional
writer who has no choice; if he didn't, he wouldn't sell and he'd
starve."[89] Within this frame, the relation between author and reader
can only be conceptualized as a commercial transaction: it is possible exclusively as a surrender of aesthetic principles to the anti-val-
ues of the marketplace. Benet's distrust toward the consumer of
fiction appears at a moment when—after the crisis of the neorealist
model—the field is left open to the struggle between alternative literary models and, consequently, to a rethinking of the connections
between the literary work and the social horizon of expectations.
As Ana María Moix said, "Benet appears and writes not to say
something but to create good literature."[90] With Benet and the
members of the experimental movement, Spanish novelists realize—as the poets had done years earlier—that literature is not a
form of communication.

It would be fallacious, however, to establish a strict dichotomy
between two goals. The difference between a literary practice that
wishes to "say something" (the position defended by the aesthetic
and political avant-garde of the 1950s) and another that aims to
"write well" (the experimentalism that dominated the late 1960s
and early 1970s) hides the fact that they both share equal suspicions
about the role of the reader. It is worth remembering that Castellet's
influential essay *La hora del lector* had not provided, in spite of its
title, a vindication of the reader. The third chapter, "A Literature
Without Readers," presented as a denunciation of the "divorce existing today between writer and reader," turns out to be an indictment of the literary public: the problem, Castellet says, does not
rest on a writer's failure to create, but rather on the deplorable state
of a readership that is not sufficiently intelligent or creative to follow the authors in the artistic investigation of reality. According to
Castellet, the divorce between author and reader is due to two factors. The first is the "resistance of readers" against innovation:
"The first [cause] refers to the intellectual inertia of men, their inevitable mental sloth in the face of novelty, their difficulties of
adapting to hitherto unknown occurrences or situations, and—in
the case that concerns us here—to the readers' resistance to new
techniques, new modes of telling that render and are justified by a
new conception of the world."[91] The second cause echoes the first:
while "the reader, in most cases, is still merely a reader," the twen-

tieth century has given birth to the "intelligent artist," one who—as the most authentic product of modernity, and differently from the nineteenth-century writer—is able not only to create but also to criticize. As creator-cum-critic, the task of the novelist is to guide the reader, and the public—no matter how much it may resist literary innovation—has no other alternative than to give in to creative authority: "Whether he does it with more or less violence depends on his subjectivity and intelligence. In any event, his defense, however stubborn it may be, will be useless, and it will only succeed in slowing down for awhile the inevitable progress of art, which—also inevitably—will follow the rhythm of humanity's general progress."[92] Castellet does caution against a "literary onanism" that would favor pure creation over the need to communicate—in the 1950s it is still required to *say something*. But these reservations are formulated in such terms that it would not be hard to discard them later in the interests of creative autonomy, as it is clear that it amounted to a tactical gesture that rested solely on an instrumental conception of the writer's social role. His messianic conception of literature, stripped of its political bent and the demand for social communication, would therefore still serve as a basis for the next generation of avant-garde writers.

In fact, ten years later, in a conference on the novel that took place in August 1967 at the Universidad Menéndez Pelayo, Castellet's avant-gardist principles were still remarkably alive. The Spanish writer Jesús Torbado contributed a lecture—"La manta a la cabeza: reflexiones urgentes sobre literatura nueva y sociedad"— that typifies the aesthetic self-congratulation we are bound to find in what Pierre Bourdieu has termed "the cultural field of restricted production," where prestige is built not on the recognition of wide audiences (which is demoted as purely commercial success) but on that of a selected group of connoisseurs.[93] For Torbado, new Spanish novelists had to face one basic problem: the reluctance of the public to accept the originality of their work. As in Castellet, this issue is raised not to question the writers' work—that is, their ability to communicate with the readers—but to deplore the public itself: "I am decided to write something 'new,' something 'original'. . . . I am sure I can say something new, but I'm also sure that novelty is not appreciated in Spain. . . . The truly 'revolutionary' novel is banned. It doesn't even please the critics. Everything new, besides being dangerous, is useless. While a *modern* book hardly has any distribution, any old story written by living novelists who cultivate traditional fields will be deserving of praise, announcements, and success."[94]

At first sight, it would appear that the experimentalist disdain for popular forms of fiction—and for the idea of popular literature itself—would place writers like Benet at a distance from the positions of the previous generation, which had championed the project of a literature both critical and realistic.[95] And yet, while important differences do exist between those two groups, what they all have in common is a twin distrust against the taste of the masses: for some, grounded on the modernist notion of autonomous creation, art is necessarily elitist, as it has to be performed against the instincts of the majority; for others—heirs to an avant-gardist tradition bent on reintegrating aesthetics and life—militant art has to shy away from the alienated commodification of massified culture.[96] In both cases, the reader is relegated to a secondary position in the literary process.

Benet's *Volverás a Región* is a text grounded on antagonism and friction that characterizes itself by the constant frustration of the reader's expectations and by the hazards of a narrative discourse that rarely accedes to grant its audience a comfortable position. The novel enigmatically opens with the presence of a anonymous traveler destined to lose his way and die in the mountains of Región:

> Es cierto, el viajero que saliendo de Región pretende llegar a su sierra siguiendo el antiguo camino real—porque el moderno dejó de serlo—se ve obligado a atravesar un pequeño y elevado desierto que parece interminable.
>
> Un momento u otro conocerá el desaliento al sentir que cada paso hacia adelante no hace sino alejarlo un poco más de aquellas desconocidas montañas. Y un día tendrá que abandonar el propósito y demorar aquella remota decisión de escalar su cima más alta. . . . O bien—tranquilo, sin desesperación, invadido de una suerte de indiferencia que no deja lugar a los reproches—dejará transcurrir su último atardecer, tumbado en la arena de cara al crepúsculo, contemplando cómo en el cielo desnudo esos hermosos, extraños y negros pájaros que han de acabar con él, evolucionan en altos círculos.

> [It's true, the traveler leaving Región who wishes to reach its mountain range by following the old king's highway—because the modern one has ceased to be such—will find himself obliged to cross a small, high desert that seems endless.
>
> At one moment or another he will get to know the discouragement of

feeling that every step forward is only bringing him a little farther away
from those unknown mountains. And one day he will have to give up
his intent and put off that remote decision to scale their highest summit.
. . . Or rather—calm, with no despair, invaded by a kind of indifference
that leaves no room for reproach—he will let his last sunset pass, lying
on the sand facing it, watching how in the naked sky the beautiful,
strange, black birds that are to finish him off maneuver in high circles.][97]

The first human figure to appear in the text, the Traveler—as
Costa and Manteiga have both argued—seems to invite the identification of the reader; but his itinerary through Región is everything
but relaxing, as he remains mute during his wanderings, and ends
up moribund "among cries of pain and tears of fright."[98] Thus, in
this text the only possible presence allowed to the public is in the
form of abandonment: the reader has no other alternative than to
surrender and follow the author's initiative toward the discovery of
a personal literary universe where there is no other will than the
writer's.[99] If there is any suggestion of communication between the
author and the reader, it is a process distorted by the noise of the
unexpected or the ineffable—the bang of a distant automobile, or
the shots fired by the Numa, the ancient watchman whose presence
is yet one more enigma in Región. To begin with, the expectations
raised by the title (the *volverás*—"you will return"—that as a com-
mand appears to address the narratee directly) turn up to be blurred
from the first line: the movement of *return* anticipated by the reader
is contradicted by the Traveler, who *is leaving* Región—and the
identification between the reader and the character thus becomes
unstable. Benet's writing parallels here the introverted drive identified by Fletcher and Bradbury in the narratives of Henry James as
a constitutive element of modernist fiction: the establishment of a
collusion between author and characters, who seem to know more
than what it is expressed in the text—which leaves the reader ostracized in the margins of the narrated world.[100] The uneasiness of the
reader is built upon an equally unstable relationship between narrative discourse and diegesis: the opening statement of certainty at
the beginning of the novel ("It's true") is gradually diminished and
eventually contradicted in the opening lines of the remaining chapters: "It certainly was," "I don't know whether it was true or not,"
"I don't know."[101]

It must be stressed, however, that the violence inflicted upon the
reader is not gratuitous. In Benet's narratives, the wandering of the

reader is designed and scripted to shatter the ideological and conceptual conventions that usually allow for a potentially deceptive recognition of appearances. In this, despite his own declarations to the contrary, Benet remains close to the programmatic intentions of *nouveau roman* writers like Nathalie Sarraute.[102] On the other hand, together with the formal and aesthetic exploration, there is also—as María Elena Bravo has noted—a profoundly moral sense in Benet's work: "Benet's literature forces us, as readers, . . . to recognize the passage from action and experience to verbalization, from memory to the present, from history and fiction to life." The reader-traveler in *Volverás a Región* is an antagonist because the narrative is an investigation that strives to disorientate, since it is against the habits and the myths of conventional wisdom that this literature is created to explore areas yet unknown to a Spanish collective will still anesthetized by postwar ideology.[103]

If Benet is the perfect example of experimental, restricted-audience writing, the position of Eduardo Mendoza could not be more different. Since the publication in 1975 of *La verdad sobre el caso Savolta*, his novels have been endorsed by a degree of commercial success that—perhaps inevitably—has also been accompanied by an ambiguous critical reception.[104] In contrast to experimental antagonism, Mendoza's novel offers the reader a relation grounded on complicity: the text appears as the expression of a collective literary world that it aims to reformulate by means of a return to its foundations—that is, a recovery of traditional narrative. While Benet seeks to surprise the readers and overcome their resistance by creating a text that antagonizes their expectations and reading habits, in Mendoza the interest of the audience is tempted by a narrative that satisfies the desire for adventure while simultaneously foregrounding the structural conventions of the tale.

The reader in *La verdad sobre el caso Savolta* cannot be further away from Benet's nebulous traveler: the novel opens with a discourse addressed to a collective group that functions as an ideological accomplice (the audience of journalist Pajarito de Soto) and before which the narrative presents itself as an act of recognition:

El autor del presente artículo y de los que seguirán se ha impuesto la tarea de desvelar en forma concisa y asequible a las mentes sencillas de los trabajadores, aun los más iletrados, aquellos hechos que, por haber sido presentados al conocimiento del público en forma oscura y difusa, tras el *camouflage* de la retórica y la profusión de cifras más propias al entendimiento y comprensión del docto que del lector ávido de verdades claras y no de entresijos aritméticos, permanecen todavía ignorados de las masas trabajadoras que son, no obstante, sus víctimas más principales.

[The author of this article and those that follow in this series has taken on the task of clarifying in a concise form accessible to the simple minds of workers, even the most ignorant among them, those events which, because they were presented to the public in diffuse, obscure fashion, camouflaged in rhetoric and a glut of figures more appropriate for experts than for readers eager to learn clear truths and not mathematical puzzles, still remain unknown to the working masses, who are, nevertheless, their principal victims.][105]

Of course, we should not confuse the "author" Pajarito de Soto with the writer who gives a title to the novel, but the semic code points out the possibility of establishing some connections between them: 1) the testimonial intent to *reveal the truth* about certain *events* or *facts*, 2) the desire to attend the needs and interests of an *avid reader* not necessarily *versed* in the *profusion of codes*, and—above all—3) the common interest in creating a collective knowledge concerning a *case* of social significance, a case in which to the dichotomy between truth and falsehood (present in the title of the novel) corresponds, in Pajarito de Soto's ideological discourse, a similar one between justice and injustice.

Since its first installment, the work of Eduardo Mendoza has been characterized by two basic traits. First, from a thematic point of view, Mendoza has concentrated his attention in tracing and reconstructing the collective memory of Barcelona and in inquiring about its present, which is also the present of the Spanish political transition to democracy—in 1981, and in reference to *La verdad sobre el caso Savolta*, the novelist declared: "I wanted to make a novel about Barcelona . . . I did not attempt a historical reconstruction but rather to capture that collective memory."[106] Whereas *Volverás a Región* attempts to explore an unknown reality buried within the abyss of individual consciousness, *La verdad sobre el caso Savolta* suggests to the reader the recovery of a common reality that is to be recognized: the social and political world of the 1920s as seen from the perspective of 1970s Spain (and vice versa).

Second, and from a structural point of view, Mendoza's texts are marked by the juxtaposition of narrative genres. The structure of *La verdad sobre el caso Savolta*, with its changing narrating voices and various but recognizable imaginary regions (the nineteenth-century realist novel, the detective novel, the picaresque), is addressed to a reader who is aware of the discursive legacy of literary tradition. Parody—the conscious recycling of past narrative forms—constitutes the axis of writing, as its mechanism is made of elements taken from public models potentially recognizable by the reader of popular literature. Thus, against the discursive practice of experimentalism—a discourse of rupture that strives for originality by means of its sheer individuality—parodic discourse appeals to the palimpsest of voices available within a common heritage. Benet's reader is forced to abandon his literary competence (habitual generic norms, traditional forms of reading), rendered useless by the diegetic intricacies of Región. With Mendoza, on the contrary, that which is already known becomes instrumental to negotiate the heteroglossia of the text.

Between 1967 and 1975—between Benet and Mendoza—the modernist construction of the reader underwent a fundamental shift. As Julio Ortega has pointed out, the turning point is García Márquez's *Cien años de soledad*, as with this novel "history is shifted, as narrative, to a reconstructed subject, to the critical consensus of popular culture."[107] Perhaps what Ricardo Gullón, in his analysis of the novel, described as a recovery of the forgotten art of storytelling was also an appeal for the forgotten pleasure to *be narrated*, in a double sense: to be both the audience of a narrating act and the object of a narration that confers meaning upon our experience of the world. It is in this direction that Manuel Vázquez Montalbán (originally identified during the 1960s as a *poeta novísimo*, roughly the generational equivalent of experimentalism in poetry) would advance in the early seventies a literary praxis purged of elitist self-indulgence and attentive to the modes of popular fiction: "What I have here ready and willing to read me is not the vast majority of people. The vast majority is devoted to Mannix, Ironside, and Corín Tellado. And from that I deduced that Mannix, Ironside and Corín Tellado must have something there. My great respect for the vast majority obliges me not to force them to read me and to try instead to find out why they read what they read."[108]

Thus, while Spanish letters during the sixties are witness to the collapse of—and the reaction against—the social novel, they are also conditioned by the crisis of the political and aesthetic foundations of modernity. Linda Hutcheon has shown how postmodernist art fashions itself as anti-elitist, making frequent and often parodic use of well-known forms in order to break away from the isolating practices of modernism.[109] In this sense, the "subliterature of agitation" promoted by Vázquez Montalbán and exemplified in Mendoza's novel represents an attempt to chart a postmodern poetics equally distant from both aestheticized anticommercialism and populist condescension. On the one hand, the strategy thus proposed aims to rescue—under the narrative turn imposed by the success of García Márquez—Spanish narrative from the predicament to which modernist experimentalism was leading it. On the other, it endeavors to create a new form of avant-garde novel (in the sense mentioned above of forging the reintegration of art and life) that would remain true to the ethical commitment of the neorealist generation and capable, at the same time, of overcoming its aesthetic limitations.[110] Far from being simply a concession to the instincts of the reader (and thus far from what in Spain has been termed *light literature*), the new narrativity advanced by Vázquez Montalbán and Mendoza resorts to parody to enact a mode of pleasant but demanding reading that requires a multiple competence—linguistic, literary, even ideological (since its comprehension presupposes also a critical awareness of social and cultural values). Parody creates a dialogical channel between the present and the past, and thus makes a basic contribution to the self-reflexive nature of literary postmodernity.[111]

If it is plausible to argue that from the mid-fifties until the mid-sixties Spanish narrative production was read against the background of testimonial poetics, during the following decade (1965–75) that central position was occupied by the Latin American new novel. However, while Spanish neorealist novels converged toward a single model and somehow substantiate the notion of a literary orthodoxy, under the aegis of the new novel there was a wide diversity of forms, and it should not surprise us that the literary landscape during that period appears to us much more fragmented than the previous one. The three central directions of autochthonous Spanish literary production during the 1970s—testimonial history (whether individual or collective), discursive experimentalism, and fictional storytelling[112]—developed in fruitful interaction with the Boom.

5
Literatures in Revolt

THE RECEPTION OF THE BOOM NOVEL IN SPAIN WAS A CONFLICTIVE process that went beyond debating fictional forms, literary theories, or aesthetic preferences—it also questioned the relationship between a former metropolis and its colonies and contributed to a remapping of Spain's cultural identities. On the one hand, while the previous reception of North American, Italian, or French models during the 1950s did not threaten the status of national writers, some of these perceived the increasing popularity of Spanish American narrative as if it were a direct attack upon their artistic and cultural authority. In this, the Boom echoed similar debates previously elicited by *modernismo* about the balance of power between Peninsular and American intellectual and literary figures.[1] On the other hand, the emergence within the world of Hispanic letters of a poetic alternative strong enough to upset not only the internal structure of the literary system in Spain, but also the hegemony of Peninsular Spanish as the legitimate medium of cultural expression, supported the struggle of other languages hitherto marginalized within Spain to gain open access to the national arena.

As I have argued so far, the Boom novel provided the dominant models in the Spanish literary system by displacing the neorealist writing of the social novel generation and taking over its functions. Such a displacement is evident in all types of activity in literary life. As far as creation is concerned, we have already seen how Latin American fiction became prominent as a textual source—of either hypotextual or intertextual nature—for Spanish writers, as the aesthetic norms of the main directions of Spanish fiction during the 1960s and early 1970s were closely affected by the contact with the Boom. The mediating role of publishing companies was equally affected by the transformation of the market—particularly in the area of what Bourdieu has defined as restricted production. The clearest example, as we have seen, is found in the publishing house

Seix Barral, which—having nurtured and supported the social novel—became the main outpost of the Latin American new novel in Spain. Literary supplements and magazines opened their pages to contributions on the Boom, often by their own protagonists, literary prizes were awarded, and chairs of Spanish American literature were soon created at Spanish universities.[2] The depreciation of the neorealist model ran parallel to the canonization of the Boom as the foremost representative of modern writing, and after 1967, with the publication of *Cien años de soledad* and the awarding of the Nobel Prize to Miguel Ángel Asturias, Latin American narrative seemed to have replaced the French *nouveau roman* as the yardstick against which contemporary fiction was to be measured.[3]

All this activity confirms the effective nature of a restructuring of the Spanish literary field, in which the writers, texts, and values of Latin American fiction became increasingly dominant over those of Spain's autochthonous production. Such a change was more than a question of aesthetic preferences. It involved a displacement of cultural and ideological capital, and eventually exploded in an open conflict of interests.

THE WHEAT AND THE CHAFF: THE POLEMICS BETWEEN SPANISH AND LATIN AMERICAN LETTERS

The canonization of the Boom novel did not go unchallenged, not only in Spain but also around the Hispanic world. Early criticism of the new trend was directed at its supposedly mimetic practices: in several occasions, critics like Manuel Pedro González and Ignacio Iglesias presented the new novel as a mere epigone of foreign modernism, even as the illegitimate product of a carefully orchestrated commercial operation (what was referred to as a "mafia" of writers and publishers).[4] Following this lead, Spanish novelist Ángel María de Lera—who had enjoyed some success after winning the 1967 Planeta Prize with *Las últimas banderas*, the first novelistic testimony of the Civil War from the Republican side to be published in Spain—questioned the growing interest in the Latin American novel. In 1968 he echoed the accusations of mimicry and formalism, and then proceeded to differentiate between Spanish and Spanish American literatures:

> I am amazed . . . at those who attempt to elevate gibberish to a supreme stylistic formula and who want to have us write now—after the healthy

purge of Azorín, Baroja, and Machado—in an archaic language which is full of echoes of our 17th century. If Spanish-American writers have only recently discovered Quevedo and Valle-Inclán or, in case they already know them, let themselves be amazed by such prose to the point of imitating them, that's their problem. This is a sea that, fortunately, we have already sailed and crossed a long time ago. . . . We don't believe any Colombian or Cuban is going to teach Spanish to Delibes, for instance. Enough is enough.[5]

The fact that writers from Spanish America were being exalted as masters of the Spanish language and outranking their Castilian counterparts became a central point of controversy in the late 1960s—the burning question of Spanish literary life. It is distinctly present in almost all literary conferences and periodicals during 1969, where the question of the Boom novel was passionately debated.

With very few exceptions, the various arguments advanced in these debates did not escape a reductive dichotomy between two groups of writers, Spanish and Latin American, and geographical differences overshadowed all other considerations. The fact that such a contraposition was established around national—not aesthetic—identities reveals the shifting balance of power in the Spanish literary field. As was noted in the earlier chapters, in terms of novelistic technique and purpose, Vargas Llosa had more in common with Martín-Santos than he had with Cabrera Infante or Cortázar; and the narrativity of García Márquez was closer to the production of Torrente Ballester than to that of Carlos Fuentes. What was at stake, however, was not the artistic value of different literary forms or models of writing, but rather the privileged position of certain literary groups within a cultural field conceived according to national categories.

Lera's comments were further elaborated by the Spanish novelist Alfonso Grosso in a lecture entitled "Rómulo Gallegos, el americanismo y la novela hispanoamericana," given in Madrid on 24 April 1969. Grosso strayed off the announced topic and set out to question the prestige awarded to Latin American writers—particularly Cortázar and Vargas Llosa—by firing off a series of whimsical blasts intended to shock the Spanish public. According to Luis Carandell, who published a chronicle of the lecture, "Grosso did not propose to give a lecture, but rather—more probably—launch a manifesto. . . . He began by saying he was not a lecturer and that he had not gone there to say anything important about Rómulo Gallegos. . . . He stated that 'we hardly have any facts about Rómulo's life' and, immediately after, read a short paragraph of *Doña Bárbara*, highliting for the audience its deep Machadian resonances. It was at that moment when, unexpectedly, he dropped the first bomb of the evening: 'This morning,' he said, 'I read Julio Cortázar's declarations in *Life* magazine, and I have to say that Julio Cortázar is a buffoon.'" In an interview given a few weeks later to clarify his position, Grosso described Cortázar as "cold" and "histrionic" and García Márquez as a "bluff," and denounced as "turbid" the political commitment of writers like Vargas Llosa.[6] This gave way for the Madrid newspaper *Informaciones* to offer its pages to the exchange of contributions on the confrontation between Latin American and Spanish narratives. The "Polémica sobre una falsa polémica" opened with Rafael Conte's response to Grosso, "Carta abierta a Alfonso Grosso" (22 May 1969), and ended in the June 26 issue. Besides Grosso and Conte, it included the participation of Martínez-Menchén, Isaac Montero, Gustavo Fabra Barreiro, Javier Alfaya, Víctor Zalbidea, Eduardo García Rico, and Juan Pedro Quiñonero. The debate was echoed in other publications.[7]

As was widely recognized, the debate lacked intellectual depth and it was often marred by personal feuds. Behind most of the positions there was the often simplistic confrontation between, on the one hand, an oppressive sense of crisis in the narrative production of Spain and, on the other, an equally overwhelming conviction of the excellence of Latin American narrative. This dichotomy was reductionist because both factors were understood in terms of a series of characteristics that remained largely undisputed, despite the initial attempt by Rafael Conte to give the debate some degree of conceptual complexity. Quiñonero's contribution to the debate paid attention to these complexities as it analyzed *La ciudad y los perros* as conforming to the principles of neorealism, but the study of these connections was displaced by more mundane interests.[8] The "Spanish novel" was made to stand for the production of neorealism— leaving aside all consideration of other novelistic attempts (experimentalism, the metaphysical "new novel" group, or Cunqueiro's fiction, for instance)—and it was mostly confined to the qualification of "cabbage generation" (*generación de la berza*), a term intended to portray its extreme, downgraded realism. Little mention was made of the post-neorealist work of Juan Goytisolo or

Juan Marsé, and it seemed as if Martín-Santos's *Tiempo de silencio* was as much of an exception in 1969 as it had been in 1962. On the other side of the coin, "Latin American narrative" signified all but the most excellent artistic writing: against the rude odors of the cabbage generation, this production was perceived to be the champion of renewal not only in Hispanic, but also in world literature, and presented the aromatic gracefulness of sandalwood.[9] Given those premises and misconceptions, it was easy to enter the fight from a self-righteous position.

The attention given to Latin American narrative was viewed by some as an ideological plot intended to silence the socially committed voice of neorealist writers.[10] For others (Grosso among them), it was the result of commercial interests and—infuriated by what they perceived as preferential treatment toward Latin American authors—many writers addressed their attacks to critics and publishers who had turned their backs to Spanish authors for commercial and/or political gain. In general, it was a question of deciding what type of realism was more appropriate for the historical conditions of Spanish society. Thus, noted Martínez-Menchén, *cabbage* literature was truer to the experience of Spaniards: "novelistically speaking, cabbage evolutions are more valid for Spaniards of my generation than the song of the Buendías' elephantiasic priapisms."[11]

A year later, José María Gironella reignited the debate, questioning once again the deification of the Boom novel and criticizing the use of a double standard in the evaluation of Peninsular and Latin American literatures:

> Much of the praise given to writers like Miguel Ángel Asturias, Carpentier, Cortázar, Vargas Llosa, Rulfo, Fuentes, etc., refers to narrative elements that—if they were to be used by those of us writing in Spain—would surely bring us a string of insults.
>
> Those writers are praised for their "idiomatic baroqueness," their "inventiveness," their "localism or rootedness of an earthy, almost vegetable quality," the "multi-leveled construction" of their stories, etc. Besides the fact that none of that sounds very original to me, if I remember correctly our critics had crossed off baroqueness as an anachronism. . . . Likewise, "inventing" was regarded as a fugitive, evasive, and swindling element. . . . Also repeatedly questioned had been the notion that "only the local is universal." . . . With regard to stratified construction and other such balancing acts, they were deemed mere contributions to technical order, with no greater transcendence.[12]

The reason for this shift, in Gironella's view, was an infatuation with Third World revolutionary movements and the resulting mimeticism of cultural forms linked to them—together with a sort of political correctness that prevented the criticism of the new literary "deities." The truth, he declared, was that he found the reading of *Cien años de soledad*, *El siglo de las luces*, or *La casa verde* to be tiring: "the book[s] fell out of my hands." As it has been the case with Grosso, the perception that the Boom writers were vain and disdainful toward their Spanish colleagues—both present and past—was also an important element in the list of reproaches addressed in the essay. Gironella promptly elicited critical responses by Baltasar Porcel and Pere Gimferrer, who in turn condemned the ignorance of Spanish writers and their arrogance toward those from Spanish America. The confrontation was the center of attention for the Spanish literary world for at least two years, and it continued to raise interest well after that. It echoed in the 1971 Salamanca Summer conference on the Spanish novel, which was held under the general theme "The Spanish and Spanish American Novel and Their Historical, Social, and Political Circumstances." The 1972 International Book Colloquium, held in Caracas, focused on the analysis of the flourishing Hispanic narrative (with the participation of Carlos Barral, J. M. Castellet, Juan Goytisolo, Ángel González, and Ángel Rama, among others), and there was a intense discussion of the continental identity of Latin American literature and its relation to that of Spain.[13]

The anecdotal evidence thus points to a pattern of national confrontation that should be considered from a larger perspective. The transformation of Spain's literary field, its reshuffling of aesthetic and commercial alliances, corresponds to a profound historical change in Spanish society. In the 1960s, Spain's postwar period came to an end, if not in institutional, at least in economic and social terms, and its impending integration into the world of neocapitalist societies came to symbolize a new opportunity for Spain to return to the "concert of nations" of the modern world. In this context, the emergence of Hispanic cultural forces that were not only autonomous but also rebellious against the traditional hegemonic status of Spanish letters could only undermine the already weakened condition of national—and nationalistic—culture in the Iberian peninsula. It was more than a matter of literary fashion: the canonization of the Boom novel was questioning the modernity of Spanish narrative.

As it is well known, a similar clash between Spanish and Spanish American writers had occurred at the beginning of the twentieth century with the surge of *modernismo*. In *De literatura contemporánea*, a 1905 collection of essays and chronicles originally published in *Razón y Fe*, the Jesuit J. M. Aicardo gave expression to a vision of Hispanic literature that illustrates some of the questions we are bound to find sixty years later. Considering the interaction between the literary tradition of Spain and its American progeny, Aicardo said: "There on the American continent there is much of Spanish, much that is ours: seeds sown by the conquering and civilizing spirit of the Catholic Kings and the House of Austria that have produced a vast wheat, which—although mixed with foreign chaff—is nevertheless essentially ours. That language, that civilization, and those habits speak of Spain; and those peoples lost on never-ending plains and difficult mountain ranges seem dormant and about to wake up asking for their Spaniards, their missionaries, their conquerors, their parents. What a great pity that some Americans search for the new American literature in exotic dialects, and that they do not look toward the very insides of their own culture, which is essentially Hispano-Catholic."[14] These two notions of "national wheat" (*mies nacional*) and "foreign chaff" (*cizaña extranjera*) make up a metaphorical frame that has often conditioned the Spanish reception of other Hispanic cultural products. During the 1960s and 1970s similar reactions materialized among those who charged Spanish American writers with pretentiously attempting to teach Spanish to Spaniards. Behind these purist positions we find an ideological conception of what should be considered Spanish literature, one that bears important consequences for the study of the processing and consumption of the Latin American new novel in Spain.

After the dissemination of Spanish language throughout the world and the realization that it is no longer a national, but a multinational language, critics are confronted with the challenge presented by a multiple Hispanic literary production that interacts—as is the case with both *modernismo* and the Boom novel—across geographical borders. Aicardo's model of colonial propagation postulates a secondary position for other literatures: from this perspective, Hispanic literatures generated outside the Iberian peninsula can only be appendices, mere transpositions and reflections of a seminal literature and whose differences would be subordinated to the identity of the original seed. Trapped by a denial of history that aims to preserve a distinction between the wheat and the chaff of cultural genealogy, such a conception can only account for literatures that either mirror or distort that which is considered primordial. Thus, any attempt to study Spanish American literature in order to illuminate our knowledge of Peninsular literature would be a superfluous activity.

This conception permeated at times the understanding of the Boom novel. Antonio Tovar's review of *Todas esas muertes*, a novel by Chilean writer Carlos Droguett, inadvertently falls into the same trap. Tovar, a philologist who devoted several studies to the linguistic diversity of America and wrote laudatory reviews of Spanish American literature, warned against a situation in which readers (and particularly jurors for literary prizes) had come to expect that every novel coming from Spanish America would be good for that reason only. In the case of Droguett's novel he disagreed with the jurors of the Alfaguara Prize; the novel, he said, made use of "non-literary" language: "Having lived for a few years in South America, the critic accepts the use of americanisms, in which we find old legacies that have been lost on the Peninsula or delicious native expressions that are deeply rooted in the South American soil. But proper expression has its limits, and certain non-literary forms—while admissible in dialogue—are inappropriate when the narrator speaks; that is the case with *denantes* or *manitos*. The construction *la quedó mirando* or *lo quedaba mirando*, without the pronoun *se*, is ungrammatical, as linguists are wont to say; and the same applies to using *le conversaré* instead of *le diré*."[15]

Tovar's concern for linguistic propriety echoes Aicardo's in what seems to point to an ideological construction of national literature according to which the literary production of other Spanish-speaking countries, that is, the former colonies, should be evaluated taking into consideration two complementary criteria of acceptability. On the one hand, this literature is understood as a secondary system that should function as a cultural reserve, a depository of the literary past of the primary center: thus, we could talk of a legacy of Peninsular literary tradition (*viejas herencias*) that is kept alive in Spanish American letters. It is then to be judged according to the standards of the original, precontaminated model. On the other hand, such a secondary system is understandably bound to acquire, by way of contamination within its geographical and cultural space, elements of local color—native expressions (*sabrosos indigenismos*) that could thus be mixed with metropolitan art forms. Such a literary production then becomes interesting not for its own potential quality, but because of its alleged portrayal of exoticism. Heritage and localism would then be the boundaries confining the acceptance of colonial literatures, and what is left beyond these limits is precisely the hybridized and evolving language resulting from its usage by new cultural producers. This colonial model is further exposed in Tovar's comment on the role of the narrator in Droguett's novel. While it seems acceptable for the language of characters to perpetrate ungrammaticalities, that is not the case with the narrator, who as representative of authority within the universe of the text is expected to abide by the rules and enforce them. Thus, the manifestations of the American otherness—indigenism and ungrammaticality—are admitted as passive components of the represented world, but they are denied access to the agency of representation itself.

Another significant example of the difficult acceptance of the autonomy of American letters appears in the manifesto of the first academic journal devoted in contemporary Spain to Latin American literature, *Anales de Literatura Hispanoamericana*, created in 1972 and published by the Universidad Complutense in Madrid. Its editor, Francisco Sánchez-Castañer, opened the very first issue with a formal declaration of principles in which he outlined the ideology and goals of the journal. He first argued against the use of *Latin America* and advocated for the justice of *Spanish America* to describe the cultural reality of the continent. According to Sánchez-Castañer, in defining the features of the "Spanish American community" the main concern should be the verification of a cultural *dependency*: "It is obviously there that the *quid* of the matter lies: whether one can demonstrate the *cultural, human, and 'living' dependence on Spain of the American people of Hispanic origin.*"[16] The interaction between Spain and Latin America was thus conceived, once again, as possible only insofar as it abided within the restrictions of a traditional understanding of *hispanidad*, as defined decades earlier by Manuel García Morente (quoted here by Sánchez-Castañer): "Hispanicity is that through which something Spanish is Spanish. It is the essence of Spanishness." According to this definition, being *Hispanic* was identical to being *Spanish*—and, in Sánchez-Castañer's view, the meaning of the latter had already been fixed by Pedro Laín Entralgo by reference to three fundamental characteristics: Spanish language, Catholic faith, and moral mettle. *Anales de Literatura Hispanoamericana*, his editor argued, was intended to study the American literary production, but this mission was framed by an ideology of *hispanidad* to the service of which is was explicitly committed: "The Hispanic world [is] the true realm of an authentic Spanish Americanism. *At its service* [is] Spanish-American Literature, to which we are devoted with enthusiasm."[17]

The colonial model, however, was certainly no longer legitimate or even useful for understanding the new world of Hispanic letters. With the impact of the Boom, the center of gravity of that creative universe had moved to Latin America. The process of autonomization of Latin American letters certainly did not begin with the new novel, but it was then that it became irrevocably evident to Spanish writers and readers, for whom the end of the control of Spain over its own language was now more conspicuous. But it was not only the hegemony of national letters that was at stake. The other side effect of the Boom was the transformation of Spain's internal system of cultural relations between the different nationalities and regional identities.

TRANSPOSING THE BOOM

In 1968, a Catalan translation of Miguel Ángel Asturias's *El señor presidente* was published by Editorial Andorra. One year later, Vargas Llosa's essay "Carta de batalla por *Tirant lo Blanc*"—praising the classic Catalan chivalric romance as a precursor of the modern novel—appeared simultaneously in Spanish and Catalan. In October 1970, *Cien años de soledad* was introduced in Catalan translation by Edhasa, the same publishing house that had issued García Márquez's novel in Spain in 1969 (the novel had been available in imported copies of the Argentinean edition of Sudamericana). The need for these translations is not obvious: after all, as the translator of García Márquez, Avel·lí Artís-Gener, put it in his preface, the intended readers of *Cent anys de solitud* "have already enjoyed it in the original." The justification given by Artís-Gener is simple: García Márquez wanted to see his novel rendered in the language of the city he had chosen to live in—"who would have the heart to deny him his wish?"[18] It is perhaps possible to explain the interest in translating Latin American literature in biographical terms: García Márquez established his residence in Barcelona in October 1967 (he stayed until 1975), and one year later he reported that a "colony of Spanish American writers" would probably be created there, as there were plans for the arrival of Vargas Llosa (who did live in Barcelona between 1970 and 1974), Octavio Paz, and Carlos Fuentes.[19] José Donoso also lived in Spain between 1967 and 1981 (he resided in Barcelona in 1969–70). It could be argued, however, that those translations also served to accommodate other purposes.

It was certainly not common for works originally in Spanish to be translated into Catalan (or any of the other languages of Spain), as even translations from foreign languages had been highly restricted during the Francoist regime. By 1972, only twenty-two Spanish literary titles were available in Catalan translation, and besides the aforementioned cases of Asturias, García Márquez, and Vargas Llosa, only seven Spanish authors had been translated in the postwar period.[20] The limited number of translations (and publications in general) was the result of a conscious effort made by the Francoist State after the Civil War to impose Spanish as the official and exclusive language of the nation, and to eradicate the use of other regional languages. The strategies to delegitimize their status included not only the prohibition against publishing in those languages (which was summarily enforced until the 1950s) but also the translation of foreign works, so that access to imported knowledge—from engineering or philosophy to cooking—could only be gained through the official language. The reprint of translations from the prewar period, usually restricted to classical texts, was occasionally permitted, but the first literary text translated and published in Catalan after the Civil War appears to have been Molière's *El misantrop*, in 1951; still in 1964, the Catalan translation of Georges Arnaud's *La plus grande pente* (*L'estimball*) had to be published under the name Jordi Arnau (that is, as if it were an original text by a Catalan author), as the publisher feared that the translation would not be authorized.[21] Translations into languages other than Spanish resumed with some regularity in the sixties, but still by the end of the decade there were suspicions, fueled by centralist forces, about their feasibility as instruments and conveyers of knowledge. In fact, after the war, it was not until 1965 that the first professorship of Catalan Language and Literature would be created at the University of Barcelona.[22]

In a 1970 lecture, intended to "explain" Catalonia to Spanish speakers, the novelist Baltasar Porcel expressed the private and marginal condition of the Catalan language in postwar Spain in the following terms: "everything superstructural, important, and grandiloquent, from politics to science to literature, would come to me from outside and in Spanish; everything basic, ordinary, and domestic, my life and that of my loved ones, occurred in Catalan." That same year, the poet and linguist Gabriel Ferrater pointed out how his courses in Catalan at the university provided some degree of surprise to his students: "Many young men and women don't know that Catalan can be used to teach metaphysics or algebra, the same as with any other language in the world, and that it's not just for ordering omelets in a restaurant." In 1973, in an attempt to rectify that condition, a group of scientists signed a manifesto declaring the possibility and the need to use Catalan as a language for scientific communication.[23]

In a context in which Spanish was the only authorized channel of communication with the outside world (in 1968 Joan Manuel Serrat, who had been selected to represent Spain in the European musical festival Eurovision, was dismissed and replaced after he insisted in singing in his native language), translation contributed to the task of rehabilitating Catalan as a language of high culture. Indeed, the importance of translation had been acutely perceived since the turn of the century, when many Catalan writers had played an active role in rendering in their language a wide selection of masterpieces from the past and the present. Joan Fuster's assessment of the interest in translation among members of the *noucentista* generation in the prewar period could equally apply to its significance in the resurgence of Catalan literature three decades later: "Speaking 'in Catalan,' the most insignificant authors of every century and every country would become the foundation and sinew of the autochthonous cultural climate, which would thus recover from the Decadent period [*Decadència*] and rise to the level of any other European literature. Translation was now done not only for the strategic purpose of adorning the language with glorious assistance, or so that native speakers may have within reach and in their own language a maximum repertoire of books, but also so that Catalan culture—understood as an organic whole—may receive the lifeblood of a tradition suppressed by the vicissitudes of History."[24] As Fuster put it, "to translate is to become universal," and the publication in Catalan of *El senyor president* and *Cent anys de solitud* was inserted in the process of linguistic normalization that was the central concern of the Catalan cultural world in the 1960s and 1970s, and which still remains nowadays one of the major sources of conflict between centralist and nationalist forces in Spain. The translating of two of the most prestigious contemporary texts—already represented and recognized in the major languages of the world—proved that Catalan was a literary language in its own right, with the same capabilities as any other. Catalan versions of literary (or scientific, philosophical, etc.) masterworks from other languages were evidence of the translatability and, therefore, the equality among those languages—that is, they proved that Catalan, as Ferrater pointed out, could be used for the same variety of purposes as any other language in the world. Translations, thus, served to expand the reach of the language beyond the boundaries of intimate or colloquial usage and into the realm of public and social discourses, and as such they carried a strong cultural and political weight.[25]

If the goal of translating other literatures was to universalize Catalan culture, the translations of Vargas Llosa and García Márquez also point in the opposite direction, as they respond also to a desire to display the universalism already present in Catalonia's own literary tradition—which, in the case of these writers, would be identified, respectively, with the chivalric romance *Tirant lo Blanc* and the "wise Catalonian" of Macondo, Ramon Vinyes. As we shall see, important differences exist between the two writers as they approach the Catalan character of their subjects: for Vargas Llosa, the Catalan of *Tirant lo Blanc* has no significance to its argument about the value of the book; in García Márquez, the cultural identity of the wise Catalonian in *Cien años de soledad* plays a fundamental role in the plot of the novel. I believe, however, that they can both be understood as taking part in a larger process of reassessment of Spain's cultural diversity.

Against the grain of officialist Spanish cultural politics, motions for a recognition of the pluralism of Hispanic culture can be seen in various forms during the 1960s. The editorial page of the first issue of *Cuadernos para el Diálogo* (October 1963) had proclaimed that the magazine would be open to a larger than usual notion of community: "its pages are open to any Spaniard, Spanish American, or well-intentioned man, no matter what his color or language, who may have something significant to tell, judge, or propose— concisely and plainly—about collective life."[26] Perhaps to show the extent of this commitment, the editors included in the same issue the Catalan text of Joan Maragall's "Oda a Espanya"—a poem originally written in 1898 and openly critical of Spanish (and Spanish language) imperialism. It is also worth remembering that the rules for the Biblioteca Breve Prize stipulated that the competition was open to "unpublished novels [written] in any of the romance languages used in the Iberian Peninsula and any of their American variants." In 1965, a new collection was created by Seix Barral, tellingly called "Nueva Narrativa Hispánica," a name that aptly displayed the dominant catchwords of the decade: *Nueva Narrativa* was clearly meant to evoke the cultural prestige of the notion of a new novel (as the *nouveau roman*), while the adjective *Hispánica* indicated a literature surpassing the limitations of Spain's national products—not surprisingly, nine of the first fifteen titles published in the collection were signed by Latin American writers.[27] At the same time, the series "Contemporary Spanish Authors" of Planeta was renamed "Spanish and Spanish-American Authors." And when in 1970 the editors of *Norte: Revista Hispánica de Amsterdam* devoted a special issue to the present condition of scholarship on Catalan language and literature, they opened with the following statement: "Precisely because *Norte* is a 'Hispanic journal,' it must be open to everything living in Spain and Spanish America, and we would be guilty of clumsy centralism or blind monolithism if we ignored that other linguistic modes of expression—Catalan, Galician, Basque, and even Quechua, Nahuatl, and Guarani—coexist with Spanish in the Hispanic world."[28]

In this historical context, Vargas Llosa's "Carta de batalla por *Tirant lo Blanc*" inserts the Catalan chivalry romance in the dialectics between the distant and the accessible that serves during the 1960s to redefine a space in which the *familiarity* of Hispanic (versus exclusively Spanish) literatures is established. For the Spanish reader, Catalan literature—as was also the case with Spanish American fiction—is presented as a distant relative, both alien and yet recognizable. On the one hand, *Tirant lo Blanc* is read as an integral part of a common tradition, one that equally embraces Spanish and Catalan letters. On the other, Vargas Llosa argues against the oblivion which that text in particular and the genre of chivalry books in general have suffered under a certain orthodoxy within the historiography of Spanish literature, an orthodoxy that demoted those texts as marginal, as illegitimate products of Hispanic culture.

It would certainly be exaggerated to think of Vargas Llosa as the exclusive force behind the contemporary interest in Joanot Martorell's *Tirant lo Blanc*, but there is no doubt that a large part of the public attention awarded to the text beyond the restricted circles of scholars of Iberian medieval literature is due to his championing the book as "one of the most ambitious, and from the point of view of its construction, perhaps the most modern among the classic nov-els."[29] Although Catalan and Spanish editions of the book by Martí de Riquer had been published in 1947, and the modernity of the chivalry romance had already been postulated by Dámaso Alonso in 1951 (in "*Tirant lo Blanc*, novela moderna"), there seems to be general agreement among critics that Vargas Llosa's essay and the 1969 paperback publication of the book—done simultaneously in the Catalan original and in Spanish translation—were instrumental in *Tirant lo Blanc*'s achieving popular status.[30] Vargas Llosa has indeed credited himself with the popularity the book was to gain after 1969: "In 1958, when I first arrived in Spain as a student, I was surprised at how unfamiliar the average Spanish reader was with a novel which, since I had discovered it in a library in Lima, had impressed me as the most outstanding of its genre. Restricted to circles of specialized scholars, there weren't even any editions—in Catalan or in Spanish—available to the wider public. From then on I tried to convince the publishers within my reach to come out with a popular edition of *Tirant lo Blanc*. It makes me proud to have overcome Carlos Barral's reluctance first to read the book and later to make a commercial edition of the novel at Seix Barral."[31]

Martorell was presented as the direct precursor of Vargas Llosa's own literary heroes—those "God-supplanters" who strive to create a "total reality": Fielding, Balzac, Dickens, Flaubert, Tolstoy, Joyce, Faulkner. Various critics have discussed Vargas Llosa's read-ing of the chivalric romance as it relates to his understanding of narrative writing.[32] Here, however, I would like to concentrate on other aspects of the prologue that have direct bearing on the percep-tion of Catalan as a literary language. Vargas Llosa's primary goal is certainly not to vindicate a Catalan national literary tradition—the fact that *Tirant lo Blanc* was originally written in that language remains in his argument secondary to its existence as a chivalric book: "What has hindered so far the encounter between *Tirant lo Blanc* and the reader? This drama cannot be explained only by the drama of the language in which the book was written . . . but, above all, by the drama of a genre: the novels of chivalry."[33] Nevertheless, his prologue calls constant attention to the linguistic materiality of the book: consistently with his own opinion that "any half-educated Spanish speaker" could read and enjoy the text in the original lan-guage, references to the text of *Tirant lo Blanc* are always in the original. Thus, by quoting in Catalan for Spanish-speaking readers (the intended audience of the Alianza edition), the prologue forces them to be aware of the mediated nature of their experience—that is, that theirs is a *translated* text.[34] The significance, in this sense, of the prologue to *Tirant lo Blanc* is very different from that of Vargas Llosa's introduction to the Spanish edition of *Madame Bovary*, also published in the same "El libro de bolsillo" series (Madrid: Alianza, 1974). While the latter is clearly perceived as one more instance of appropriation of a *foreign* model (which inserts itself among other contemporary attempts to familiarize the Spanish reader with other national literatures), the former identifies a model of writing that is national and yet is not quite Spanish—thus raising the issue of the multiculturalism, and multilingualism, of Hispanic letters.

By legitimizing chivalry books as the source of a consummate form of realism, Vargas Llosa also contributed to reshuffling the canonical values of Spanish literary tradition. It is through his reading of *Tirant lo Blanc* that he develops in detail the notion of a "total realism" or "total novel":

> Novel of chivalry, fantastic, historical, military, erotic, psychological: all of these and none of them exclusively, no less than reality itself. Being multiple, it admits different and conflicting readings, and its nature varies according to the point of view adopted to order its chaos. Being a verbal object that communicates the same impression of plurality as the real, it is—like reality—both an act and a dream, objectivity and subjectivity, reason and wonder. This is the essence of "total realism"— the supplantation of God. . . . The understanding of reality of the authors of chivalry romances embraces in one single perspective various orders of human existence and, in this sense, their concept of literary realism is broader, more complete than that of later writers.[35]

This ideal of total realism calls for the novel to incorporate testimonial documentation but also transcend it by drawing upon the power of narrativity—the novelist is required not to indoctrinate but to indulge in the pleasure of storytelling and thus involve the reader in a "jungle of stories."[36] By advocating such a recovery of narrativity, Vargas Llosa—as a critic—does for the new Spanish novel what Juan Goytisolo had done in the fifties for the social novel movement with his exaltation of the picaresque novel: they both offer a new model of realism equally grounded on the common Spanish literary tradition.

But the recovery of chivalric romance is explicitly inserted in the midst of a conflict between dogma and imagination: chivalric romances, argues Vargas Llosa, have remained ostracized because they give a subversive view of reality—the Inquisition, the scholastic orthodoxy of the literary establishment and the "academic catacombs," have all conspired to forget those books out of "fear of imagination, natural enemy of dogma and source of all rebellion."[37] By reading *Tirant lo Blanc* as an exemplar of heterodox literature, Vargas Llosa points to a polarized tradition, thus acknowledging the existence of *another* lineage of Spanish literature, one that—in contrast to the much criticized stagnation of contemporary forms—could serve as a foundation for the remodeling of fiction. Such a heterodox legacy has been often claimed as integral to the formation of Latin American literature, and it was now presented as the alternative to the perceived orthodoxy of Peninsular letters (we should recall here the "sacred" language of Spain that was the aim of the destructive writing of Juan Goytisolo).[38]

Cashing in the claim to heterodoxy of Latin American narrative, the *other* languages (and literatures) of Spain—Catalan, Galician, Basque, and also some regional varieties of Spanish, like those of Andalusia or the Canary Islands—were also granted, by association, a privileged status as *new* narratives. Thus, in the same way Spanish letters from across the Atlantic could claim to be alternatives to peninsular Spanish, others within Spain could equally aspire to gain recognition as literatures in their own right. The tension between center (identified as dogmatic) and periphery (claiming heterodoxy), one of the central features of the Latin American imagery of Spain, was also applied to the contrast between Spain's centralist culture and its regional diversity. And the hope for an authentic literary renewal seemed to rest with the cultures marginalized by the Spanish state.

The condition of being cultures of dissent runs parallel to an equally common desire for autonomy. It is perhaps in the case of Catalan culture that the collusion with Latin American interests against Spain has been most commonly established. There is in fact a tradition among Latin American intellectuals—at least since the independence of the Spanish American republics—that links the oppression experienced by the former colonies to the condition of peripheral regions within Spain. In his *Viajes* (1849), Domingo F. Sarmiento's impressions of Barcelona established a clear parallel between Latin America and Catalonia, as both aspired to liberate themselves from the yoke of the Spanish government. Upon his arrival in Barcelona, Sarmiento declared to be relieved at "leaving

Spain": "I am, at last, outside of Spain. As you know, we are Latin American and Barcelonans are Catalan, and thus we can gossip at ease about those who are on Montjuich, with their cannons aimed over the city."[39] In *España contemporánea*, which chronicles the impressions of his visit to Spain at the turn of century, Darío also contrasted Castilian tradition and Catalan modernity: while "Madrid is invariable in spirit, today the same as yesterday," in Barcelona "triumphs a modern wind that brings something of the future."[40] The desire for regional autonomy in early twentieth-century Spain was also compared by José Enrique Rodó to the independence of Spanish American colonies a century earlier: "The colonial system maintained in the Antilles by the will not of Spain but of those who rule in Spain, was fundamentally, up till the last moment, the same one that had provoked the Spanish-American revolution a century earlier. The same can be said regarding the regional autonomies, which are in essence an aspiration no different from the one that motivated the colonies."[41] It should be pointed out, however, that in Rodó, Darío, and many others, the recognition of Catalan identity is not at odds with the calls for an integration with the rest of Spain: as Ricardo Rojas put it in 1938, "it is not necessary for Americans to vilify the rest of Spain in order to recognize the merits of Catalan culture. For Payró and myself—two Argentines who perceived Catalonia's greatness within the unity of eternal Spain—Catalonia belongs so indisputable to this unit that if it were separated from Spain, it would see its destiny wane."[42]

The appreciation of Catalan culture as belonging to the heterodox lineage of Hispanic culture is also a central component of the representations of Spain present in García Márquez's *Cien años de soledad*. It is perhaps no coincidence that *Cent anys de solitud* remains until today the only translation of the novel in any of the other languages of Spain. Besides the factors already mentioned above—the author's personal wishes and the state of literary translation—we should here consider the presence in the novel of explicit references to Spain which are associated with significant characters or events in the narrative. These representations, I will argue, replicate in fiction the polarization of Spanish culture, and serve to explain the interest in a Catalan translation of García Márquez's novel.

Fernanda del Carpio and the wise Catalonian are the only characters in *Cien años de soledad* to have a direct connection with Spain: while Fernanda claims to be "la ahijada del Duque de Alba, una dama con tanta alcurnia . . . que tenía derecho a firmar con once apellidos peninsulares" [the godchild of the Duke of Alba, a lady of such lineage that she . . . had the right to sign eleven peninsular names], the wise Catalonian is overcome by nostalgia and, as the end of Macondo looms, decides to return to Barcelona.[43] Readers of the novel will remember that Úrsula Iguarán's great-grandfather was also a Spaniard, from Aragon, but this ancestry does not play a significant role for the identity of the character—while Fernanda clings to her lineage, Úrsula's seems so removed that in fact the Aragonese merchant is referred later in the same page as her great-great-grandfather.[44] In this sense, Úrsula's Spanish roots belong to the prehistory of Macondo and, like the Spanish artifacts found in its surroundings—the fifteenth-century armor and the galleon—have little effect in the present life of its inhabitants.

Fernanda del Carpio enters the story of Macondo as an "intruder," an antidote against subversion brought to the village by the enemies of the Buendías in order to avert the possibility of Remedios being chosen the beauty queen in the carnival: "La noticia de que Remedios Buendía iba a ser la soberana del festival rebasó en pocas horas los límites de la ciénaga, llegó hasta lejanos territorios donde se ignoraba el inmenso prestigio de su belleza, y suscitó la inquietud de quienes todavía consideraban su apellido como un símbolo de la subversión" [The news that Remedios Buendía was going to be the sovereign ruler of the festival went beyond the limits of the swamp in a few hours, reached distant places where the prestige of her beauty was not known, and it aroused the anxiety of those who still thought of her last name as a symbol of subversion].[45] Later, she will become the antagonist of Úrsula in the struggle for the control over the Buendía house, and she will indeed serve the cause of Catholic traditionalism against the subversive strain of the tribe. She is a representative of a decadent dynasty—"una catástrofe familiar que había tardado dos siglos en consumarse" [a family catastrophe that had been two centuries late in its fulfillment][46]—with a close resemblance to the Spanish declining empire:

Fernanda era una mujer perdida para el mundo. Había nacido y crecido a mil kilómetros del mar, en una ciudad lúgubre por cuyas callejuelas de piedra traqueteaban todavía, en noches de espantos, las carrozas de los virreyes. Treinta y dos campanarios tocaban a muerto a las seis de la tarde. En la casa señorial embaldosada de losas sepulcrales jamás se conoció el sol. . . . Su madre, sudando la calentura de las cinco, le hablaba del esplendor del pasado. . . . Hasta el día de la boda soñó con un reinado de leyenda, a pesar de que su padre, don Fernando, tuvo que hipotecar la casa para comprarle el ajuar.

[Fernanda was a woman who was lost in the world. She had been born and raised in a city six hundred miles away, a gloomy city where on ghostly nights the coaches of the viceroys still rattled through the cobbled streets. Thirty-two belfries tolled a dirge at six in the afternoon. In the manor house, which was paved with tomblike slabs, the sun was never seen. . . . Her mother, perspiring with five-o'clock fever, spoke to her of the splendor of the past. . . . Until the day of her wedding she dreamed about a legendary kingdom, in spite of the fact that her father, Don Fernando, had to mortgage the house in order to buy her trousseau.][47]

Fernanda's death opens a new world for Aureliano Babilonia, who had been forced by his grandmother to spend his life hidden in Melquíades's room, as it signals the possibility of direct contact with the outside world and its discoveries, and leads to his association with the wise Catalonian and his circle.[48]

The segments of *Cien años de soledad* devoted to Aureliano Babilonia's comrades at the bookstore have been read as a sort of roman à clef—a reading encouraged by García Márquez himself, who claimed that in writing the final sections of the novel he inserted a series of private jokes intended for his friends in Barranquilla: "there are pranks, private jokes, secret messages for my friends; I knew the book wasn't getting away from me, so I started to play, purely out of happiness." Following this lead, the figure of the wise Catalonian has been largely considered a fictional transposition of Ramon Vinyes, to whom the character, according to García Márquez, pays homage.[49] That there indeed existed a wise Catalonian to whom García Márquez wanted to pay tribute in his novel—and therefore that there is a relevant *autobiographical* component to his presence in the text—should not overshadow the fact that such a character plays also an important *functional* role in the novel. It is thus not the historical Vinyes, but rather the fictional role of the wise Catalonian, that should concern us here.

The most obvious function of the bookseller in the novel is to fill the void left by the final departure of Melquíades.[50] While the narrative of Macondo opens with the memory of Melquíades and his tribe, who bring to Macondo the latest discoveries and marvels of the world, at its end we have the departure of another sort of merchant and his circle, who had introduced Aureliano to a last invention, literature:

> Para un hombre como él, encastillado en la realidad escrita, aquellas sesiones tormentosas que empezaban en la librería a las seis de la tarde y terminaban en los burdeles al amanecer, fueron una revelación. No se le había ocurrido pensar hasta entonces que la literatura fuera el mejor juguete que se había inventado para burlarse de la gente, como lo demostró Álvaro una noche de parranda. Había de transcurrir algún tiempo antes de que Aureliano se diera cuenta de que tanta arbitrariedad tenía origen en el ejemplo del sabio catalán, para quien la sabiduría no valía la pena si no era posible servirse de ella para inventar una manera nueva de preparar los garbanzos.

> [For a man like him, holed up in written reality, those stormy sessions that began in the bookstore and ended at dawn in the brothels were a revelation. It had never occurred to him until then that literature was the best plaything that had been invented to make fun of people, as Álvaro demonstrated during one night of revels. Some time would have to pass before Aureliano realized that such arbitrary attitudes had their origins in the example of the wise Catalonian, for whom wisdom was worth nothing if it could not be used to invent a new way of preparing chick peas.][51]

Once Melquíades disappears for the last time, it is thanks to the wise Catalonian that Aureliano is able to gather the necessary information to interpret the parchments that reveal the history and the destiny of Macondo. Like Melquíades, the bookseller writes manuscripts of his own, which—being written in Catalan—will also require translation.[52] And the bookshop serves as substitute for Melquíades's room—the space where reading and interpretation are achieved.

The wise Catalonian, however, is also a counterpart of Fernanda. Both of them share and are tormented by "the same elves," but their presence in the text points in two different directions.[53] The last Aureliano, who cannot communicate nor share his solitude with Fernanda, nevertheless finds companionship in the bookstore. While Fernanda is a force of repression and religious indoctrination, the wise Catalonian serves the cause of freedom and culture:

> A pesar de su vida desordenada, todo el grupo trataba de hacer algo perdurable, a instancias del sabio catalán. Era él, con su experiencia de

antiguo profesor de letras clásicas y su depósito de libros raros, quien los había puesto en condiciones de pasar una noche entera buscando la trigesimoséptima situación dramática, en un pueblo donde ya nadie tenía interés ni posibilidades de ir más allá de la escuela primaria.

[In spite of their disordered life, the whole group tried to do something permanent at the urging of the wise Catalonian. It was he, with his experience as a former professor of classical literature and his storehouse of rare books, who got them to spend a whole night in search of the thirty-seventh dramatic situation in a town where no one had any interest any more in going beyond primary school.][54]

In contrast with Fernanda's tendency to use euphemisms, which was the object of constant mockery by Amaranta, the Catalonian's last words are a string of expletives and blasphemies: *"Collons—maldecía—. Me cago en el canon 27 del sínodo de Londres. . . . ¡Ahí les dejo esa mierda!"* [*"Collons,"* he would curse. "I shit on Canon Twenty-seven of the Synod of London. . . . All that shit there I leave to you people!"].[55]

Assuming it is possible—and wise—to extrapolate a larger cultural significance to the individual characterization of Fernanda del Carpio and the bookseller, the picture that emerges from the pages of *Cien años de soledad* is critical of a sacralized Spanish official tradition, and clearly favorable to Catalonia's contribution to Hispanic culture. I would thus argue that not only the physical presence in Barcelona of Latin American writers like Vargas Llosa or García Márquez, but also their interest in Catalan literature and culture, provided additional substance to the claims for autonomy from the stagnant condition of the centralist Spanish state. The revolt against canonical Spanish Peninsular literature represented by the new novel from Latin America and the interest it elicited in restoring and forging a space for heterodoxy within the Hispanic world facilitated the uprising in Spain of national and regional literatures.[56]

The contrast between Latin American and Spanish literatures—which served to question the hegemony of peninsular Spanish—was mirrored by a similar opposition between Catalan and Castilian, where the concern for the legitimation of an autonomous cultural production found an ally in the Latin American resurgence. Thus, in a 1971 interview, asked to comment on the differences between Peninsular and American Spanish—a matter of heated debate in those years—Gabriel Ferrater declared that from the perspective of a Catalan writer the terms of the polemic should be focused on the differences between Spanish and Catalan: "you have insisted on that issue of difference between Spanish-American and Spanish literatures, and actually it is something that is quite removed from me. You should rather question me about the differences between Catalan and Spanish Peninsular literatures. There is a great deal of difference between Catalan and Spanish."[57] Commenting on the "literary war" being fought in Spanish periodicals over the values of different narratives in Spanish language, Baltasar Porcel vauntingly declared the disengagement of the Catalan writer from the malaise of Castilian literature: "As a novelist writing originally in Catalan, all this history of the ups and downs of narrative in the Spanish language is as foreign to me as the palm trees of Pernambuco. . . . What is really happening (and this is the foremost cause of the Spanish–Latin American War) is that Spanish writers have practiced a strict and frenetic literary separatism, but now find themselves hounded and even suffocated by what we could call a provincial rebellion. They discover to their astonishment that their hegemony, so often proclaimed by history (especially native history, of course), has ceased to exist and they are now the ones relegated to provincial obscurity."[58]

Other hitherto marginalized or "peripheral" literatures of Spain, I believe, shared a similar transformation. The boom of the new novel was echoed by various *booms* across the Spanish literary geography, not only in terms of an increase in book production (since, as we have seen, book printing in other languages of Spain also expanded during the sixties), but also in terms of a growing consciousness of distinct cultural identities—obvious cases being the coinage of labels like "narraluces" and "narraguanches" to designate the new crop of young writers from Andalusia and the Canary Islands, respectively. It is arguably in Canarian letters that the association with the Latin American Boom appears to have had its most lasting impact. In this case, the strategy applied in the struggle for autonomy called for a closer connection: more than simply sharing with American novelists similar interests and grievances (as was the case in Catalan letters), Canarian writers claimed the right to appropriate a common history and poetics. Thus, according to Alfonso Armas Ayala, while the Boom novel was appreciated in Catalonia because of the "editorial sensitivity" of that region, its reception in the Canaries was a "natural" phenomenon, since Canarian literature is "impregnated with America."[59]

Up to the 1960s, Canarian literature had a long and recognized tradition in poetry, but few would have been able to point to more than a few of samples of narrative. The transformation of the literary field produced by the emergence of the Latin American new novel, however, gave impetus in the Canaries to a surge in the production—and, equally important, in the circulation—of autochthonous fiction. As with other regional literatures in Spain, increasing critical attention was paid to Canarian authors in the late sixties, and the creation of a new literary prizes (the Premio de Novela Benito Pérez Armas, in 1970, and the Premio Canarias, in 1973) and the foundation of two publishing houses (Inventarios Provisionales, in Las Palmas de Gran Canaria, in 1970; and Taller de Ediciones JB, in Madrid, in 1973) provided the breeding ground for yet another *boom*, this time corresponding to the *nueva novela canaria*.[60] Encouraged by the Latin American Boom, young Canarian writers sized their opportunity to claim the possibility of writing another Hispanic literature autonomous from Spanish Peninsular letters: "It is undeniable that the 1970s are one of the most creative periods, not only because of the prosperity attained by narrative in the Canary Islands, but also because of the polemical context in which this develops. . . . A Spanish-American literature exists, differentiated from the rest of Hispanic writing. Why not, then, claim the existence of a Canarian literature equally differentiated? Such seems to be the reasoning of the period."[61] As Sabas Martín has acknowledged, the writer from Canary Islands finds self-recognition in the 1960s in the new Latin American literature; this recognition is based in a common historical condition—what García Ramos, echoing Octavio Paz, identifies as a experience of orphanhood.[62]

Significantly, several historical studies have been devoted to the comparison of the colonization process in the Canaries to that of Latin America, and the fact that the Islands served as a testing ground and a platform for the colonization of the New World—not to speak of the linguistic similarities between the Spanish spoken in those areas as different from the accent of Peninsular Spanish, or the intense migrations from the Islands across the Atlantic—has prompted the analysis of close historical and cultural ties. As Carlos Alberto Morales has noted, "the Antilles should have been christened 'New Canaries.' . . . The conquest and settlement of the Canarian archipelago was the first chapter in the conquest and settlement of the Americas. The Creole—the Spaniard born in the overseas provinces—is a Canarian invention."[63]

It is perhaps no coincidence then that the area of Spain referred to in positive terms in *Cien años de soledad* is the Canary Islands, the "Fortunate Isles" where Amaranta Úrsula goes, on her return from Europe, searching for the birds intended to "repopulate the skies of Macondo."[64] In "Las Islas Afortunadas en *Cien años de soledad*"—a lecture given in the course of a seminar on Canarian Studies in 1969—Gregorio Salvador read this episode of the novel in terms of the symbolism of the islands as utopian space, and critics like García Ramos have since then furthered the notion that the archipelago belongs not so much to Spanish but rather to Atlantic culture, as part of an Atlantic imaginary: "because of its mythology, history, literature, and culture in general, the Canary Islands belong to a cultural region that is not strictly Spanish but rather, Atlantic."[65] J. J. Armas Marcelo, a publisher and novelist himself closely linked to several of the main figures in the canonization of Latin American literature in Spain (particularly Barral and Vargas Llosa), has also postulated a poetics of eccentricity that—corresponding to a space in the "ultraperiphery of Spanish national literature" that is shared by writers from both sides of the Atlantic—would represent the proper tradition of Canarian literature. It is in this context that, according to Armas Marcelo, Canarians have a rightful claim to be "imaginary Americans": "we are imaginary and imagined Latin Americans because we are Spaniards, and are Spaniards since then because we are *the first America* and the last Spain looking at itself toward the south, toward the Archipelago that the geological arbitrariness of time stranded on this side of the Atlantic, but which is glimpsed at by Latin American imagery in its geographical, linguistic, idiosyncratic, and historical proximity."[66]

The Boom novel gave the archipelago the chance to claim legitimate status for its particular linguistic usage of Spanish, and it was thanks to the impact of the Latin American writers that the Canarian novel attained visibility. While figures like Isaac de Vega or Rafael Arozarena had been active for more than a decade, it was not until the early seventies that they began to receive widespread attention, and it was also then that a new generation of young writers—known as the "generation of the seventies"—began to have a real chance at getting their work published. The Canarian accent, often identified as Latin American by Peninsular speakers, became in the early seventies as *respectable* as the accents of the Boom novelists. Therefore, more than a question of imitation or epigonism, Canarian writers seem to have experienced the discovery of a linguistic and poetic harmony with their Spanish American colleagues.[67]

In reference to Benito Pérez Galdós, who left his native island to become a successful novelist in Madrid, José F. Montesinos once claimed that the Canary Islands could not produce anything more than provincial literature because they lack a language of their own—a condition Montesinos extended also to other regions of Spain, as if there the Spanish language could be regarded as just a sort of loan from Castile.[68] After the Boom, Spanish language and literature definitely ceased to be the exclusive property of central Spaniards. Like Catalan writers, who declared their work outside of the area of control of Spanish literature and its ailments, those from Canary Islands saw the condition of Peninsular letters as something equally distant, positioning themselves in direct lineage with their American colleagues and thus claiming a status that was equally emergent and defiant of both literary and linguistic orthodoxy.

Epilogue

In July 1974, Mario Vargas Llosa ended his residence in Spain and went back to his native Peru. Almost at the same time, Barral Editores announced the termination of its literary prize (1971–74), which had continued the tradition of the Biblioteca Breve Prize (1958–73), and the publishing house was eventually sold to Editorial Labor. Those events could mark a symbolic end to the phenomenon of the Boom novel in Spain: on the one hand, with Vargas Llosa's departure—which would be followed soon afterwards by that of García Márquez from Barcelona to Mexico—the direct contact between Latin American and Spanish writers began to fade; on the other hand, with the end of Carlos Barral's publishing career, the main supporter of that literary exchange disappeared. Other factors contributed to the transformation of the literary landscape: in 1972 Planeta and Barral had launched a new generation of Spanish writers, hoping to tap into the commercial potential of a resurgence of autochthonous creativity; in 1973, the revolutionary experiences in Latin America began to be destroyed by the force of dictatorial regimes; also in 1973, the world entered in a recession that greatly diminished the growth of Latin American economies (which in turn affected the interest of Spanish publishers, who found that their publications would reach prohibitive prices in the transatlantic markets); last but not least, the death of Franco in 1975 created the expectation of dramatic changes in Spain's political life, and critical attention turned to the possibilities of post-Francoist culture. By the mid-seventies, and although novels by the most famous authors continued to have great success, it became increasingly difficult for new Latin American writers to enter the Spanish literary market.[1]

The years of the Boom novel stand out as unique for both the overall quality of its production and—perhaps more importantly from our perspective—for the international recognition it gained for the Spanish language as a literary medium. While it would be wrong to reduce the whole of Latin American fiction to the Boom, as if nothing of interest or importance had come before or after, there is no doubt it represented a momentous event in the history of Hispanic literatures—after all, it is no coincidence that of the ten Nobel Prizes awarded to literature in Spanish, six have been given in the last three decades.[2] Here I have limited my study to a few central figures and events, and thus this is not—it never pretended to be—a complete history of the Boom novel in Spain. While I have centered my attention on what I consider the most canonized texts and authors of the period in Spain, similar research could and should be done on the reception of Carlos Fuentes, José Donoso, or Manuel Puig, just to name a few, and there is no doubt that this sort of study would also benefit from a detailed analysis of the impact of the previous generation (I am thinking here of Jorge Luis Borges and Juan Rulfo, who were given attention in Spain as part of the Boom phenomenon). These limitations notwithstanding, my contention is that the picture presented is applicable to the Spanish reception of the Boom novel at large. This novel was consequential not only for its impact on narrative art but also for the changes it helped effect on Spanish literary life: the refurbishing of the publishing industry; the mobilization across national lines of a reading public that had remained until then fragmented in local markets; the establishing of a sense of modernity in Spanish letters, which had long suffered from the stigma of epigonism as secondary imitations of other, more advanced literatures; and, finally, the relaxation of linguistic and poetic norms, which served to legitimize areas of Spain's literary map hitherto marginalized by officialist culture.

I have argued that the reception of Latin American narrative in Spain transcended individual biographies and resulted from the conjunction of three parallel developments in the economy, politics, and the arts: the expansion of the Spanish book industry and its literary markets; the turn to Latin America as the primary site of revolutionary hopes for the European (and Spanish) left; and the crisis of social realism as the dominant model for Spanish fiction. This historical constellation made possible the canonization of Latin American literature in the Spanish literary field, to the extent that it could be said that Peninsular letters were for a few years in a state of dependency in relationship to the transatlantic Hispanic production, which provided and legitimized models (and counter-models) for the renewal of fiction in Spain.

The preeminence of the Boom novel in Spain's literary field emerged during a phase of transition from the postwar documentary poetics—best represented by the neorealism of the social novel—

and toward an updating of literary forms demanded by the new social and economic configuration of the country in the sixties.
Thanks to the weakness of the social novel as the dominant model
in Spain, the Boom novel was able to occupy a central position in
the Spanish literary system. Latin American fiction benefited as
well from the expansion of the Spanish publishing industry, which
found in the Boom novel a strategic element in its efforts to reach
a wider market. The rare combination of critical praise, commercial
success and ideological appeal some of the authors came to enjoy
turned them into valuable objects and justified the special attention
conferred to them by Spain's cultural producers. The Latin American new novel thus functioned as an essential intertext for the renewal of the Spanish novel, particularly for the younger generation
of writers. Such a centrality is attested not only by its influence on
the new writing, but also by the impact Latin American narratives
had in the establishing of literary values and norms for Spanish
readers. Their success created a paratextual landscape against
which every new attempt to regenerate the ailing Spanish novel was
measured and evaluated, and it thus determined the processing and
experience of literary products.

This process can be summarized in three different moments. The
first one evolves around the problem of realism. Spanish neorealist
novelists tried to build upon the social language of everyday speech
in order to create a picture of reality, a documentary of Francoist
Spain. This concern led to an impoverished literary form whose
overhaul was the central focus of writers in the early sixties. In this
context, Vargas Llosa's *La ciudad y los perros* should be placed
together with Martín-Santos's *Tiempo de silencio* as founding
blocks of the renewal of Spanish realism. A second moment of the
Spanish reception of the Boom novel can be identified in the experimentalist trend of the mid-sixties. In contrast with the French *nouveau roman*, which also elicited this reaction against traditional
diegesis, Latin American experimentalism—through the incorpora-
tion of parody and irony—seemed able to animate textual elabora-
tion with intellectual and/or humorous elements. Works like
Cortázar's *Rayuela* and Cabrera Infante's *Tres tristes tigres* were
thus consequential in establishing an alternative direction away
from the outmoded practices of neorealism. After the rage of experimentalism, which was basically antinarrative, a third movement
would gravitate around the recovery of storytelling that is best represented in García Márquez's *Cien años de soledad*. The reception

of this variety of Latin American new novel can be seen as playing an essential role in overcoming the document/poem dichotomy that dominated the literary debate during the 1960s and, eventually, in reestablishing for Spanish literature the legitimacy of romance. This last direction, however, is better understood not only as a reaction against other literary trends, but also as a result of the crisis of modernism. The excesses of both documentary and experimental poetics in Spain were part of a hasty updating of the literary system at a time of increasing contacts between a society still coping with industrialization on the one hand and, on the other, the cultural production of late capitalism. In conclusion, what can be considered the most significant change in Spanish narrative during the sixties and early seventies—that which transformed the documentary poetics of the previous decade into, first, an aesthetics of textual experimentation and eventually into a recovery of openly fictional storytelling—is a process that can hardly be understood without considering the Latin American production as an active component of Spain's literary life.

It is thus surprising that, given its historical importance, this phenomenon has received minimal attention among scholars. The place of the Boom novel in the course of Latin American letters has been and continues to be the subject of numerous studies and debates, but those of us who devote ourselves to so-called "Peninsular" studies (a somewhat misleading label, that forgets—or dismisses as irrelevant—the actual boundaries of Spain's territory) have managed so far to keep a certain distance. My contention has been that this lack of attention to the presence of Latin American fiction in Spain's literary life is the result of two factors. The first is a genealogical notion of national literature, which has limited the scope of study to the autochthonous production of a nation and a language, usually ignoring the presence of foreign, imported literary works and values. I believe those who study Hispanic letters are in a privileged position to question this notion and advance the study of interliterary relationships and communities, not only because of the international presence of the Spanish language, but also because of the multilingualism of the national units of study themselves.

The second factor, historical rather than theoretical, is the fact that the international acclaim of the Boom novel forced a reshuffle in the literary exchange between Spain and Latin American countries, which threatened the privileged position of Spanish writers as leading producers of fiction in the Spanish language. History seems to repeat itself today in academic circles (particularly in the United States), as increasing interest in Latin American literatures has displaced Peninsular studies from a dominant position within most departments of Spanish. Therefore, it is perhaps no coincidence that there is a certain reluctance to poke around such sensitive issues. But these displacements and dependencies move back and forth, and they are the stuff of literary history; there is no use in veiling them, and much is to be gained from a closer scrutiny of their dialectical shifts.

Notes

PREFACE

1. Mario Paoletti, *El Aguafiestas: La biografía de Mario Benedetti* (Buenos Aires: Seix Barral, 1995), 113.
2. David K. Herzberger, "An Overview of Postwar Novel Criticism of the 1970's," *Anales de la Narrativa Española Contemporánea* 5 (1980): 36.
3. Nora Catelli, "Atlántico desdén: la vieja América vista desde la España nueva," in *La crítica literaria española frente a la literatura hispanoamericana*, ed. Leonor Fleming and María Teresa Bosque Latra (Mexico: UNAM, 1993), 11–18.

1. ON NATIONAL AND NATIONALIZED LITERATURES

1. *Cuestión palpitante* is the expression used by Pere Gimferrer in "De una guerra literaria: ¿combatir en dos frentes?," *Destino* 1697 (11 April 1970): 41, and Juan García Hortelano in Fernando Tola de Habich and Patricia Grieve, *Los españoles y el boom* (Caracas: Tiempo Nuevo, 1971), 154. The Spanish reception of Latin American letters has been the subject of many contemporary studies, and I believe the interested reader will profit here from a brief bibliographical account. The case of *modernismo* has been documented by Donald F. Folgelquist in *Españoles de América y americanos de España* (Madrid: Gredos, 1968). A more ambitious study by Anna Wayne Ashhurst, *La literatura hispanoamericana en la crítica española* (Madrid: Gredos, 1980), sets out to analyze the critical reception of Latin American letters by Spaniards from the sixteenth century to 1970; for the postwar period (1940–70), however, Ashhurst concentrates on commentaries by Spaniards in exile—whose relation with Hispanic literatures in America was undoubtedly more direct and fruitful—and thus leaves aside the consideration of the literary interaction within Spain. José María Martínez Cachero's "La recepción española de la literatura hispanoamericana posterior al modernismo: primeras notas para su estudio," in *XVII Congreso del Instituto Internacional de Literatura Iberoamericana* (Madrid: Centro Iberoamericano de Cooperación, 1978), vol. 3: 1499–509, focuses also on the reception of Spanish American writers during the decades of the 1920s and 1930s. For the analysis of the interliterary relations as seen from a Latin American perspective, see the various studies by Emilia de Zuleta, particularly useful for the first decades of this century. Her *Relaciones literarias entre España y la Argentina* (Madrid: Cultura Hispánica, 1983) studies the presence of Spanish letters in Argentinean literary journals between 1907 (when

the magazine *Nosotros* was first published) and 1949 (the year *Realidad* ceased publication), while in "Relaciones literarias entre Hispanoamérica y España," in *Relaciones literarias entre España y la Argentina: Seminario 1991*, ed. E. de Zuleta (Buenos Aires: Oficina Cultural de la Embajada de España, 1991), 11–28, she gives a historical account of the development of Hispanism (mostly in Latin America, with less detailed attention to its history in Spain), with particular attention to personal and institutional contacts.

    Closer to the concerns of this book are José Antonio Fortes's "La novela hispanoamericana en España: apunte bibliográfico, años setenta," *Ínsula* 388 (March 1979): 11, which offers a bibliographical listing of articles and reviews on the topic, and "En la historia intelectual de postguerra civil española (Para una lectura del 'Boom' de hispanoamericanos en España: años 60)," *Cuadernos de ALDEEU* 9, 1 (April 1993): 9–24, where Fortes concentrates on the ideology of Spanish literary periodicals during the decade. In "La recepción de la literatura hispanoamericana en España," Enrique Ruiz-Fornells summarily reviews the editorial production and academic activity (dissertations, conferences, journals, prizes) during the 1970s and 1980s. The contribution of literary magazines and reviews is also the object of study of Nuria Prats i Fons in "La narrativa hispanoamericana en el suplemento *Informaciones de las Artes y las Letras*," *Antagonía: Cuadernos de la Fundación Luis Goytisolo* 2 (1997): 75–88. Rafael M. Mérida's "La difusión de la literatura hispanoamericana en España: datos para *otra* recepción," in *Actas del XXIX Congreso del Instituto Internacional de Literatura Iberoamericana* (Barcelona: PPU, 1994), vol. 3: 429–37, studies the presence of Latin American literature, and particularly the Boom novel, in the catalogue of Spanish book club "Círculo de Lectores." Finally, as I write these pages I receive notice of the publication of Pablo Sánchez López's "La alternativa hispanoamericana: Las primeras novelas del 'boom' en España," *Revista Hispánica Moderna* 51 (1998): 102–18, where he gives detailed accounts of some of the early Spanish reviews of Vargas Llosa's *La ciudad y los perros* and *La casa verde*, Alejo Carpentier's *El siglo de las luces*, and Cabrera Infante's *Tres tristes tigres*.

    2. See Claudio Guillén, *Literature as System: Essays Toward the Theory of Literary History* (Princeton: Princeton University Press, 1971), 502.

    3. For an overview of some of the issues addressed from this perspective, see the collection of essays edited by Homi Bhabha, *Nation and Narration* (London: Routledge, 1990).

    4. Mikhail M. Bakhtin and P. N. Medvedev, *The Formal Method in Literary Scholarship: A Critical Introduction to Sociological Poetics* (Cambridge: Harvard University Press, 1985), 26. For a survey of the development of the concept of literary life, see Peter Scherber, "'Literary Life' as a Topic of Literary History," in *Issues in Slavic Literary and Cultural Theory*, ed. Karl Eimermacher, Peter Grzybek, and Georg Witte (Bochum, Germany: Norbert Brockmeyer, 1989), 571–92.

    5. See Reingard Nethersole, "From Temporality to Spatiality: Changing Concepts in Literary Criticism," in *Proceedings of the XIIth Congress of the ICLA*, ed. Roger Bauer and Douwe Fokkema (Munich: Iudicium, 1990), vol. 5: 59–65. The XIIth Congress of the International Comparative Literature Association (Munich, 1988) was devoted to the general theme "Space and Boundaries." The geography of literature has also received attention in the work of Franco Moretti (whose re-

search aims at mappings of both the diegetic content of historical narratives and the expansion of literary genres), the sociological analysis of the "literary field" by Pierre Bourdieu, and Itamar Even-Zohar's dynamic structuralism and his concept of the "polysystem." See also José Lambert, "In Quest of Literary World Maps," in *Interculturality and the Historical Study of Literary Translations*, ed. Harald Kittel and Armin Paul Frank (Berlin: Erich Schmidt, 1991), 133–44.

6. Christopher Clausen, " 'National Literatures' in English: Toward a New Paradigm," *New Literary History* 25 (1994): 61.

7. Carlos Fuentes, "Mi patria es el idioma español," in *Tres discursos para dos aldeas* (Mexico: Fondo de Cultura Económica, 1993), 35. Fuentes has often criticized the compartmentalization of literatures in the Spanish language: "I don't accept the division among Peruvian, Argentine, Cuban, Mexican, or Spanish literature. I don't accept the Atlantic as a dividing line. I think that [Juan] Goytisolo, for instance, belongs to the same enterprise as we do, not because he became Latin American or we became Spaniards, but because we are part of the same undertaking of imagination and language" (in "Mesa redonda: la experiencia de los novelistas," by Jorge Edwards et al., *Revista Iberoamericana* 116–17 [1981]: 313); see also Fuentes, "Discurso de recepción del Premio Rómulo Gallegos," in *Premio Internacional de Novela Rómulo Gallegos 1972–1976* (Caracas: Consejo Nacional de Cultura, 1978), 18. The same opinion was advanced by García Márquez in 1968: "Let us speak no longer of Latin American literature and Spanish literature as separate entities but simply of literature in Spanish. . . . Not only are we writing in the same language, but continuing the same tradition" ("Gabriel García Márquez," interview by José Domingo, *Ínsula* 259 [June 1968]: 6, 11).

8. Carlos Barral, "Puntualización de motivos: enfrentamientos novelísticos de continente a continente," *Triunfo* 522 (30 September 1972): 36.

9. Washington Irving, *Bracebridge Hall, or The Humorists: A Medley by Geoffrey Crayon, Gent.* (Boston: Twayne, 1977), 3.

10. See Claudio Guillén, *The Challenge of Comparative Literature* (Cambridge: Harvard University Press, 1993), 37–45.

11. Julian Hawthorne, "The American Element in Fiction," *The North American Review* 139 (1884): 167.

12. Naftoli Bassel, "National Literature and Interliterary System," *Poetics Today* 12 (1991): 773–74.

13. Georg M. Gugelberger, "Decolonizing the Canon: Considerations of Third World Literature," *New Literary History* 22 (1991): 507–8.

14. Ibid., 515.

15. "Borges is a typical colonial writer. . . . He is not a European writer; there is no European writer like Borges. . . . European writers belong to very concrete and provincial traditions—reaching the extreme case of a Péguy, for example, who boasted of never having read anything but French authors. Apart from a few professors of philology, who receive a salary for it, there is only one type of person who really knows in its entirety the literature of Europe: the colonial. Only in the case of mental imbalance can a learned Argentine writer ever boast of having read nothing but Argentine—or even Spanish-language—authors. And Borges is not imbalanced" (Roberto Fernández Retamar, *Caliban and Other Essays* [Minneapolis: University of Minnesota Press, 1989], 28).

16. An example of this generalized approach is found in the *History of World*

Literature projected by the Gorky Institute, where national literatures, considered the "basic units" of study, are understood in native terms and international connections are restricted to "literary influences and typological semblances;" see Yuri B. Vipper, "National Literary History in *History of World Literature*: Theoretical Principles of Treatment," *New Literary History* 16 (1985): 545–58.

17. The notion of literary system has been offered as the key to a new definition of national literatures by José Lambert in "L'éternelle question des frontières: littératures nationales et systèmes littéraires," in *Langue, dialecte, littérature: Etudes romanes à la mémoire de Hugo Plomteux*, ed. C. Angelet et al. (Louvain, Belgium: Leuven University Press, 1983), 355–70. For a brief historical overview of the notion of literary system, see Milan V. Dimić's "Space and Boundaries of Literature According to Russian Formalism, The Prague School, and the Polysystem Theory," in *Proceedings of the XIIth Congress of the ICLA*, ed. Roger Bauer and Douwe Fokkema (Munich: Iudicium, 1990), vol. 5: 30–35. A useful summary of contemporary approaches is given by Steven Tötösy de Zepetnek in "Systemic Approaches to Literature: An Introduction with Selected Bibliographies," *Canadian Review of Comparative Literature* 19, 1–2 (March-June 1992): 21–93.

18. Roland Barthes, *On Racine* (Berkeley: University of California Press, 1992), 158–59.

19. Ibid., 161.

20. Guillén, *The Challenge of Comparative Literature*, 7.

21. André Lefevere, "Théorie littéraire et littérature traduite," *Canadian Review of Comparative Literature* 9, 2 (June 1982): 144–45.

22. In fact, according to Guillén himself, "traductology shows, or rather confirms, that language is not everything in a work of literary art" (*The Challenge of Comparative Literature* 284); see also Lefevere, "Théorie littéraire et littérature traduite," 145. In this context, it is interesting to note how, in the last decades, the field of poetics has displaced its focus away from an inquiry linguistically centered on the intrinsic properties of texts and toward one semiotically concerned with the institutional character of literature; see C. J. van Rees, "Advances in the Empirical Sociology of Literature and the Arts: The Institutional Approach," *Poetics* 12 (1983): 285–86. A similar development—and one to which we shall return later in this book—is also indicated in Gérard Genette's *Paratexts: Thresholds of Interpretation* (Cambridge: Cambridge University Press, 1997).

23. See Itamar Even-Zohar, *Polysystem Studies*, special issue of *Poetics Today* 11, 1 (spring 1990): 45–51.

24. Felix Vodička, "Response to Verbal Art," in *Semiotics of Art: Prague School Contributions*, ed. Ladislav Matejka and Irwin R. Titunik (Cambridge: MIT Press, 1976), 199. For the notion of concretization (or actualization), see Vodička's "The Concretization of the Literary Work: Problems of the Reception of Neruda's Works," in *The Prague School: Selected Writings, 1929–1946*, ed. Peter Steiner (Austin: University of Texas Press, 1982), 103–34.

25. Vodička, "Response to Verbal Art," 203–4.

26. Mario J. Valdés and Linda Hutcheon, *Rethinking Literary Theory—Comparatively* (n.p.: American Council of Learned Societies, 1994), 3–4.

27. The same argument could be applied, for instance, in favor of a *Spanish* Kafka, who became prominent in the mid-sixties as a model for young writers and whose works were published in popular pocket-book editions (*La metamorfosis*

was the first work of fiction included in Alianza Editorial's "El libro de bolsillo" series). For a similar point made regarding the reception of Italo Calvino in the United States, see Rebecca West, "L'identità americana di Calvino," *Nuova Corrente* 34 (1987): 363–74.

28. Vodička, "Response to Verbal Art," 207.

29. David Perkins, *Is Literary History Possible?* (Baltimore: Johns Hopkins University Press, 1992), 25.

30. See Jan Mukařovský, "Art as Semiotic Fact," *Semiotics of Art: Prague School Contributions*, ed. Ladislav Matejka and Irwin Titunik (Cambridge: MIT Press, 1976), 4–6.

31. István Sötér, "L'application de la méthode comparative a l'histoire d'une littérature nationale," in *Proceedings of the VIIIth Congress of the ICLA*, ed. Béla Köpeczi and György M. Vajda (Stuttgart: Erich Bieber, 1980), vol. 2: 452.

32. Anthony D. Smith, *National Identity* (London: Penguin, 1991), 143.

33. It is interesting to note that, while Italian publisher Mondadori established itself during the early 1990s as one of the most active publishers in Spain's literary industry, its Italian and Spanish catalogues are not identical—international expansion still has to pay tribute to the peculiarities of national life.

34. On the notion of literary interference, see Even-Zohar, *Polysystem Studies*, 93. This view of the dynamics of literary borrowings is supported by Roman Jakobson's understanding of the processes of linguistic borrowings; see F. W. Galan, *Historic Structures: The Prague School Project, 1928–1946* (Austin: University of Texas Press, 1985), 15–16. For a critique of the one-sided notion of influence in Czech structuralism, see Jan Mukařovský, "On Structuralism," in *Structure, Sign, and Function: Selected Essays by Jan Mukařovský*, ed. John Burbank and Peter Steiner (New Haven: Yale University Press, 1978), 15–16. On the notion of paratext, which I borrow from Genette with some modifications, see chapter 3.

2. Book Trade and Literary Production in Spain

1. Ángel Rama has thus described the "synchronic leveling" (*aplanamiento sincrónico*) of the history of Latin American narrative as seen from Spain and, later, the United States, where the label Boom novel lost its historical specificity and came to designate also a wide spectrum of writers active since the 1940s; see "El 'boom' en perspectiva," in *Más allá del boom: literatura y mercado*, by Ángel Rama, et al. (Mexico: Marcha, 1981), 52. John S. Brushwood has also noted this juxtaposition of periods and the contrast between the North American perception of the Boom and that of Spanish Americans in "Two Views of the Boom: North and South," *Latin American Literary Review* 29 (January-June 1987): 15–16. For the reception of Latin American literature in the United States, see also Neil Larsen, *Reading North by South: On Latin American Literature, Culture, and Politics* (Minneapolis and London: University of Minnesota Press, 1995). An analysis of the marketability of the Boom novel and its role in the German reception of Latin American literature is offered by Meg H. Brown in *The Reception of Spanish American Fiction in West Germany, 1981–1991: A Study of Best Sellers* (Tübingen: Max Niemeyer, 1994).

2. Ángel Rama, "El 'boom' en perspectiva," 51–52. See interview with Car-

los Barral in Tola de Habich and Grieve, *Los españoles y el boom*, 16–17. An important testimony in this respect is given by José Donoso in his own history of the Boom, where he remembers that even though his novel *Coronación* became a moderate success after its publication in Chile in 1957 (where it sold three thousand copies and went out of print), the publisher did not care to reprint it, since "everyone" had already read it in Chile and no attention was being paid to either the exporting or the importing of books (Donoso, *Historia personal del boom* [Buenos Aires: Sudamericana/Planeta, 1984], 29).

3. "During the 1950s, the Spanish economy had still been one of the poorest economies in Western Europe. In 1953, the gross domestic product of Spain amounted to only 14% of that of France and 23% of that of Italy. By 1965, these percentage figures were respectively 22% and 39%. . . . Evaluated in real terms, Spain's GNP grew at an average annual rate of about 7% in the period 1959 to 1971. This was one of the highest growth rates recorded by advanced countries of that time. Only Japan recorded a higher rate of economic growth in that period. Even though in 1972 Spain's GNP was still relatively small when compared to that of the major industrial nations of Western Europe, it doubled in value in the 1960s" (Sima Lieberman, *Growth and Crisis in the Spanish Economy: 1940–93* [London and New York: Routledge, 1995], 97). The expansion of the Spanish economy has been throughly documented in numerous works; concise accounts of the phenomenon can be found in Raymond Carr and Juan Pablo Fusi, *Spain: Dictatorship to Democracy* (London and New York: Routledge, 1991), 49–78; and in José Antonio Biescas and Manuel Tuñón de Lara, *España bajo la dictadura franquista (1939–1975)* (Barcelona: Labor, 1983), 71–104.

4. See Ramón Tamames, *La República/La Era de Franco (1931–1970)* (Madrid: Alianza/Alfaguara, 1976), 467–70.

5. See Carr and Fusi, *Spain: Dictatorship to Democracy*, 118–19.

6. See Salvador García, *Las ideas literarias en España entre 1840 y 1850* (Berkeley: University of California Press, 1971), 166.

7. Celestino del Arenal, *Política exterior de España hacia Iberoamérica* (Madrid: Complutense, 1994), 15–18. The critical bibliography on the diplomatic, economic, and cultural relations between Spain and Latin America has grown notably in the last two decades; see Carlos M. Rama, *Historia de las relaciones culturales entre España y la América Latina: Siglo XIX* (Mexico: Fondo de Cultura Económica, 1982); Lorenzo Delgado Gómez-Escalonilla, *Diplomacia franquista y política cultural hacia Iberoamérica: 1939–1953* (Madrid: CSIC, 1988), and *Imperio de papel: Acción cultural y política exterior durante el primer franquismo* (Madrid: CSIC, 1992); Montserrat Huguet Santos et al., eds., *La formación de la imagen de América Latina en España: 1898–1989* (Madrid: Organización de Estados Iberoamericanos, 1992); Pedro Pérez Herrero and Nuria Tabanera, eds., *España/América Latina: un siglo de políticas culturales* (Madrid: AIETI/Síntesis, 1993); Isidro Sepúlveda Muñoz, *Comunidad cultural e hispano-americanismo: 1885–1936* (Madrid: Universidad Nacional de Educación a Distancia, 1994); and Marina Pérez de Mendiola, ed., *Bridging the Atlantic: Toward a Reassessment of Iberian and Latin American Cultural Ties* (New York: State University of New York Press, 1996).

8. Rufino Blanco-Fombona, "El libro español en América," in *El libro español: Ciclo de conferencias* (Barcelona: Cámara Oficial del Libro de Barcelona,

1922), 176. In 1914, Blanco-Fombona founded in Madrid the Editorial América precisely to publish and popularize among Spanish readers the works of Latin American writers.

9. Hipólito Escolar, *Historia del libro* (Madrid: Fundación Germán Sánchez Ruipérez, 1984), 512. Whether the promotion of Latin American fiction from Barcelona in the 1960s should be linked to the rise of nationalistic consciousness within the margins of the Spanish State is an issue that will be considered in more detail later in this book. It is interesting to note, in any case, that the untapped potential of the Spanish American market was also a matter of commercial concern for publishers established in the Basque Country; see Julio de Lazúrtegui, *El libro español en América* (Bilbao: Centro de la Unión Ibero-Americana en Vizcaya, 1919).

10. That is the image described by José Miguel Oviedo: "During my years at the university I remember the Spanish editions of foreign books, covered with dust on the shelves. We preferred to read the Germans or English or Russians in versions coming from Buenos Aires or Mexico. . . . Peninsular editions were lethally academic and solemn: parchment paper, leather bindings, red bookmarks— desperate luxuries of a weakening culture" ("La cultura española desde América," *Cuadernos para el Diálogo* extraordinario 42 [August 1974]: 64–65).

11. See Valeriano Bozal, "La edición en España: notas para su historia," in *Treinta años de literatura: narrativa y poesía española, 1939–1969*, special issue of *Cuadernos para el Diálogo* extraordinario 14 (May 1969): 85.

12. José Manuel Galán Pérez, *Análisis estructural del sector editorial español* (Madrid: Fundación Germán Sánchez Ruipérez and Ediciones Pirámide, 1986), 232.

13. "Throughout its forty years of existence, [the INLE] has been a good tool favoring the development of the Spanish publishing industry. . . . The intervention of professional publishers varied through the years, since it was always dependent on the Administration, but in the same way that censors were the Administration's left hand, in charge of unpleasant deeds, the INLE came to represent the right hand, the paternal or compensatory one. Although certain political or religious sectors saw in the book a possible destabilizing or revolutionary influence, in the end there prevailed the idea of protecting it in order to both maintain Hispanic cultural unity and at the same time compensate publishers for the damaging effects of censorship, which prohibited the publication of so many easily salable books. This would eventually favor the emerging book industry in Argentina and Mexico" (Escolar, *Historia del libro*, 522–23).

14. Critics have given different dates to mark the beginning of the Boom: 1959 (Joseph Sommers, "Literatura e ideología: la evaluación novelística del militarismo en Vargas Llosa," in *Cultura y dependencia* [Jalisco: Departamento de Bellas Artes, 1976], 88); 1960 (Sara Castro-Klarén and Héctor Campos, "Traducciones, tirajes, ventas y estrellas: el boom," *Ideologies and Literature* 17 [1983]: 322); 1963 (Brushwood, "Two Views of the Boom," 13), or 1964 (Rama, "El 'boom' en perspectiva," 87). There is more consensus in regard to its ending in 1973, "the dark year for Latin American democracies" (Rama, 85).

15. There are three major sources of information on book production for the years that concern us here: the National Institute of the Spanish Book (INLE), Spain's National Statistics Institute (Instituto Nacional de Estadística, or INE), and

UNESCO. Since the 1940s, the INLE has provided statistical information on the production of books that is based on titles registered by commercial publishers in their catalogues; given its time range, this information will be used here to establish a larger picture of the development of the book industry in the postwar period. Starting in 1959, however, the official source for this sort of data has been the yearly reports by the INE, which record the information taken from the copyright office (Depósito Legal) and follow the guidelines established by UNESCO in 1964. INLE and INE do not provide identical data, since UNESCO guidelines require the inclusion of a larger range of publications (not only books of commercial value, but also official publications, textbooks, or dissertations); thus in 1960, for instance, the INLE seems to have covered only 50 percent of the production reported by the INE—the range of coverage, however, improves with the years (69 percent in 1970, 98 percent in 1980). One advantage of the INE is that it not only reports on the number of titles published, but also on the number of copies, a feature that will prove useful in this inquiry. Finally, data in the *UNESCO Statistical Yearbook* usually correspond to the information provided by the Spanish INE, although there are occasional differences; I will use UNESCO figures for the purpose of comparing Spain's book production with other nations. The development of the Spanish publishing industry has been documented by Fernando Cendán Pazos in *Edición y comercio del libro español: 1900–1972* (Madrid: Editora Nacional, 1972) and by José Manuel Galán Pérez in *Análisis estructural del sector editorial español*. Neither of them, however, sets out to consider in detail the specificity of literary production, a subject that has remained hitherto marginal to literary scholarship.

16. See Galán Pérez, *Análisis estructural del sector editorial español*, 17.

17. For data on the production of books in contemporary Spain, see the current series *Panorámica de la edición española de libros*, published by Spain's Ministry of Culture.

18. Interestingly enough, the situation was very different in 1950, when the total number of titles in Argentina was 4,291, which was 18 percent higher than the total produced by Spanish publishers (3,633). UNESCO gives no data on copies printed in Mexico; as for Argentina, the only figure is for 1966, with a total of about 25 million copies (some 5 million of them in literature); in contrast, that same year Spain printed 115 million copies (52 million in literature).

19. See Galán Pérez, *Análisis estructural del sector editorial español*, 197.

20. See Cendán Pazos, *Edición y comercio del libro español: 1900–1972*, 149; and Galán Pérez, *Análisis estructural del sector editorial español*, 208. Foreign trade was one of the main forces behind the economic recovery of Spain during the 1960s—between 1961 and 1973, total Spanish exports exploded from $150 million to $5.225 billion. One of the biggest increases took place in the book industry: while publication exports represented 1.1 percent of the total in 1962, by 1970 that figure was 2.7 percent; and it remained at over 2 percent until 1976. See Biescas and Tuñón de Lara, *España bajo la dictadura franquista (1939–1975)*, 83 and 86–87; and Galán Pérez, *Análisis estructural del sector editorial español*, 202.

21. Galán Pérez, *Análisis estructural del sector editorial español*, 199.

22. Rodrigo Rubio, *Narrativa española, 1940–1970* (Madrid: EPESA, 1970), 30; Bozal, "La edición en España: notas para su historia," 87.

23. Carr and Fusi, *Spain: Dictatorship to Democracy*, 123.

24. During the period 1990–96, in contrast, translated titles in literature average 38 percent of Spain's literary production; see *Panorámica de la edición española de libros: 1994*, 58; and *Panorámica de la edición española de libros: 1996*, 145.

25. There are important discrepancies between UNESCO and the INE in regard to translations, since INE statistics on titles published give a higher share to translations, placing them at 20–25 percent of total production of literature during the period 1965–80 (no data are given for translations for 1960–64). If this were the case, and contrary to our hypothesis, there would be no significant disparities in the evolution of translated and nontranslated literary titles produced during the sixties and seventies in Spain. However, INE data on copies printed do show that the print run of translated literary titles actually *decreases* in the years 1966–1967, down to a historic 4 percent of copies in that category. For the period 1965–80, copies of translated works represent an average of about 20 percent of all literary copies printed, and it is even lower than that in five significant years: 1966, 1967, 1979, 1970, and 1971 (I have found no INE data on translated titles in literature for 1972). In other words, as far as the distribution of titles (indicated by the size of printing) is concerned, translations of literary works become less important during the years of the Boom; consequently, the increase in the production of literary titles has to be associated with an increase in the publication of titles and copies of works of Hispanic literature. Whether this booming literature originates from within Spain or from Latin America is an essential issue, but one that we will have to address through other means.

26. Joan Fuster, "Literatura en lengua catalana," in *Treinta años de literatura*, 20–21. The same year, 1962, is also mentioned as the beginning of a Catalan editorial recovery by Josep Maria Puigjaner, "La producció actual de llibres en català," in *El llibre i la llengua catalana* (Barcelona: Curial, 1986), 70. According to Josep M. Capdevila Bassols, "Algunas consideraciones sobre la industria editorial," *Banca Catalana* 3 (December 1966): 20, and using INLE data, in 1960 titles in Catalan represented 0.83 percent of the total number of titles published in Spain; by 1965, the figure was up to 4.35 percent. It will take, however, one more decade, until 1976, for the production of Catalan books to reach the pre–Civil War level, which was 20 percent of Spain's total output in 1933. See also Antoni M. Güell and Modest Reixach, *La producció editorial a les àrees lingüístiques restringides: el cas català* (Barcelona: Fundació Jaume Bofill, 1978), 82–85.

27. "Carlos Barral o el límite de la heterodoxia," interview by F. Monegal, *La Vanguardia* [Barcelona] 6 September 1973: 49.

28. A list of participants in the "Conversaciones Poéticas" is given by José María Espinás in "Notas al margen de las Conversaciones," *Destino* 1138 (30 May 1959): 38. José Luis Cano offers a chronicle of the sessions in "Las Conversaciones Poéticas de Formentor," *Ínsula* 151 (15 June 1959): 10. See also Luis Ripoll, "Postal de Mallorca: Las Conversaciones Poéticas de Formentor," *Destino* 1137 (23 May 1959): 39–40; and Juan Ramón Masoliver, "Poética agitación en la isla de la calma, o las Conversaciones de Formentor," *Destino* 1138 (30 May 1959): 38–39. The significance of the event for Spanish poets has been highlighted by Carme Riera, *La Escuela de Barcelona: Barral, Gil de Biedma, Goytisolo* (Barcelona: Anagrama, 1988), 221–25.

29. Reports of this colloquium appeared in various publications: J. M. Espinás,

"El I Coloquio Internacional de Novela, en Formentor;" *Destino* 1139 (6 June 1959): 13–15; J. M. Castellet, "El Primer Coloquio Internacional sobre Novela," *Ínsula* 152–53 (July–August 1959): 19, 32 (the text appeared later in almost identical form as "Coloquio Internacional sobre Novela en Formentor," *Cuadernos del Congreso por la Libertad de la Cultura* 38 [September-October 1959]: 82–86); and Joan Fuster, "El I coloquio internacional de novela en Formentor," *Papeles de Son Armadans* 41 (August 1959): 207–12.

30. Espinás, "El I Coloquio Internacional de Novela, en Formentor," 14; Fuster, "El I coloquio internacional de novela en Formentor," 208.

31. Rama, "El 'boom' en perspectiva," 66–67. For a chronicle of the sessions, see Espinás, "Cita en Formentor: El II Coloquio Internacional de la Novela," *Destino* 1188 (14 May 1960): 43–44; and Castellet, "El Segundo Coloquio Internacional de Novela en Formentor," *Ínsula* 163 (June 1960): 4.

32. Barral has given an account of the history of this group in *Los años sin excusa* (Madrid: Alianza, 1982), 221–51; and *Cuando las horas veloces* (Barcelona: Tusquets, 1988), 29–40. For Einaudi's version, see his *Frammenti di memoria* (Milan: Rizzoli, 1988), 126–29; and G. Einaudi and Severino Cesari, *Colloquio con Giulio Einaudi* (Rome: Theoria, 1991), 180–91.

33. Barral, *Los años sin excusa*, 221; *Cuando las horas veloces*, 29.

34. Einaudi, *Frammenti di memoria*, 126.

35. Barral, *Los años sin excusa*, 233.

36. Jorge Luis Borges, "Autobiographical Essay," in *The Aleph and Other Stories, 1933–1969* (New York: E.P. Dutton, 1978), 254. See chronicles of the third Formentor meeting by Enrique Canito, "Crónica de Formentor: los premios internacionales de novela," *Ínsula* 174 (May 1961): 5; and J. R. Masoliver, "Formentor: Por una literatura sin fronteras," *Destino* 1240 (13 May 1961): 41–43. For the French reception of Latin American literature, see Sylvia Molloy, "El descubrimiento de la literatura hispanoamericana en Francia," *Cuadernos del Congreso por la Libertad de la Cultura* 60 (May 1962): 50- 57; and, especially, *La difussion de la littérature hispanoaméricaine en France au XXe siècle* (Paris: PUF, 1972), which analyzes the reception between 1900 and 1967, with particular attention to literary periodicals and the publishing world. By 1961, and although Borges had been translated into French, relatively few people were familiar with his texts in Europe; according to Umberto Eco, Borges was still largely unknown to Italian critics in 1965, at the time of the Gruppo 63 meeting (*Postscript to The Name of the Rose* [New York: Harcourt Brace Jovanovich, 1984], 64). In Spain, Borges was known among very restricted circles mostly because of his association with Spanish *ultraísmo* in the 1920s, but it was not until four decades later that he was recognized by a larger audience. According to Castellet (who declared this in 1968), "Borges did not really began to be known in Spain until six or seven years ago. . . . Borges is now known in Spain through what has been said about him by writers like Cortázar" ("La actual literatura latinoamericana vista desde España," in *Panorama actual de la literatura latinoamericana* [Madrid: Fundamentos, 1971], 54). Andrés Amorós, reminiscing about his experiences as a university student in Madrid in those same years, confirms the observation: "when I was in my fifth year at the university . . . don Rafael Lapesa . . . said to me: 'Look, a Spanish-American writer is coming to Madrid to give a lecture on Hispanic culture. I'm afraid nobody will be there to hear him, and that would be a pity. See if you can

convince your friends and tell them a really good writer is coming to speak, believe me, he's very good, you won't get bored, and even if you haven't read him and he's not known around here, he's a wonderful gentleman. His name is Jorge Luis Borges.' And the truth is none of my friends, no one in Madrid knew him, and he was in danger of speaking to an almost deserted lecture hall" ("Narrativa latinoamericana," in *Hispanoamérica: La sangre del espíritu*, ed. Victorino Polo [Murcia: Universidad de Murcia, 1992], 21).

37. Antonio Martínez-Menchén, *Del desengaño literario* (Madrid: Helios, 1970), 97. An optimistic view of the international reception of the Spanish novel in the late 1950s appears in the anonymous notes "Las novelas de Miguel Delibes en el extranjero," *Destino* 1210 (15 October 1960): 49; and "Ana María Matute y su obra en el extranjero," *Destino* 1235 (8 April 1961): 34–35; see also Juan Cano Ballesta, "Décadas de conquista para las letras españolas: poesía y novela (1953–1963)," *Ínsula* 210 (May 1964): 6. A somewhat erratic history of Spanish social realism in France can be found in José Antonio Fortes, "Gallimard y la novela española de postguerra: años 1957–1968," *Letras Peninsulares* 1, 2 (fall 1988): 182–99.

38. Ricardo Muñoz Suay, "Operación Realismo: precisiones para un debate histórico," *Imprévue* 1–2 (1979): 177. See also Joan Estruch Tobella, "Un intento de realismo socialista español: la literatura y el PCE en la década de los 50," in *Actas del I Simposio para profesores de Lengua y Literatura Española*, ed. Ricardo Velilla Barquero (Madrid: Castalia, 1981), 133–51. For a general view of the culture of dissidence in postwar Spain, see Shirley Mangini, *Rojos y rebeldes: la cultura de la disidencia durante el franquismo* (Barcelona: Anthropos, 1987).

39. Fernando Morán, *Novela y semidesarrollo: una interpretación de la novela hispanoamericana y española* (Madrid: Taurus, 1971), 355.

40. Carlos Barral has commented on the convergence of his editorial interests and the Communist Party's cultural strategy in *Los años sin excusa*, 187–93. For a somewhat different view of these developments, see Muñoz Suay, "Operación Realismo."

41. Juan Goytisolo, *Realms of Strife: The Memoirs of Juan Goytisolo, 1957–1982* (San Francisco: North Point Press, 1990), 12; original Spanish in *En los reinos de taifa* (Barcelona: Seix Barral, 1986), 15- 16. See also the dossier "Spécial Espagne: Jugez sur pièces 'le nouveau' roman espagnol," *Les Lettres Françaises* 936 (19–25 July 1962): 1 and 4–7, where this generation of novelists is presented as representative of a "pre-revolutionary period" in Spanish history. In a lecture given in 1964, Antonio Iglesias Laguna analyzed the historical, linguistic, literary, and political causes for the declining international interest in Spanish literature, and—from the standpoint of Francoist anti-Communism—criticized the almost exclusive attention given to the social novel in other countries: "Those battling us with pen and sword still maintain a propagandistic and publishing network that on the one hand dodges any knowledge of Spanish writers who do not share their ideas, and on the other translates, disseminates and inflates those who present the picture of contemporary Spain that is most convenient for them. As we have already noted, it is symptomatic that the Spanish writers most widely read abroad are Juan Goytisolo, Juan García Hortelano, José Soler Puig, Rafael Alberti, and Jesús López Pacheco" (*¿Por qué no se traduce la literatura española?* [Madrid: Editora Nacional, 1964], 33).

42. See Maurice Edgar Coindreau, "Homenaje a los jóvenes novelistas españoles," *Cuadernos del Congreso por la Libertad de la Cultura* 33 (November-December 1958): 44–47. The Gallimard collection eventually concentrated on novels published before 1962; for a list of titles published in the collection, see Fortes, "Gallimard y la novela española de postguerra: años 1957–1968."

43. Gonzalo Torrente Ballester, *Panorama de la literatura española contemporánea*, 3rd ed. (Madrid: Guadarrama, 1965), 530. On the "indulgence" of publishers in the Formentor group toward the Spanish novel, see Barral, *Cuando las horas veloces*, 59–60.

44. While, according to the Russian Formalist conception of literary evolution, literary models age and become automatized (with time and exposure), it must be also taken into consideration that artistic evaluation has little to do with objective analysis of internal properties of works. As it has been pointed out by Even-Zohar, the main concern of the literary historian is not the study of *canonical*, but rather of *canonized* literature: "While 'canonical' may suggest (and so it does in the writings of many English- or French-speaking critics) the idea that certain features are *inherently* 'canonical,' . . . 'canonized' . . . clearly emphasizes that such a state is a result of some act(ivity) exercised on certain material, not a primordial nature of this material 'itself' " (*Polysystem Studies*, 16 n. 4).

45. See Carr and Fusi, *Spain: Dictatorship to Democracy*, 86–90. *Cuadernos para el Diálogo*, one of the most influential periodicals of the period, began publication in 1963; by 1966, the pressure of sociological changes rendered the 1938 censorship obsolete, and a new Press Law opened the door to some deregulation of state control: "Whatever limitations the law of 1966 placed on the freedom of the press, newspapers now increasingly exposed the conflicts of Spanish society. Their language changed: bombs were called bombs; strikes, strikes" (ibid., 167).

46. The social novelists' loathing for the new Spanish condition is conveyed in the final pages of Juan Goytisolo's 1966 novel, where crowds of tourists take pictures of a distorted image of the Civil War in Montjuich while the United States Sixth Fleet docks its warships at the Barcelona seaport: "Everything has been futile" (*Todo ha sido inútil*), concludes the narrator of *Marks of Identity* (New York: Grove Press, 1969), 350; original Spanish in *Señas de identidad* (Barcelona: Seix Barral, 1979), 420.

47. See Rama, "El 'boom' en perspectiva," 60–63.

48. Francisco Fernández Santos, "Desde Cuba: Premios Casa de las Américas 1967," *Índice* 217–18 (1967): 79. On the function of Casa de las Américas during the 1960s and 1970s, and in particular of its homonymous journal, see Nadia Lie, *Transición y transacción: La revista cubana "Casa de las Américas" (1960–1976)* (Louvain, Belgium: Leuven University Press and Hispamérica, 1996).

49. Castellet, "La actual literatura latinoamericana vista desde España," 55–56.

50. See Jorge Schwartz, ed., *Las vanguardias latinoamericanas: textos programáticos y críticos* (Madrid: Cátedra, 1991), 552–61.

51. Goytisolo, *Realms of Strife*, 132; *En los reinos de taifa*, 156. On the Padilla affair, see the various dossiers published in *Libre* 1 (1971), and *Índice* 288–89 (April 1971) and 292–95 (July–August 1971).

52. Barral, "Reflexiones acerca de las aventuras del estilo," in *Treinta años de literatura*, 39.

53. Seix Barral was not the only publisher of Spanish neorealism, although it was the one visibly promoting it not only commercially but also ideologically. An important group of these novels were published by Destino, some of them having been awarded its Nadal Prize (among them, Luis Romero, Carmen Martín Gaite, Rafael Sánchez Ferlosio and Ana María Matute); but the 1968 prize given to Álvaro Cunqueiro's *Un hombre que se parecía a Orestes* indicated also a departure from its interest in traditional Spanish realism.

54. "Carlos Barral, contra el indigenismo," interview by Baltasar Porcel, *Destino* 1677 (22 November 1969): 27.

55. For a review of the critical reappraisal of social realism see Santos Sanz Villanueva, *Historia de la novela social española (1942–1975)* (Madrid: Alhambra, 1980), vol. 1: 212–23.

56. "Examen de conciencia," in *El furgón de cola* (Barcelona: Seix Barral, 1977), 253; "Literatura y eutanasia," in *El furgón de cola*, 84. Significantly, both essays by Juan Goytisolo were first published in Uruguay—in *Número* 1 (April–June 1963), and in *Marcha* 1307–8 (June 1966), respectively. See also his "Destrucción de la España sagrada," interview by Emir Rodríguez Monegal, *Mundo Nuevo* 12 (June 1967): 47–48.

57. For a more detailed analysis (and defense) of neorealism as a proper response to the cultural conditioning of postwar Spain, see Fernando Morán, *Explicación de una limitación: la novela realista de los años cincuenta en España* (Madrid: Taurus, 1971).

58. Castellet, "Tiempo de destrucción para la literatura española," in *Literatura, ideología y política* (Barcelona: Anagrama, 1976), 152, 154–55. The essay was first published in French in *Les Nouvelles Lettres* (March-April 1968) and later in its original Spanish version in *Imagen* [Caracas] 28 (1–15 July 1968).

59. The exchange between Torrente Ballester and Amorós appears in Andrés Amorós et al., *Novela española actual* (Madrid: Cátedra/Fundación Juan March, 1977), 292 and 297–98. For Juan Goytisolo's comments, see his "La novela española contemporánea," in *Disidencias* (Barcelona: Seix Barral, 1977), 155–56.

60. Antonio Martínez-Menchén complained of this situation: "The dialectic of realism vs. Latin American novel was certainly not raised by the Spanish realists. For several years they have had to endure the annoying comparison with Latin American novelists, and from all sorts of angles—reactionary and progressive, more or less traditional enemies, and old stalwart, renegate friends. . . . Ever since Goytisolo, with a laudable sense of self-criticism and intellectual honesty, considered the problem in *El vagón de cola* [sic], there have hardly been any critics or fault-finders, whether young or old, who write about the topic without repeating those already-clichéd insults about the Spanish novel in general, and about realists in particular, and then who don't propose to follow the Latin American route as a panacea for so many ills" ("El mismo Martínez-Menchén contra . . . Guelbenzu y Vázquez Montalbán," *Informaciones* [Madrid] 29 May 1969, sec. "Informaciones de las Artes y las Letras": 1–2).

61. Manuel Vázquez Montalbán, "Experimentalismo, vanguardia y neocapitalismo," in *Reflexiones ante el neocapitalismo* (Barcelona: Ediciones de Cultura Popular, 1968), 107. Vázquez Montalbán has later reconsidered this position and acknowledged the value of social realism as the only possible and even authentic avant-garde in Spain during the late fifties and early sixties: "young writers had

within reach at that time . . . the existence of a real avant-garde, the only real avant-garde then at our disposal: those writers who had tried to present—apart from and against the production of the official literary culture—a code of conduct as writers and a code of expression, a language of rupture. This group of writers, so highly complex and oftentimes so falsely characterized, is usually called social literature. I insist on its avant-garde character, in spite of my being one of the people responsible for attempting to bury that sector in my youth" ("Literatura y transición," in *Política y literatura*, ed. Aurora Egido [Zaragoza: Caja de Ahorros y Monte de Piedad de Zaragoza, Aragón y Rioja, 1988], 128).

62. Juan Benet, "Una época troyana," in *En ciernes* (Madrid: Taurus, 1976), 99–101. The initial confrontation between Issac Montero and Benet took place in 1970 in the context of a roundtable together with José Manuel Caballero Bonald, José María Guelbenzu, Carmen Martín Gaite, and Antonio Martínez-Menchén; see Montero et al., "Mesa redonda sobre novela," in *Literatura española a treinta años del siglo XXI*, special issue of *Cuadernos para el Diálogo* extraordinario 23 (December 1970): 45–52; see also Montero's "Acotación a una mesa redonda" and Benet's "Respuesta al señor Montero," which appear in the same issue, 65–74 and 75–76, respectively. Benet also questioned the notion of a functional interaction between culture and society in a 1972 lecture, "La crítica en cuanto antropología," in *En ciernes*, 63–84.

63. See Luis Núñez Ladeveze, "Polémica sobre la novela española," *Nuestro Tiempo* 200 (February 1971): 33–48.

64. Daniel Sueiro, "Silencio y crisis de la joven novela española," in *Prosa novelesca actual: segunda reunión*, ed. Francisco Ynduráin (Madrid: Universidad Internacional Menéndez Pelayo, 1969), 177–78.

65. The Barral Prize was given for the last time in 1974, when Mauricio Wácquez reached the final round with *Paréntesis*; see Vázquez Montalbán, "Muere el Premio Barral," *Triunfo* 617 (27 July 1974): 46.

66. See José María Martínez Cachero, *La novela española entre 1936 y 1980: historia de una aventura* (Madrid: Castalia, 1985), 274–81. Contrary to other contemporary awards, the Critics' Prize was not related to any publishing houses; created in 1956 by the Association of Spanish Critics, it was decided by the vote of literary critics working in different newspapers accross the country, although not all geographical areas were always equally represented (the critics were mostly from Barcelona and Madrid). Given this partial representation, it was noted that the name of the award should be "premios de Crítica," as opposed to "premios de la Crítica" (see "Los premios de Crítica 1964," *Destino* 1394 [25 abril 1964]: 65–66). For a history of the prize, see Enrique Molina Campos, "Los Premios de la Crítica," *Camp de l'Arpa* 2 (July 1972): 7–11; and Florencio Martínez Ruiz, "Pequeña historia de un gran premio," *ABC* [Madrid] 19 April 1980: 25. On the polemical deliberations of the 1969 prize, see Leopoldo Azancot, "Premio de la Crítica 1969: las desventuras de la democracia," *Índice* 246 (1 May 1969): 30–31; and Ángel María de Lera, "Los Premios de la Crítica," *ABC* 29 May 1969, sec. "Mirador Literario": 3.

On the Nadal Prize, see Rafael Vázquez Zamora, "El Eugenio Nadal, pionero de los premios novelísticos en la posguerra," *La Estafeta Literaria* 251 (October 1962): 5; Eduardo Godoy Gallardo, "Índice crítico-bibliográfico del Premio Nadal: 1944–68," *Mapocho* [Santiago de Chile] 22 (1970): 109–36; and Antonio Vilanova, "El Premio Nadal en las letras españolas," in *50 años del Premio Nadal* (Barcelona: Destino, 1994), 13–32. On the Planeta Prize during the 1950s and 1960s, see Carlos de Arce, *Grandeza y servidumbre de veinte Premios Planeta* (Barcelona: Picazo, 1972). For a comparative view of the Nadal, Planeta, and Biblioteca Breve, see Samuel Amell, "Los premios literarios y la novela de la postguerra," *Revista del Instituto de Lengua y Cultura Españolas* 1, 2 (1985): 189–98.

The list of Spanish publications that help bring to the foreground the newly discovered Spanish American literature is quite extensive. The literary journal *Índice* published several dossiers: "Julio Cortázar," in 221–23 (July-September 1967): 9–24; "José Lezama Lima," 232 (June 1968): 22–42; and "Gabriel García Márquez," 237 (November 1968): 21–37. *La Estafeta Literaria* devoted a complete issue to a "Presentación reunida de escritores argentinos" 379–80 (23 September–7 October 1967), followed by the dossier "Veinte escritores argentinos más," 381–82 (21 October–4 November 1967): 5–36. *Ínsula* had special issues devoted to "Literatura cubana actual," 260–61 (July–August 1968); "Arte y letras de Venezuela," 272–73 (July–August 1969); and "Letras de América," 303 (February 1972). Alianza Editorial published a series of introductory anthologies, beginning with José Manuel Caballero Bonald's *Narrativa cubana de la revolución* in 1968—other titles included: Emmanuel Carballo's *Narrativa mexicana de hoy* (1969), Roberto Yahni's *Setenta años de narrativa argentina: 1900–1970* (1970), Rafael di Prisco's *Narrativa venezolana contemporánea* (1971), and Abelardo Oquendo's *Narrativa peruana 1950–1970* (1973). To these, and by other publishing houses, we should add *Nueva poesía cubana*, ed. José Agustín Goytisolo (Barcelona: Península, 1970), and Arturo Berenguer Carisomo, *Literatura argentina* (Barcelona: Labor, 1970). Finally, the first book-length studies by Spanish authors on the new Latin American narrative appear in the early 1970s: Andrés Amorós, *Introducción a la novela hispanoamericana actual* (Salamanca: Anaya, 1971); Fernando Morán, *Novela y semidesarrollo: una interpretación de la novela hispanoamericana y española* (Madrid: Taurus, 1971); Rafael Conte, *Lenguaje y violencia: introducción a la nueva novela hispanoamericana* (Madrid: Al-Borak, 1972); and Antonio Rodríguez Almodóvar, *Lecciones de narrativa hispanoamericana, siglo XX: orientación y crítica* (Sevilla: Universidad de Sevilla, 1972). Joaquín Marco's *La nueva literatura en España y América* (Barcelona: Lumen, 1972) and Antonio Tovar's *Novela española e hispanoamericana* (Madrid: Alfaguara, 1972) are both collections of previously published reviews.

67. Itamar Even-Zohar, *Papers in Historical Poetics* (Tel Aviv: The Porter Institute for Poetics and Semiotics, 1978), 80.

3. The Search for Poetic Realism

1. Pierre Bourdieu, "The Market of Symbolic Goods," *Poetics* 14 (1985): 21.

2. Gérard Genette, *Paratexts*, 1–2. Genette's paratextuality represents—together with intertextuality, metatextuality, hypertextuality, and architextuality—one of the basic types of transtextuality, that is, "all that sets the text in a relation, whether obvious or concealed, with other texts" (*Palimpsests: Literature in the Second Degree* [Lincoln and Nebraska: University of Nebraska Press, 1997], 1).

3. Genette, *Paratexts*, 407; on the paratextual quality of reviews and recommendations, see 3.

4. It should be noted that, notwithstanding this distinction, Genette himself admits that the boundaries between presentation and interpretation are not completely sealed; see *Paratexts*, 270.

5. Ibid., 409.

6. Ibid., 346.

7. Ibid., 7.

8. Ibid., 5–6.

9. On the role of prejudices in the hermeneutical process, see Hans Georg Gadamer, *Truth and Method* (New York: Continuum, 1975), 235–74.

10. An academic commentary of a novel published in a learned journal can and must legitimately assume that readers will be familiar with the object of the reading; a review published in the press as a book hits the stores, however, does not presuppose such familiarity. These differences are clearly illustrated by some of the reviews of *La ciudad y los perros*. Luis Ponce de León's review, in *La Estafeta Literaria* 284 (February 1964): 19, intentionally avoids giving away the surprise about the identity of one of the narrators—a surprise that he announces but does not reveal—undoubtedly not to ruin the device's effect for the first-time reader. In contrast, Raúl H. Silva Cáceres's review, in *Cuadernos Hispanoamericanos* 173 (May 1964): 416–22, which gives away the secret, is closer in tone and content to an academic textual analysis (including footnotes with references to theoretical works by Kayser or Wellek and Warren).

11. The previous winners of the Leopoldo Alas Prize had been: Lauro Olmo, *Doce cuentos y uno más* (1956); Jorge Ferrer-Vidal, *Sobre la piel del mundo* (1957); and Ramón Nieto, *Los desterrados* (1958). The jury in 1959 was made up by Martín Garriga, Manuel Carreras Roca, Manuel Pla y Salat, Gonzalo Lloveras, Miguel Dalmau, Enrique Badosa, Esteban Padrós de Palacios, and Juan Planas Cerdá; see Planas Cerdá, "Prólogo," in *Los jefes*, by Mario Vargas Llosa (Barcelona: Rocas, 1959), ix–xi.

12. As José Miguel Oviedo pointed out in 1970, "The [Leopoldo Alas] prize has little or no resonance outside of Spain (anthologies of Peruvian short stories appearing around that time frequently omitted his [Vargas Llosa's] name), and the Spanish edition [of *Los jefes*], humble in appearance and with a limited printing, is today a collector's item" (*Mario Vargas Llosa: la invención de la realidad* [Barcelona: Barral, 1970], 29).

13. Planas Cerdá, "Prólogo," ix–x.

14. The jury was formed by such prestigious critical and literary figures as José María Salaverría, Ramón Pérez de Ayala, Eduardo Gómez de Baquero, Gabriel Miró, Enrique Díez-Canedo, Ricardo Baeza, and Pedro Sáinz Rodríguez; see Amorós, *Introducción a la novela hispanoamericana actual*, 32. The novel was simultaneously published in Madrid (by Espasa-Calpe) and Barcelona (by Araluce).

15. Planas Cerdá, "Prólogo," x.

16. The jury of the 1962 Biblioteca Breve was formed by publishers Carlos Barral and Víctor Seix, critic Josep Maria Castellet, poet and university professor José María Valverde, and philologist Joan Petit. Vargas Llosa's novel, originally entitled *La morada del héroe* and later announced in the press as *Los impostores*,

was finally published in October 1963 under its definite title, *La ciudad y los perros* (the original title was partly preserved in the English translation, *The Time of the Hero*).

The Biblioteca Breve Prize was quickly identified with the Boom novel by most critics both inside and outside Spain. See Ignacio Iglesias, "Novelas y novelistas de hoy," *Mundo Nuevo* 28 (October 1968): 84–88, where the prize appears as one of the institutional supporters of the Boom; cf. also the critical view presented in "Venturas y desventuras de un conocido premio literario," *Mundo Nuevo* 38 (August 1969): 93–94. Unquestionably, the Biblioteca Breve became a showcase for the Boom novel, as six Latin American writers were awarded the prize: Vargas Llosa (1962), Vicente Leñero (*Los albañiles*, 1963), Cabrera Infante (*Tres tristes tigres*, 1964), Carlos Fuentes (*Cambio de piel*, 1967), Adriano González León (*País portátil*, 1968), and Nivaria Tejera (*Sonámbulo de sol*, 1971). To that list we should add no less than seven finalists: Carlos Droguett (*Eloy*, 1959), Carlos Martínez Moreno (*El Paredón*, 1961), Mario Benedetti (*Gracias por el fuego*, 1963), Manuel Puig (*La traición de Rita Hayworth*, 1965), Jorge Guzmán (*Tirante el Negro*, 1967), José Donoso (*El obsceno pájaro de la noche*, 1970), and Emilio Díaz Valcárcel (*Figuraciones en el mes de marzo*, 1971). The prize was not awarded in 1960, 1966, 1970, and 1973 (when it was terminated). Donoso was expected to receive it in 1970, but the competition was canceled that year after the turmoil created by Carlos Barral's departure from Seix Barral.

17. In 1964, the Critics' Prize was decided by critics from Barcelona (Juan Ramón Masoliver, Ángel Marsá, Fernando Gutiérrez, Lorenzo Gomis, Esteban Molist, Enrique Sordo, Rafael Vázquez Zamora, and Julio Manegat), Zaragoza (Luis Horno Liria), Palma de Mallorca (Baltasar Porcel), Valencia (Joan Fuster and Miguel Dolç), and Bilbao (Javier de Bengoechea). Leopoldo Azancot reviews the deliberations of the 1970 prize in "Premios de la Crítica 1970: fin del 'realismo social' español y revisión de la narrativa latinoamericana," *Índice* 267 (15 April 1970): 34–35.

18. Other prominent Latin American writers were also jurors of those literary prizes: García Márquez (Biblioteca Breve 1970, Barral 1971–73), Guillermo Cabrera Infante (Biblioteca Breve 1971–73), Juan Rulfo (Biblioteca Breve 1971–73), Cortázar (Barral 1972). The critical work of some Boom novelists was an important force behind the recovery and legitimation of forgotten areas of the literary tradition, both national and foreign. In the case of Vargas Llosa, the influence is evident in the rehabilitation of the Catalan classic of chivalric romance, *Tirant lo Blanc* (to which we will return later in this book), as well as through an extensive production of essays and prologues on Fielding, Balzac, Flaubert, Joyce, and others; see comments by Joaquín Marco in Vargas Llosa et al., *Semana de autor: Mario Vargas Llosa* (Madrid: Ediciones Cultura Hispánica, 1985), 42–43.

19. The outcome of the 1963 Formentor Prize, which was awarded to Jorge Semprún for *Le long voyage*, gave rise to a rather juicy story by Carlos Barral, featuring Juan Goytisolo as conspirator against the intentions of the Spanish members of the jury; see Barral, *Cuando las horas veloces*, 45–46. As it was later stated by Seix Barral in the editorial note inserted with the first edition of the novel, *La ciudad y los perros* was the only manuscript submitted to the Formentor by the Spanish committee.

20. The insert ran a total of nine unnumbered pages; references to these pages

will be given here in roman numerals. For an overview of the functions of original prefaces, see Genette, *Paratexts*, 196–236 and 263–75.

21. Many of the works associated with the social novel were published by Seix Barral, where the most important manifestoes of the movement—J. M. Castellet's *La hora del lector* (1957) and Juan Goytisolo's *Problemas de la novela* (1959)— had also been published.

22. José María Valverde, "Carta informativa sobre un prologuillo a *La ciudad y los perros*," in *Asedios a Vargas Llosa*, ed. Luis A Díez (Santiago de Chile: Editorial Universitaria, 1972), 102.

23. Juan Goytisolo, "La novela española contemporánea," in *Disidencias*, 167; the essay was originally published in *Libre* 2 (December 1971–February 1972) 33–40. Other Latin American texts, however, were not so fortunate with Spanish censorship. Manuel Puig's *La traición de Rita Hayworth*, the runner-up of the 1965 Biblioteca Breve Prize, could not be published in Spain until 1971, "presumably because of the comic candor of certain sexual episodes" (Emir Rodríguez Monegal, "A Literary Myth Exploded," *Review* 72 [1971–1972]: 61). And there was a fierce debate between Carlos Fuentes and Carlos Robles Piquer, the Spanish official in charge of censorship, over the publication of Fuentes's *Cambio de piel*, winner of the 1967 Biblioteca Breve (the novel was first published in Mexico in 1968 and had to wait until 1974 to appear in Spain). The exchange between Fuentes and Robles Piquer—together with a fragment of the report of the censors and under the heading "La inquisición española todavía quema libros mexicanos"—was published in *Siempre* [Mexico] 741 (6 September 1967): 5. See also "Fuentes y la censura española," *Mundo Nuevo* 17 (November 1967): 90–91; and "Un episodio literario de 1967: el caso Fuentes," *La Estafeta Literaria* 387 (13 January 1968): 4–7.

24. Genette, *Paratexts*, 224.

25. By the early 1960s, the national novel was seen by many of its contemporaries as a genre in crisis that had produced mainly testimonial texts that risked alienating its intended public; see Isaac Montero, "La novela española desde 1955 hasta hoy: una crisis entre dos exaltaciones antagónicas," *Triunfo* 507 (June 1972): 88–89. As we have already noted, a severe generational self-criticism can also be seen in Juan Goytisolo's essays "Examen de conciencia" and "Literatura y eutanasia," where he describes how Spanish intellectuals had trimmed the analysis of reality according to Manichean designs and remained oblivious of the social changes taking place in the country.

26. In Tola de Habich and Grieve, *Los españoles y el boom*, 21.

27. Ibid., 176; see also Luis Goytisolo, "Carta sobre Vargas Llosa," in *El autor y su obra: Mario Vargas Llosa* (Madrid: Universidad Complutense, 1990), 139–41.

28. Armas Marcelo, *Vargas Llosa: el vicio de escribir* (Madrid: Temas de Hoy, 1991), 27–28 and 250; see also his "¿Qué hubo, poeta?," *Letra Internacional* 20 (1990): 22–23.

29. Fernando Álvarez Palacios, *Novela y cultura española de postguerra* (Madrid: Edicusa, 1975), 60–61.

30. "Javier Alfaya contra el confusionismo," *Informaciones* 12 June 1969, sec. "Informaciones de las Artes y las Letras": 2.

31. Jorge Campos, "Otra gran novela: *La ciudad y los perros*," *Ínsula* 209 (April 1964): 11; emphasis added.

32. Morán, *Novela y semidesarrollo*, 316.

33. Andrés Sorel, "La nueva novela latinoamericana: Costa Rica y Perú," *Cuadernos Hispanoamericanos* 201 (September 1966): 726. See also José Escobar's review of *La ciudad y los perros*, *Revista de Occidente* 26 (May 1965): 261–67.

34. Fernando Gutiérrez, "Dos novelistas hispanoamericanos," review of *La ciudad y los perros*, by Vargas Llosa, and *El día señalado*, by Manuel Mejía Vallejo, *La Prensa* [Barcelona] 31 March 1964.

35. José Batlló, review of *La ciudad y los perros*, *Cuadernos Hispanoamericanos* 178 (October 1964): 200. Together with the reviews of the novel already indicated, we should also mention one by Juan de Castro y Delgado, in *Razón y Fe* 807 (April 1965): 435–36. The list, of course, is not complete.

36. Among the many examples of this conviction, there is of course John Barth's "The Literature of Exhaustion" (1967), of special interest to those concerned with the reception of Latin American literature in the United States as it declared the arrival of postmodernism apropos of "some aspects of the Argentinean writer Jorge Luis Borges, whose fiction I greatly admire" (*The Friday Book: Essays and Other Nonfiction* [New York: G.P. Putnam's Sons, 1984], 64). See also Leslie Fiedler's declaration in 1970: "the kind of literature which had arrogated to itself the name Modern . . . is *dead*" ("Cross the Border— Close the Gap," in *A Fiedler Reader* [New York: Stein and Day, 1977], 270). Across the Atlantic, in 1965 the Gruppo 63 met in Palermo to certify the decline of modernist writing and consider whether literature could be more fun without ceasing to qualify as art; for the papers debated at the meeting, see Nanni Balestrini, ed., *Gruppo 63: Il romanzo sperimentale* (Milano: Feltrinelli, 1966). According to Umberto Eco's recollection of the meeting, Renato Barilli voiced a generalized consensus when he called for a recovery of plot: "Barilli [said] that till then the abolition of plots and action had been encouraged, in favor of the pure epiphany in its extreme form of 'materialistic ecstasy.' . . . But now a new phase of narrative was beginning: action was being sanctioned again, even though it was an *autre* action." Significantly enough, the figure of Borges also appears here—although in the negative—in connection with this change: "Barilli mentioned the rediscovered Roussel, who loved Verne, but he did not mention Borges, because *his* rediscovery was yet to come" (*Postscript to The Name of the Rose*, 62).

37. For a general overview, see Pablo Gil Casado, *La novela social española: 1920–1971* (Barcelona: Seix Barral, 1973); Santos Sanz Villanueva, *Historia de la novela social española (1942–1975)* (Madrid: Alhambra, 1980); and Darío Villanueva, "La novela social: Apostillas a un estado de la cuestión," in *Literatura contemporánea en Castilla y León* (Valladolid: Junta de Castilla y León, 1986), 329–48. The general tendency tends to approve of social realism's progressive ideology but criticize its outdated aesthetic practices; as we mentioned earlier, a different interpretation, which highlights the values of this narrative as a true artistic avant-garde, can be found in Manuel Vázquez Montalbán, "Literatura y transición." See also David K. Herzberger, "Social Realism and the Contingencies of History in the Contemporary Spanish Novel," *Hispanic Review* 59.2 (Spring 1991): 153–73. Constantino Bértolo argues for a reading of social realism as "civil literature" and questions the traditional idea that it failed as a literary movement: "To speak nowadays of the failure of realism seems to me an aesthetic simplifica-

tion that either reveals mere ignorance or involves a self-interested blindness. Realist literature more than fulfilled the role that every literature performs in every age, that of contributing to the creation or dissemination of a certain cultural sensibility; and it provided the necessary tools for collective subjectivities to have their appropriate symbolic referents. . . . Realism was able to be the conscience of its time, and it is not too generous to state that, as a whole, it represents one of the most solid blocs of recent literary history" ("Introducción a la narrativa española actual," *Revista de Occidente* 98–99 [July–August 1989]: 32–33).

38. Juan Goytisolo, *Problemas de la novela* (Barcelona: Seix Barral, 1959), 16.

39. See Juan Goytisolo, "Ortega y la novela," in *Problemas de la novela*, 79–86; and "Para una literatura nacional popular," *Ínsula* 146 (January 1959): 6 and 11.

40. Goytisolo, *Problemas de la novela*, 18–19.

41. Both essays were included in *Problemas de la novela*, 87–94 and 95–106, respectively. See also Gonzalo Sobejano, "Cervantes en la novela española contemporánea," *La Torre* 3–4 (July-December 1987): 552. Interestingly, years later (in 1967) Camilo José Cela was still advocating *Lazarillo de Tormes* against *Madame Bovary* (Vargas Llosa's own favorite) as the model for the Spanish novel: "The novelist nowadays has an obligation to disregard Madame Bovary and pay attention, a lot of attention, to Lazarillo. The analysis of those scatterbrained, sentimental and dreamy-eyed wives who go about whoring—with their bodies or their souls—on the outskirts of the province is no longer a novelistic problem; but the hunger, bad faith, defenselessness, and frustration experienced by the serf with a hundred masters are still prevalent" ("Sobre el concepto de novela," in *Prosa novelesca actual*, ed. Francisco Ynduráin [Madrid: Universidad Internacional Menéndez Pelayo, 1968], 52).

42. Castellet, *La hora del lector: notas para una iniciación a la literatura narrativa de nuestros días* (Barcelona: Seix Barral, 1957), 25.

43. For a self-criticism of social realism in the 1950s and its "performative illusion," see Juan Goytisolo, "La novela española contemporánea," 159–60.

44. Castellet, *La hora del lector*, 36.

45. "El Mestre: Josep Maria Castellet," in Jochen Heymann and Montserrat Mullor-Heyman, *Retratos de escritorio: Entrevistas a autores españoles* (Frankfurt am Main: Vervuert, 1991), 162. According to Castellet, who took part in the organization and selection of participants, the conference was openly intended to debate the theoretical foundations of Spanish realism—"a debate on realism to try to qualify the schematic approaches we Peninsular writers observed"—and it was then that he began to question his own aesthetic creed: "there opened up a deep crisis that forced me to rethink many theoretical positions I had been defending at the time" (*Els escenaris de la memòria* [Barcelona: Edicions 62, 1988], 233, 212).

46. "Two tendencies quickly appeared among the writers who took part in the debate: on the one hand, those who supported social realism, albeit with nuances going from a properly socialist realism (Castellet, Celaya, García Hortelano, López Salinas, José María de Quinto, Sastre, López Pacheco) to the continuing, modernizing realism of the Spanish realist tradition that starts with Cervantes and passes through Galdós (Torrente Ballester); and on the other, the defenders of a non-engagé literature, uncommitted to a society understood in terms of a historical situa-

tion in need of the writer's help. This last line was advocated by Miguel Delibes and almost all the foreigners in attendance, especially Chiaromonte (Italy), Nathalie Sarraute (France), and Mary McCarthy (United States)" ("Coloquios sobre el realismo," in *Ínsula* 204 [November 1963]: 2). Other accounts of the conference are given by Martín-Santos, "Realismo y realidad en la literatura contemporánea," in Juan Luis Suárez Granda, *Tiempo de silencio, de Luis Martín-Santos: Guía de lectura* (Madrid: Alhambra, 1986), 141–42; first published in *El mundo en español* [Paris] (December 1963); and by Torrente Ballester, "Un congreso de escritores," in *Panorama de la literatura española contemporánea*, 3rd edition (Madrid: Guadarrama, 1965), 558–59. For a recollection of the ideological and political context of the conference, see Castellet, *Els escenaris de la memòria*, 211–12 and 226–42.

47. Martín-Santos, "Realismo y realidad en la literatura contemporánea," 142.

48. Ibid., 141.

49. Ibid., 142.

50. See Castellet, "Tiempo de destrucción para la literatura española," 145. For Martín-Santos's notion of dialectics, see Juan Luis Suárez Granda, "La 'poética' de Luis Martín-Santos de Ribera," in *Luis Martín-Santos*, ed. Iñaki Beti Sáez (San Sebastián: Universidad de Deusto, 1991), 27–31.

51. The connection, however, was not lost to Mario Benedetti, who had found some affinities between Martín-Santos and Fuentes; see Benedetti, "Luis Martín-Santos: nueva invasión del personaje," in *Sobre artes y oficios* (Montevideo: Alfa, 1968), 221.

52. See Gonzalo Sobejano, "Testimonio y poema en la novela española contemporánea," in *Actas del VIII Congreso de la Asociación Internacional de Hispanistas*, ed. A David Kossoff et al. (Madrid: Istmo, 1986), vol. 1: 89–115.

53. "To state, as Robbe-Grillet does, that '*the world signifies nothing, it simply is*,' is equivalent to pointing out in man a congenital inability to understand external reality, that is to say, nature and history. . . . And it is not accurate to say that 'objective theory' guarantees the writer's independence vis-à-vis reality; on the contrary, it subjects him, bound hand and foot, to it. Because upon deliberately turning himself into a screen that only reflects the sensorial world, the writer mutilates reality, depriving it of those specifically human dimensions—the rational and the emotive—where it acquires meaning. . . . Robbe-Grillet's consideration of the novel seems arbitrary to me, but interesting; like all iconoclastic theories, his is full of irreverence and vibrations, of vitality. His novels, on the other hand, immediately suggest the idea of still lifes" (Vargas Llosa, "Alain Robbe-Grillet y el simulacro del realismo," *Cinema Universitario* 19 [January–March 1963]: 24); *Cinema Universitario*, published in Salamanca, was a Spanish journal devoted to larger cultural issues than its name seems to denote, and we find there collaborations by other members of the social realist literary scene like Juan García Hortelano or Armando López Salinas. For similar contemporary comments on the French *nouveau roman* by other Latin American writers, see Mario Benedetti, "El *nouveau roman* o la nueva retórica" (originally published in 1963), in *Sobre artes y oficios*, 241–47; and Ernesto Sábato, *El escritor y sus fantasmas* (Buenos Aires: Aguilar, 1963), 106–32. For the view of Spanish neorealist writers, see Sanz Villanueva, *Historia de la novela social española*, 130–32.

54. In Eduardo García Rico, *Literatura y política: en torno al realismo español* (Madrid: Edicusa, 1971), 21.

55. In Tola de Habich and Grieve, *Los españoles y el boom*, 19.

56. Benedetti, "Luis Martín-Santos," 220. The second edition of *La ciudad y los perros* was issued immediately after the first, in October 1963, and by 1965 it had been printed at least five times. In 1971, as the publisher was eager to announce in the press, the novel had reached sixteen printings: nine in the Biblioteca Breve series, plus seven more in the Biblioteca Breve de Bolsillo, with a total of 135,000 copies (see Seix Barral's advertisement in *Informaciones*, 25 February 1971, sec. "Informaciones de las Artes y las Letras": 4). In contrast, the second edition of *Tiempo de silencio* did not come out until 1965 (after the first edition in the Biblioteca Formentor, the novel was subsequently published within the Biblioteca Breve series), and by 1971 it had only been printed a total of eight times.

57. In Tola de Habich and Grieve, *Los españoles y el boom*, 19; emphasis added.

58. Guelbenzu, "Literatura, una insoportable soledad," *Cuadernos para el Diálogo* extraordinario 7 (February 1968): 48.

59. José Antonio Gómez Marín, "Literatura y política: del tremendismo a la nueva narrativa," *Cuadernos Hispanoamericanos* 193 (January 1966): 109. The dialogue with Vargas Llosa took place in 1967 in Barcelona, with the participation of Enrique Badosa (a member of the 1958 Leopoldo Alas jury), Carlos Barral, Josep Maria Castellet, Joaquín Marco, Juan Ramón Masoliver, and Esther Tusquets; see Vargas Llosa et al., " 'Realismo' sin límites: Vargas Llosa, diálogo de amistad," *Índice* 224 (October 1967): 21–22. Note that even the printed title of the dialogue presents the word "realism" in quotation marks, as if to indicate that normal assumptions about the meaning of the word should be reconsidered.

60. Mejía Vallejo declared he had unsuccessfully submitted his novel to the Nadal Prize on five previous occasions; see "Preocupación social y religiosa de *El día señalado*, último Premio Nadal," interview by Miguel Fernández, *El Diario Vasco* [San Sebastián] 12 April 1964. After being awarded to *El día señalado*, the Nadal Prize has recognized transatlantic letters in only three other occasions: *El buen salvaje*, in 1965, by Eduardo Caballero Calderón (Colombia); *Culminación de Montoya*, in 1974, by Luis Gasulla (Argentina); and *La ocasión*, in 1987, by Juan José Saer (Argentina). Founded in 1944 by the publishing house Destino, the Nadal Prize is the oldest and arguably the most prestigious of literary prizes in postwar Spain, and it had gained a well deserved reputation for discovering some of the most valued writers of the period; see Antonio Vilanova, "El Premio Nadal en las letras españolas." The prize is awarded each sixth of January for novels submitted during the previous year, which has created some confusion between the year designated by the award and the year when the actual decision is made (which is, consequently, the year of publication of the novels). Thus, *El día señalado* was awarded the "1963 Nadal Prize" in 1964 (beginning with 1990, the year indicated in the prize is the same in which the award is decided.) According to Vilanova (ibid., 26–27), the creation of the Biblioteca Breve Prize in 1958 and the publication by Seix Barral of Martín-Santos's *Tiempo de silencio* (1962) put an end to the central position the Nadal Prize had on the Spanish literary scene, and during the 1960s the attention of young novelists turns towards the Biblioteca Breve, perceived as more progressive both aesthetically and ideologically. The Nadal, however, remained a very coveted award, with as many as 149 manuscripts submitted in 1963; in contrast, the Biblioteca Breve received 81 originals in 1962 and 98 in

1968. Only the Planeta prize, which catered to a more commercial market, could claim a greater interest (386 submissions in 1968).

61. Gutiérrez, "Dos novelistas hispanoamericanos."

62. Review of *El día señalado*, *La Estafeta Literaria* 288 (28 March 1964): 19.

63. Review of *El día señalado*, in *Mundo* [Madrid] 28 June 1964.

64. See the dossier on the award of the 1964 Nadal Prize published in *Destino* 1379 (11 January 1964), which did not include the traditional photo of the winner, since Mejía Vallejo was not even in Spain at the time of the award. Readers were able to see his picture in the following issue, in "Así es el ganador del Nadal 1963: Manuel Mejía Vallejo," *Destino* 1380 (18 January 1964): 27.

65. See Masoliver, "Y ahora, el público: *El día señalado*," *La Vanguardia* 11 March 1964: 13. Masoliver himself had already published a chronicle on the competition at the Nadal Prize, where he advanced the main elements of his later review of *El día señalado*; see his "Desde el jurado: Mejía, Viguera y compañeros," *La Vanguardia* 8 January 1968.

66. José Giménez Aznar pointed to such a displacement as he captured the reactions that the outcome of the Nadal Prize provoked among other Spanish literati: "I've had the occasion to feel out the opinion that this 1963 Nadal prize has caused in such important cities within the literary world as Barcelona and Madrid. . . . In the majority of these literary cliques, for all their grand virtues and defects, the opinion prevailed that the prize never should have been given to a South American writer. There are still in Spain numerous novelists who deserve to be known, they said, and we should not expand this objective to a continent as huge as Spanish-speaking America" (*"El día señalado*, de Manuel Mejía Vallejo," in Radio Popular of Zaragoza, *Por el mundo de los libros y del teatro*, broadcast on 18 March 1964).

67. Masoliver, "Y ahora, el público: *El día señalado*," 13.

68. In Tola de Habich and Grieve, *Los españoles y el boom*, 17.

69. Josep M. Huertas Clavería and Lluís Bassets, "Con el adiós de Vargas Llosa: pequeña historia de los escritores americanos en Barcelona," *Tele/Exprés* [Barcelona] 15 June 1974: 3. See also Manuel Vázquez Montalbán, "Adiós a Vargas Llosa," *Triunfo* 613 (29 June 1974): 64.

70. Rafael Conte, review of *El día señalado*, *Tele Radio* [Madrid] 11 May 1964.

71. Antonio Muñoz Molina has pointed to Marsé as the Spanish writer who profited the most from the impact of Vargas Llosa's novels: "The technical style of *Conversación en la Catedral* was best understood in Spain by Juan Marsé, who wrote with it a wonderful novel, *Si te dicen que caí*" ("Simulacros de realidad," in Heymann and Mullor-Heymann, *Retratos de escritorio*, 111). For an analysis of similarities between Vargas Llosa and Marsé, see M. Celia Romea Castro, "Aspectos intertextuales entre *La ciudad y los perros* de M. Vargas Llosa y *Si te dicen que caí* de J. Marsé," in *Actas del XXIX Congreso del Instituto Internacional de Literatura Iberoamericana*, vol. 3: 551–62.

72. Sobejano, "Testimonio y poema en la novela española contemporánea," 93.

4. Experimentalism and Narrativity

1. Paul Valéry, *Introduction a la Poétique* (Paris: Gallimard, 1938), 15.

2. Nathalie Sarraute, "Novela y realidad," *La Voz de Galicia* [La Coruña] 20 December 1963, sec. "Artes y Letras": 11. Sarraute had defended the same idea against social realism in "Les deux réalités," *Esprit* 329 (July 1964): 72–75, her contribution to still another conference on "Reality and the Novel" that took place in Leningrad in the summer of 1963; see also another lecture given by Sarraute that same year in Brussels: "the work of the novelist is indeed a research. And this research tends to unveil the existence of an unknown reality" ("Nouveau roman et réalité," *Revue de l'Institute de Sociologie* 2 [1963]: 432).

3. The reception of the French *nouveau roman* is still another uncharted territory of Spanish literary history that deserves detailed analysis; the notes that follow are intended to provide only a brief and partial account.

4. Other titles published by Seix Barral included: Marguerite Duras's *Días enteros en las ramas*, *El Square* (both in 1957), and *Una tarde de M. Andesmas* (in 1963); Michel Butor's *El empleo del tiempo* (1958), *Sobre literatura* (1960), and *La modificación* (1969); Claude Ollier's *Garantía de orden* (1962); Robbe-Grillet's *La celosía* (1958), *El año pasado en Marienbad* (1962), and *Por una novela nueva* (1964). Seix Barral was the exclusive provider of French new novelists in Spain until 1967, when Lumen published Claude Simon's *La ruta de Flandes*, and Guadarrama translated critical works by Jean Bloch-Michel (*La nueva novela*) and Nathalie Sarraute (*La era del recelo*). In 1970, Robbe-Grillet's *Instantáneas* appeared in Tusquets, while Barral Editores issued, by the same author, *La casa de citas* and—in a new translation—*La celosía*. For the early critical reception in Spain, see J. M. Castellet, "De la objetividad al objeto: a propósito de las novelas de Alain Robbe-Grillet," *Papeles de Son Armadans* 15 (June 1957): 309–32; Jaime Gil de Biedma, "Las novelas de Alain Robbe-Grillet," *Ínsula* 132 (November 1957): 12; and Juan Goytisolo, "Novela francesa, novela americana" (1957) and "El caso Robbe-Grillet" (1958), both included in *Problemas de la novela*, 45–53 and 63–70, respectively. Castellet also included an essay by Robbe-Grillet, "Un camino para la novela futura," as an appendix to his book *La hora del lector*. Both Alain Robbe-Grillet and Michel Butor had participated in the 1959 First International Colloquium on the Novel, in Formentor. Butor was back in 1960, where he gave a lecture on "Novela y poesía" at the French Institute in Madrid; see "Michel Butor y sus claves," interview by Enrique Canito, *Ínsula* 159 (February 1960): 5.

5. See José Corrales Egea, *La novela española actual: ensayo de ordenación* (Madrid: Edicusa, 1971), 209–16; and Pablo Gil Casado, *La novela deshumanizada española: 1958–1988* (Barcelona: Anthropos, 1990), 64–67.

6. Corrales Egea, *La novela española actual*, 208. A similar argument against the imitative use of foreign forms in experimental novels, and particularly in Benet, has been more recently presented by José Antonio Fortes, who sees it as a manifestation of the ideological retreat of Spanish writers during the 1960s, in "La joven novelística del traduccionismo," *Novelas para la transición política* (Madrid: Ediciones Libertarias, 1987), 111–19.

7. Leo Pollman offered a first comparative study of these two movements in *La "nueva novela" en Francia y en Iberoamérica* (Madrid: Gredos, 1971), a topic

he has recently reviewed in "La Nueva Novela en Francia e Iberoamérica," *New Novel Review* 1, 1 (October 1993): 41–57.

8. Antonio Vilanova, "De la objetividad al subjetivismo en la novela española actual," in *Prosa novelesca actual*, ed. Francisco Ynduráin (Madrid: Universidad Internacional Menéndez Pelayo, 1968), 147–48.

9. See Bozal, "La edición en España: notas para su historia," 92.

10. "The history of the *nouveau roman* during the sixties presents itself . . . as a series of last or next-to-last accomplishments of the laboratory of the novel. . . . Little by little it loses its novelistic space of patient adventure, because its authors, without beating around the bush, pursue ends which are exclusively extranovelistic" (Pollmann, "La Nueva Novela en Francia e Iberoamérica," 54–55). See also Corrales Egea, *La novela española actual*, 204–5, who sees the debate in the 1963 conference in Madrid as confronting two literary models which were already about to become extinct. For some parallelisms between prewar and postwar narrative strategies, see Robert C. Spires, *Beyond the Metafictional Mode: Directions in the Modern Spanish Novel* (Lexington: University Press of Kentucky, 1984).

11. Michel Butor, "The Novel as Research," in *Inventory* (New York: Simon and Schuster, 1968), 27; this essay first appeared in French in the volume *Repertoire I* (1959), which was published in Spain as *Sobre literatura: estudios y conferencias 1948–1959* (Barcelona: Seix Barral, 1960).

12. Germán Sánchez Espeso, *Experimento en Génesis* (Barcelona: Seix Barral, 1967), 191.

13. Ibid., 6.

14. "Metaphor, as a matter of fact, is never an innocent figure of speech. . . . The choice of an analogical vocabulary, however simple, already does something more than account for purely physical data, and what this *more* is can scarcely be ascribed only to the credit of belles-lettres. . . . In almost the whole of our contemporary literature, these anthropomorphic analogies are repeated too insistently, too coherently not to reveal an entire metaphysical system" (Alain Robbe-Grillet, "Nature, Humanism, Tragedy," in *For a New Novel: Essays on Fiction* [Freeport, NY: Books for Libraries, 1970], 53). Robbe- Grillet's essay had appeared in Spanish as "Naturaleza, humanismo, tragedia," *Papeles de Son Armadans* 51 (June 1960): 373–402.

15. Within indicial narrative units, Barthes differentiates between "informants" (which supply "bits of information used to identify or pinpoint certain elements of time and space") and "indices proper" (which convey personality traits, feelings, atmosphere or philosophy); while "an index always signifies implicitly . . . informants do not, at least at the level of the story: they provide pure, locally relevant data" ("An Introduction to the Structural Analysis of Narrative," *New Literary History* 6 [1975]: 249).

16. Sánchez Espeso, *Experimento en Génesis*, 27.

17. Compare, for instance, the summaries of the novel given by José Domingo, review of *Experimento en Génesis*, *Ínsula* 256 (March 1968): 5; and by Gil Casado, *La novela deshumanizada española*, 167.

18. Sánchez Espeso has indicated how the critical attention paid to the Boom novel in the 1960s hindered the reception of writers like Ramón Hernández—who also published his first novel, *El buey en el matadero*, in 1967—and himself (interview by author, New York, 29 April 1992).

19. See Pollmann, *La "nueva novela" en Francia e Iberoamérica*, 345.

20. Donald L. Shaw, *Nueva narrativa hispanoamericana* (Madrid: Cátedra, 1981), 119–21. See also Luis Alemany, "Una concepción lúdica en la novelística hispanoamericana," in *Una aproximación a la moderna literatura hispanoamericana* (Santa Cruz de Tenerife: Aula de Cultura, 1974), 11–55.

21. See Jorge Campos, "*Rayuela*, de Julio Cortázar," *Ínsula* 250 (September 1967): 11. *Índice* issued a dossier on the Argentinean writer in its July–September 1967 issue, and the publication of *Ceremonias* was celebrated in the pages of the literary supplement of *Informaciones*, which was devoted to Cortázar on 5 December 1968. Surprisingly, although *Rayuela* was hugely popular among Spanish readers, it appears that it was for many years available only in imported copies, as the first Spanish edition by Edhasa was published in 1977. The reception of Cortázar in Latin America was briefly discussed by Ángel Rama in "El 'boom' en perspectiva," 87–88, and has been the subject of analysis in greater detail by Graciela Montaldo, "Destinos y recepción," in *Rayuela*, ed. Julio Ortega and Saúl Yurkievich (Buenos Aires: Fondo de Cultura Económica/Colección Archivos, 1992), 597–612.

22. See Cabrera Infante, "Lo que este libro debe al censor," in *Tres tristes tigres* (Caracas: Biblioteca Ayacucho, 1990), xi. The discarded title of the novel was recycled for a different book published in 1974. The earliest appearance of Cabrera Infante in Spain, as far as I know, is an interview by José Corrales Egea conducted in Paris in December 1962 and published two months later in *Ínsula*, on the occasion of the French translation of *Así en la paz como en la guerra*. Presented then as a representative of the new generation of Cuban revolutionary writers, Cabrera Infante proclaimed the admiration of his colleagues for contemporary Spanish literature: "I don't think it is necessary to insist on how important it is to us and to all of Spanish-speaking America . . . to see now in Spain a literature which is not only exemplary but also lively, up-to-date, and capable of serving as a guide for us" ("Tres escritores hispanoamericanos en París, I: Con Guillermo Cabrera Infante," *Ínsula* 195 [February 1963]: 7). The Spanish novelists mentioned in this context are Juan Goytisolo, Sánchez Ferlosio, Matute, and Cela.

23. Pere Gimferrer, "Notas sobre Julio Cortázar," in *Julio Cortázar*, ed. Pedro Lastra (Madrid: Taurus, 1981), 253–55; originally published in *Ínsula* 227 (October 1965): 7. After this early text, the first essay devoted to Cortázar in Spain seems to be Osvaldo López Chuchurra, ". . . Sobre Julio Cortázar," *Cuadernos Hispanoamericanos* 211 (July 1967): 5–30.

24. Gimferrer, "Notas sobre Julio Cortázar," 256. At this point (in 1965), Gimferrer considered *Los premios* and *Final del juego* to be above *Rayuela* as Cortázar's "masterpieces" (ibid., 255). He later amended what he termed an "insufficient evaluation" of the 1963 novel; see his 1981 postscript to the essay (ibid., 257).

25. Jorge Campos, "*Rayuela*, de Julio Cortázar," 11.

26. Valeriano Bozal, "Novela hispanoamericana: la estructura narrativa," *Informaciones* 5 December 1968, sec. "Informaciones de las Artes y las Letras": 1.

27. "Con Dámaso Alonso: Hay que respetar el castellano de América," interview by Francisco Umbral, *Informaciones* 12 December 1968, sec. "Informaciones de las Artes y las Letras": 3. The "injustice" of Cortázar towards Galdós has also been deplored by Julio Rodríguez Puértolas, who criticizes the Argentin-

ean writer for a lack of historical perspective and the failure to see the anticonventional character of Galdós's work; see "Galdós y Cortázar," in *Galdós: burguesía y revolución* (Madrid: Turner, 1975), 212–18. See also Germán Gullón, *El narrador en la novela del siglo XIX* (Madrid: Taurus, 1976), 114.

28. Jerome S. Bernstein, "*Rayuela*, Chapter 34: A Structural Reading," *Hispanófila* 52 (September 1974): 62. See Andrés Amorós, "*Rayuela*: nueva lectura," *Anales de Literatura Hispanoamericana* 1 (1972): 287; and his "Introducción" to *Rayuela* (Madrid: Cátedra, 1988), 57. In an even more optimistic reading of chapter 34, Randolph D. Pope has argued that what it shows is rather a hidden complicity between Cortázar and Galdós: "it is naive to accept Horacio's first reaction of rejection toward Galdós's novel. . . . The characters in *Lo prohibido* could be founding members of the cronopios club" ("Cgoarltdaozsar: el Galdós intercalado en Cortázar en *Rayuela*," *Anales Galdosianos* 21 [1986]: 142–43). For other views on the intertextual connections between *Rayuela* and *Lo prohibido*, see Debra Castillo, "Reading over Her Shoulder: Galdós/Cortázar," *Anales Galdosianos* 21 (1986): 147–60; and Hernán Castellano-Girón, "Lo galdosiano en Cortázar, lo cortazariano en Galdós: a propósito del capítulo 34 de *Rayuela*," in *Los ochenta mundos de Cortázar: ensayos*, ed. Antonio Burgos (Madrid: EDI-6, 1987), 129–35. Myron I. Lichtblau attempts to establish some parallelisms in the psychological characterization of the protagonists in both novels, in "Horacio Oliveira and Pérez Galdós: A Strange Textual Convergence in Cortázar's *Rayuela*," in *La Chispa '87: Selected Proceedings*, ed. Gilbert Paolini (New Orleans: Tulane University, 1987), 161–67.

29. Cortázar, "Un gran escritor y su soledad," *Life en español* 33.7 (7 April 1969): 50; "Alfonso Grosso explica algunas cosas," interview by Antonio Bernabeu, *Informaciones* 15 May 1969, sec. "Informaciones de las Artes y las Letras": 1. Amorós saw it differently: "Cortázar rejects didactic art and socialist realism, which is leftist in message, but deeply traditional and reactionary as art" ("*Rayuela*: nueva lectura," 305). A similar argument is presented by Robert Brody: "Cortázar does not attack Galdós the man or even Galdós's language in itself. What he does offer is a critique of a tradition—the Realistic, the Descriptive—and he criticizes Galdós's language as representative of that tradition. . . . Cortázar does not criticize Galdós; he criticizes the twentieth-century inheritors and imitators of Galdosian language" (*Julio Cortázar: Rayuela* [London: Grant and Cutler, 1976], 63). See also Jaime Alazraki, "España en la obra de Julio Cortázar," in *Actas del XXIX Congreso del Instituto Internacional de Literatura Iberoamericana*, vol 3: 5–7.

30. The features identified by García Viñó for the production of this group are clearly intended to contrast with the poetics—and the ideology—of neorealism: "this new Spanish novel can be unquestionably credited with two characteristics which summarize the rest. First: a conception of the novel as a way of knowing man rather than history; in other words, as the contemplation of a universal, invisible reality more than as the photographic reflection of what is immediate and visible. Second: an aesthetic, educated, academic concern for the genre, which is understood as a means of intellectual expression, as an art that is therefore independent from any sort of political servitude" (*Novela española actual* [Madrid: Guadarrama, 1967], 221). García Viñó's criticism of Martín-Santos appears on pp. 232–38.

31. Andrés Bosch et al., "La nueva novela: coloquio," in *Papeles sobre la "nueva novela" española*, ed. Manuel García Viñó (Pamplona: Universidad de Navarra, 1975), 104–5; first published in *Índice* 225 (November 1967): 54–57. A year later Rojas reiterated the same idea by contrasting what he described as the social determinism of neorealism (Martín-Santos, Sánchez Ferlosio, Goytisolo) with the essential humanism of "the most representative novels of the twentieth century," among which he mentioned the work of Robbe-Grillet, Faulkner, and Cortázar; "Problemas de la nueva novela española," in *La nueva novela europea* (Madrid: Guadarrama, 1968), 124. See also his 1972 lecture "Novela y humanismo," where he again turned to Cortázar to substantiate the notion of a humanistic novel detached from the here and the now of neorealism: "we must reclaim the definition of the modern novel given by Julio Cortázar. . . . The search and contemplation of the *cause* and *purpose* [*por qué* y *para qué*] for man's existence in his world and time, or if you prefer it backwards, which ends up being the same, the search for the *cause* and *purpose* of the world and time man gets to live—this seems to me to be the only attitude possible for the contemporary writer. This contemplative search, or inquisitive rapture, always begins in an act of doubt or radical distrust before the first appearances of ourselves and our *here* and *now* given to us by the immediate reality" (in *Novela y novelistas: Reunión de Málaga 1972*, ed. Manuel Alvar [Málaga: Diputación Provincial, 1973], 41).

32. Herzberger, "Experimentation and Alienation in the Novels of José María Guelbenzu," *Hispania* 64 (September 1981): 368. In 1971 Guelbenzu declared that his novelistic work "began to develop in exact opposition to" the tradition of social realism: "its existence forced me to try to use a means of expression that would cover the serious defects that, at least for me, were involved in that way of understanding narrative" (in García Rico, *Literatura y política* 35). For the early critical attention given to his novel, see Valeriano Bozal, review of *El mercurio*, *Cuadernos Hispanoamericanos* 223 (July 1968): 250–55; Andrés Amorós, "Carta a José María Guelbenzu y a un posible lector," and Juan Carlos Curutchet, "Una lectura de *El mercurio*," both in *Cuadernos Hispanoamericanos* (January 1969): 172–74 and 174–77, respectively. *El mercurio* and *Tirante el Negro*, by Chilean writer Jorge Guzmán, reached the final round of 1967 Biblioteca Breve Prize, eventually won by Carlos Fuentes's *Cambio de piel* (which received three votes against one each for the other two novels). The five members of that jury were Carlos Barral, Josep M. Castellet, Salvador Clotas, García Hortelano and Vargas Llosa; see note appeared in *Índice* 217–18 (1967): 81.

33. José María Guelbenzu, *El mercurio* (Barcelona: Seix Barral, 1968), 13.

34. For the notion of chronotope see Bakhtin's "Forms of Time and of the Chronotope in the Novel: Notes Toward a Historical Poetics," in *The Dialogic Imagination* (Austin: University of Texas Press, 1981), 84–258. For the relationship between the notion of chronotope and the tasks of historical poetics, see Michael Holquist, *Dialogism: Bakhtin and His World* (London and New York: Routledge, 1990), 106–48; Holquist gives a tentative definition of the chronotope as "the total matrix that is comprised by both the story and the plot of any particular narrative" (113). Tomás Yerro Villanueva, in *Aspectos técnicos y estructurales de la novela española actual* (Pamplona: Universidad de Navarra, 1977), argues that *El mercurio* is an anti-novel, following Sartre's characterization of "anti-romans" as works in which "it is a matter of questioning the novel in itself, of de-

stroying it even as we seem to construct it, of writing the novel of a novel that is not to be written, and that cannot be written" ("Préface" to Nathalie Sarraute's *Portrait d'un inconnu*; quoted in Yerro, 85).

35. Guelbenzu, "Literatura, una insoportable soledad," 48. The canonized status of *El Jarama*—and the singularity of Guelbenzu's comment—was evidenced in a poll conducted by *Cuadernos para el Diálogo* a year later, in which twenty Spanish novelists ranked Sánchez Ferlosio's novel as the most important text of postwar Spanish literature, closely followed by Cela's *La familia de Pascual Duarte* and Martín-Santos's *Tiempo de silencio*; see "Encuesta: poesía, novela," in *Treinta años de literatura*, 63–70. It is interesting to note, however, that all those polled were writers of older generations—having been born between 1897 (Llorenç Villalonga) and 1935 (Luis Goytisolo)—who were already well established as novelists when Guelbenzu (born in 1944) published his first novel.

36. Guelbenzu, "Literatura, una insoportable soledad," 48.

37. Guelbenzu, *El mercurio*, 133–34.

38. See Herzberger, "Experimentation and Alienation in the Novels of José María Guelbenzu," 368–69. Sanz Villanueva, *Tendencias de la novela española actual (1950–1970)* (Madrid: Edicusa, 1972), 269, and Yerro Villanueva, *Aspectos técnicos y estructurales*, 89, both quote the same passage given here from *El mercurio* without preserving the original lines, and therefore obliterate the syntactic structure that sustains the sequence of words.

39. Goytisolo, "La novela española contemporánea," 164.

40. This experimental writing fully participates of many of the characteristics of what Janet W. Díaz considers the dominant mode of Spanish fiction between 1970 and 1975, which she describes as post–neorealism: complex vocabulary and linguistic renovation; formal considerations and metaphysical thematics removed from any utilitarian (that is, sociopolitical) preoccupations; temporal experimentation; devaluation of plot; see Díaz, "Origins, Aesthetics and the 'Nueva Novela Española,'" *Hispania* 59.1 (March 1976): 114–15.

41. See Sobejano, "Cervantes en la novela española contemporánea," 556.

42. Goytisolo, "A Cervantine Reading of *Three Trapped Tigers*," in *Saracen Chronicles: A Selection of Literary Essays* (London: Quartet Books, 1992), 141–42; original Spanish in "Lectura cervantina de *Tres tristes tigres*," in *Disidencias*, 205.

43. Guillermo Cabrera Infante, *Tres tristes tigres* (Barcelona: Seix Barral, 1983), 225–58; *Three Trapped Tigers*, trans. Donald Gardner and Suzanne Jill Levine (New York: Harper and Row, 1971), 235- 78. On puns in Cabrera Infante's novel, see Alfred Mac Adam, *Modern Latin American Narratives: The Dreams of Reason* (Chicago: University of Chicago Press, 1977), 66–67.

44. Goytisolo, "A Cervantine Reading of *Three Trapped Tigers*," 143; "Lectura cervantina de *Tres tristes tigres*," 207.

45. On the importance of the dialogical as part of Cervantes's legacy, see Sobejano, "Cervantes en la novela española contemporánea," 550.

46. See Shaw, *Nueva narrativa hispanoamericana*, 224.

47. "Entrevistas a Juan Goytisolo," interview by Julio Ortega, in Goytisolo, *Disidencias*, 293.

48. Goytisolo, "Literatura y eutanasia," 89.

49. Baquero's intention is clearly stated in the "Advertencia" that opens the

volume: "The purpose of this book is to present, especially to young Spanish students, a parade of names and works worth remembering. Knowledge of those names and works is, in our opinion, of paramount importance for the education of Spanish students, because it is well known that their own world—Spain's peculiar world—is not complete without a broad view of the Hispanic scene, which transcends the Peninsula and adopts forms that are rich and meaningful in Spanish America or in American Spain . . . Such is the degree of mutual unfamiliarity, the lack of news and directions, that it is no exaggeration to state that even those great Latin American authors who have been recognized by the evidence of their work and the test of time, have not been brought to the attention of current Spanish generations" (Gastón Baquero, *Escritores hispanoamericanos de hoy* [Madrid: Instituto de Cultura Hispánica, 1961], 7–8). The book is divided in individual entries on each of the twenty authors selected, in the following order: Rubén Darío, José Vasconcelos, Gabriela Mistral, Vicente Huidobro, Alfonso Reyes, Porfirio Barba Jacob, Alberto Hidalgo, Pablo Neruda, Fernando González, César Vallejo, Francisco Romero, Alfonso Junco, Erico Verissimo, Jorge Luis Borges, Alejo Carpentier, Ignacio B. Anzoategui, Eduardo Caballero Calderón, Gabriel García Márquez, Juvencio Valle, Germán Arciniegas.

50. Vargas Llosa referred to those changes inflicted by the Spanish copyeditors as a process of *madrileñización*: "The company sponsoring the prize, trying to do their best, sent the winning book to be printed in Spain. The proofreaders at Imprenta Luis Pérez, in Madrid, proceeded—without consulting the author—to put the text into 'correct Castilian.' They madrilenized it, removing all Americanisms, replacing phrases or words they found to be obscure, and, as if that weren't enough, they poisoned the novel with typographical errors" (*García Márquez: Historia de un deicidio* [Barcelona: Barral, 1971], 74). In the second edition of the novel, published in Mexico in 1966, García Márquez included the following note: "The first time *La mala hora* was published, in 1962, a proofreader took the liberty of changing certain expressions and starching the style in the name of linguistic purity. On this occasion, in turn, the author has allowed himself to restore linguistic inaccuracies and stylistic atrocities, in the name of his sovereign and arbitrary will" (quoted in Vargas Llosa, ibid., 75).

51. Gimferrer, "Sobre *Cien años de soledad*," *Destino* 1575 (14 October 1967): 125. The review by Gimferrer was accompanied by a general introduction to García Márquez's life and previous works; see Joaquín Marco, "Gabriel García Márquez: Un joven maestro de la literatura colombiana," ibid., 124–25. This rather limited view of García Márquez as a somewhat traditional narrator, which permeates the reception of *Cien años de soledad* in Spain, overshadowed other qualities of his work. Although Ricardo Gullón, in *García Márquez o el olvidado arte de narrar* (Madrid: Taurus, 1970), and Carmen Arnau, in *El mundo mítico de Gabriel García Márquez* (Barcelona: Península, 1971), also paid attention to the importance of myth in the novel, the main interest of reviewers remained focused on the value of storytelling. This reception—as I hope will become clear in my analysis—is clearly marked by the condition of the Spanish novel, which framed the reading of the novel according to its specific needs. A different and more complex view of García Márquez has emerged from within the Latin American literary field, which sees in *Cien años de soledad* not simply a return to narrativity, but rather a sort of *summa narratologica* in which all previous dominant discourses

about Latin America are contained and revisited thanks to what Roberto González Echevarría has characterized as the archival nature of the novel: "*Cien años de soledad* contains, as in a blow-up, a map of narrative possibilities or potentialities of Latin American fiction. If Carpentier's [*Los pasos perdidos*] is the founding archival fiction, García Márquez's is the archetypical one" (*Myth and Archive* [Durham and London: Duke University Press, 1998], 4).

52. Andrés Amorós, Review of *Cien años de soledad*, *Revista de Occidente* 70 (January 1969): 58–59. A similar assessment in given by Antonio Tovar, who argues that García Márquez "doesn't tire of narrating; the pleasure of story-telling, the pleasure of the narration takes over and absorbs him, and the reader is dragged along in this chariot of fire—and it is the same with critics, who would let themselves be carried away by the pleasure of repeating, copying, and commenting these incredible pages. Surprises happen, and in the lengthy narration everything is unexpected" (*Novela española e hispanoamericana*,226; the review was originally published in *La Gaceta Ilustrada* in August 1968). Jorge Campos, however, warned not to confuse imagination with the absolute reversal of realism: "We think of story and of the ability to tell a story as the first attribute to grant the author. He wants to tell us what his country and people are like, but he cannot do it by describing. He has to invent constantly, like those pathological swindlers who are repelled and made allergic by truth. . . . Nonetheless, that fantastic or fabulous country is not pure imagination. It has constant and powerful ties to a geographical and political reality—as if a child put a transparent piece of paper over a map and, after beginning to trace, gave free rein to his imagination and began to invent" ("García Márquez: fábula y realidad," *Ínsula* 258 [May 1968]: 11).

53. "*Cien años de soledad* . . . forced everyone writing a novel to rethink yet again all the problems of language and structure . . . or possibly to put it to bed or even throw it into what is rightly called a purifying fire. . . . Dear García Márquez: like Cortázar with *Rayuela* a few years ago, you are responsible today for having forced writers of our language to resume the old watchfulness over their work tools, to aspire to more ambitious projects in which some will rise to the challenge and succeed while others will split their heads open" (Félix Grande, "Con García Márquez en un miércoles de ceniza," *Cuadernos Hispanoamericanos* 222 [June 1968]: 637). The title of the interrupted novel, *Curiosa manera de ocupar un lugar en el espacio: Crítica de la razón epiléptica*, seems to attest to the dominance of experimentalist poetics in the mid-sixties.

54. Castellet, *La hora del lector*, 59.

55. See Joset, "Introducción," in *Cien años de soledad* (Madrid: Cátedra, 1984), 23. Philip Swanson has argued that *Cien años de soledad*, with its "movement away from complexity toward more popular forms" ("Boom or Bust?: Latin America and the Not So New Novel," *New Novel Review* 1 [October 1993]: 83), is in fact an element of the post-Boom (closer to Puig or Cabrera Infante than to Vargas Llosa, Fuentes or Cortázar), which he interprets as a sign of the market's power over the condition of post-modern fiction in Latin America and its ability to dilute its potential for aesthetic and political renewal. In this sense, a parallel can be explored with the production of what has been termed "light" literature in Spain (a phenomenon of the 1980s), which should nevertheless be also analyzed within the context of the new political ascendancy and accommodation of Spanish intelligentsia after 1982.

56. Ynduráin, "Para una estética del *nouveau roman*," *Revista de Ideas Estéticas* 22 (1964): 113. The recovery of narrativity in Hispanic letters could be traced back to Borges and the foundational program he outlined in his 1940 prologue to Adolfo Bioy Casares's *La invención de Morel*, vindicating the value and the pleasure to be gained from the narrative of adventure. See Emir Rodríguez Monegal, *El boom de la novela latinoamericana* (Caracas: Tiempo Nuevo, 1972), 64–66.

57. According to Rafael Conte, "the new novelists possess an obvious tradition—a tradition where one must first recognize that of Spanish literature, especially the classical one. One finds traces of Góngora in Lezama Lima; and those of Ramón Gómez de la Serna, Gabriel Miró, or chivalric literature in Vargas Llosa and especially in Gabriel García Márquez. The Quixote is a permanent theme in Jorge Luis Borges' obsessions, and the entire work of a writer like Alejo Carpentier breathes linguistic classicism of the highest quality. It is very possible that Carpentier's style is the most archaic of all contemporary literature written in Spanish, including that from Spain. Valle-Inclán's mark hovers over Miguel Ángel Asturias and at the same time over the young Severo Sarduy." Conte pointedly notes also that this attention to tradition does not conflict with the assimilation of universal literature: "the entry of the South American continent into Western culture, achieved on all levels, . . . has turned Spanish America into a true crossing of cultures" (*Lenguaje y violencia*, 22).

58. Gabriel García Márquez and Mario Vargas Llosa, *La novela en América Latina: diálogo* (Lima: Carlos Milla Batres, [1967]), 17.

59. Álvarez Palacios, *Novela y cultura española de posguerra*, 73.

60. See Darío Villanueva, "La novela," in *Letras españolas 1976–1986* (Madrid: Castalia, 1987), 33–35. In what should be considered one of the first manifestos of the new Spanish romance, *La infancia recuperada* (1976)—a collection of essays explicitly conceived under the aegis of Borges and clearly against the tradition of Ortega or Castellet—Fernando Savater differentiated between *pure narration* (romance) and *novel*, and proclaimed the "immortality" of storytelling; see *La infancia recuperada* (Madrid: Taurus, 1976), 179–83.

61. José Domingo's "Los caminos de la experimentación," *Ínsula* 312 (November 1972): 6, accordingly presented these two authors as the two main alternatives for the renovation of Spanish fiction. Gérard Genette has defined hypertextuality as "any relationship uniting a text B (which I shall call the *hypertext*) to an earlier text B (I shall, of course, call it the *hypotext*), upon which it is grafted in a manner that is not that of commentary" (*Palimpsests*, 5).

62. See his comments on some of the Latin American sacred names: "Unfortunately I have read Cortázar . . . *malheureusement* I have read Borges," "Carlos Fuentes is the prototype of the pedestrian writer," "Cortázar does not care about literature," (in Tola de Habich and Grieve, *Los españoles y el boom*, 28, 31, 33). A few years later (1975), he added: "Literary works are most convincing when they combine two categories: pleasure and interest. When only one exists, you see too many flaws. I don't know of any Spanish-American writer who both pleases and interests me. . . . So I read those Spanish-American writers only at the insistence of my friends, but friends are annoying and force you to read Cortázar. Vargas is an honest writer, and that has its drawbacks—being an honest writer takes away the interest. García Márquez is a flowery and brilliant writer, but he plays a melody that was composed—very well—centuries ago. And Carpentier is a man

of much talent, but I don't know if he distributes it well" (in Amorós et al., *Novela española actual*, 187).

63. Juan Benet, *Una meditación* (Barcelona: Seix Barral, 1970), 95; *A Meditation*, trans. Gregory Rabassa (New York: Persea Books, 1982), 104–5.

64. Ken Benson, "Autenticidad y pureza en el discurso de Juan Benet," *Ínsula* 559–60 (July–August 1993): 12.

65. See Genette, *Palimpsests*, 343–50. It should be mentioned that in an interview originally published in 1969, Benet declared he began writing *Una meditación* in 1965, although—he added—"I have interrupted my writing a lot" ("Encuentro con Juan Benet," in Kathleen M. Vernon, ed., *Juan Benet* [Madrid: Taurus, 1986], 22). Such an early date, together with the much publicized image of the novel being written on a continuous roll of paper—which its implication of a linear, unidirectional writing process, the product of which would have thus avoided the reshuffling of pages—should not be enough to prevent us from positing hypertextual links between Benet's and García Márquez's texts. According to Pere Gimferrer: "written on a roll of continuous paper that made rereading impossible, the original of *Una meditación* had only the memory of its author to rely on in order to proceed. One should not exaggerate the importance of this procedure, which was undoubtedly crucial for Benet's work but in no way the total determining factor of the results. In fact, Benet did not publish the gross product of his experience, but instead, once the text was finished, submitted it to an extensive revision" ("Notas sobre Juan Benet," in Vernon, ed., *Juan Benet*, 51). An early attempt to contrast the narrative models represented by García Márquez and Benet is found in Francisco Carrasquer, "*Cien años de soledad* y *Volverás a Región*, dos polos," *Norte: Revista Hispánica de Amsterdam* 11, 6 (November–December 1970): 197–201.

66. Benet, *Una meditación*, 11; *A Meditation*, 11–12.

67. Benet, *Una meditación*, 17 and 9; *A Meditation*, 19 and 10.

68. In Tola de Habich and Grieve, *Los españoles y el boom*, 33.

69. Juan Benet, "De Canudos a Macondo," *Revista de Occidente* 70 (January 1970): 49.

70. In Amorós et al, *Novela española actual*, 187.

71. See Benet, *Una meditación*, 77; *A Meditation*, 85.

72. Benet, *Una meditación*, 274; *A Meditation*, 304.

73. On the confrontation of history and mythical thought in Benet, see Jo Labanyi, *Myth and History in the Contemporary Spanish Novel* (Cambridge: Cambridge University Press, 1989), 95–96.

74. "Contrary to the case of intertextuality, as it has been so aptly described by Riffaterre, a simple understanding of the hypertext never necessitates resorting to the hypotext. Every hypertext, even a pastiche, can be read for itself without becoming perceptibly 'agrammatical'; it is invested with a meaning that is autonomous and thus in some manner sufficient. But sufficient does not mean exhaustive" (Genette, *Palimpsests*, 397).

75. Torrente summarized his understanding of Cervantes's legacy (and also played down the alleged influences of Latin American fiction) in "Conversación con Gonzalo Torrente Ballester sobre *La saga/fuga de J.B.*," interview by Andrés Amorós, *Ínsula* 317 (April 1973): 4, 14–15.

76. Dionisio Ridruejo, "Gonzalo Torrente Ballester busca y encuentra: una

lectura de *La saga/fuga de J.B.*," in *Sombras y bultos* (Barcelona: Destino, 1977), 198; the essay was originally published in *Destino* 1820 (19 August 1972): 8–9. Torrente declared that when he read García Márquez in 1970 he had already completed his own novel; see *Cuadernos de La Romana* (Barcelona: Destino, 1975), 200. The published text of novel is signed "En los Prados Cubillos, El Escorial, 3 de agosto de 1971" (*La saga/fuga de J.B.* [Barcelona: Destino, 1973], 585).

77. Torrente Ballester, *La saga/fuga de J.B.*, 579.

78. Ibid., 463–505.

79. Martín Vilumara, "El desafío de Torrente Ballester," *Camp de l'Arpa* 6 (March 1973): 22.

80. Torrente Ballester, *Cuadernos de La Romana*, 198, 200.

81. Félix Grande, "El 'boom' en España," in *Once artistas y un dios: ensayos sobre literatura hispanoamericana* (Madrid: Taurus, 1986): 58–59. The essay was first published in the newspaper *Madrid* in 1969, and reprinted in *Imagen* [Caracas] in February 1970.

82. The English translation was published as the preface ("Author's Note") to *Return to Región*. Benet has explained the circumstances that forced the eventual exclusion of the novel from the catalogue of Alianza Editorial in "La historia editorial y judicial de *Volverás a Región*," in *La moviola de Eurípides y otros ensayos* (Madrid: Taurus, 1981), 31–44.

83. See Robert C. Spires, *La novela española de posguerra* (Madrid: Cupsa, 1978), 237; Malcolm Alan Compitello, *Ordering the Evidence: "Volverás a Región" and Civil War Fiction* (Barcelona: Puvill, 1983), 100, 142–43; Randolph D. Pope, "Benet, Faulkner and Bergson's Memory," in *Critical Approaches to the Writings of Juan Benet*, ed. Roberto C. Manteiga et al. (Hanover: University Press of New England, 1984), 147 n. 4; Stephen J. Summerhill, "Prohibition and Transgression in *Volverás a Región* and *Una meditación*," in ibid., 58; and Jo Labanyi, *Myth and History in the Contemporary Spanish Novel*, 95, 125.

84. Benet, "Author's Note," in *Return to Región*, trans. Gregory Rabassa (New York: Columbia University Press, 1985), viii; Spanish original in "Prólogo a la segunda edición," *Volverás a Región*, 2nd ed. (Madrid: Alianza, 1974), 10.

85. Guelbenzu, "Dos libros de Juan Benet," *Cuadernos para el Diálogo* 73 (October 1969): 48; Gimferrer, "En torno a *Volverás a Región*, de Juan Benet," *Ínsula* 266 (January 1969): 14.

86. Benet, "Author's Note," viii; Spanish original in "Prólogo a la segunda edición," 10.

87. In Marie-Lise Gazarian Gautier, *Interviews with Spanish Writers* (Elmwood Park, Ill.: Dalkey Archive Press, 1991), 35.

88. In 1966, when the series "El libro de bolsillo" was inaugurated by printing an average of ten-thousand copies per title—at the speed of one title per week—the average print run for a literary title in Spain was 6,476 copies (according to the data provided by the INE; see also Bozal, "La edición en España," 92). By those counts, the 3,080 copies of the first edition of *Volverás a Región* (Destino, 1967) amounted to a modest figure. In 1974, however, when Alianza Editorial launched 15,000 copies of the second edition of Benet's novel, the national average print run was 8,023; see Benet, "Historia editorial y judicial de *Volverás a Región*."

89. "Juan Benet o el azar," in Federico Campbell, *Infame turba* (Barcelona: Lumen, 1994), 261; the interview was first published in 1971.

90. Quoted in María Elena Bravo, *Faulkner en España: perspectivas de la narrativa de postguerra* (Barcelona: Península, 1985), 215.

91. Castellet, *La hora del lector*, 69–70.

92. Ibid., 71.

93. For Bourdieu, the field of restricted production is defined by an autonomous principle of hierarchization, according to which art is justified in itself, and not by reference to external elements; such a principle "brings its most radical defenders to understand temporal failure as a sign of being among the elect, and success as a sign of compromise with the world" ("Le champ littéraire," *Actes de la Recherche en Sciences Sociales* 89 [September 1991]: 6).

94. Jesús Torbado, "La manta a la cabeza: reflexiones urgentes sobre literatura nueva y sociedad," in *Prosa novelesca actual*, ed. Francisco Ynduráin (Madrid: Universidad Internacional Menéndez Pelayo, 1968), 87–88.

95. See Goytisolo, "Para una literatura nacional popular."

96. See Andreas Huyssen, "Mapping the Postmodern," in *A Postmodern Reader*, ed. Joseph Natoli and Linda Hutcheon (Albany: State University of New York Press, 1993), 120. It is important here to recall the suspicions popular culture used to generate in those same years among the leaders of the Francoist regime, who failed in their attempts to control from above the values and tastes of the masses—for the example of soccer, see John London, "The Ideology and Practice of Sport," in *Spanish Cultural Studies: An Introduction*, ed. Helen Graham and Jo Labanyi (Oxford: Oxford University Press, 1995), 204–7. The same mistrust could help explain the limited presence of many forms of popular culture in both social novels and experimentalist narratives. It is in the 1970s when—in contrast with the classical mythologies found in the works of Martín-Santos, Juan Goytisolo, or Benet, for instance—the myths of mass culture appear in Marsé (who pays constant homage to film), Martín Gaite (popular songs or *coplas*, fashion and romance magazines) or Vázquez Montalbán (soccer, *cine negro*, popular music). For a contrast between the representation of mass culture in Goytisolo's *Reivindicación del conde don Julián* and Martín Gaite's *El cuarto de atrás* (1978), see Stephanie Sieburth, *Inventing High and Low: Literature, Mass Culture, and Uneven Modernity in Spain* (Durham: Duke University Press, 1994).

97. Benet, *Volverás a Región*, 13; *Return to Región*, 1.

98. Benet, *Volverás a Región*, 201; *Return to Región*, 195. See Luis F. Costa, "El lector-viajero en *Volverás a Región*," *Anales de la Narrativa Española Contemporánea* 4 (1979): 9–18; and Roberto Manteiga, "El lector-viajero de Juan Benet," *Ínsula* 559–60 (July–August 1993): 23–24.

99. "Benet shows little respect—even verging on disdain—towards the reader-critics of his literary work and enjoys seeing them lost in the labyrinthine paths of his fictional world" (Roberto Manteiga, "El lector-viajero de Juan Benet" 23). We should recall Benet's judgment against the notion of an "open work," about which he confessed to have "many reservations, and even true distaste" (in Amorós et al, *Novela española actual*,177). In my reading of the novel I differ here with Manteiga, who argues for an "openness" in Benet's work that, in my opinion, goes against the central core of Benetian writing.

100. See John Fletcher and Malcolm Bradbury, "The Introverted Novel," in *Modernism, 1890–1930*, ed. M. Bradbury and J. McFarlane (Sussex: Harvester Press, 1978), 396–97. Although I deem it important to differentiate between the

positions assigned to the reader in modernist and postmodernist texts, it is not my purpose here to attempt a detailed characterization of those two movements. In the case of Benet—whom I would include in the modernist mold—critics have differed over whether he should be considered a modern or a postmodern writer. See, for example, the contrasting opinions of María Elena Bravo, "Juan Benet: de modernismo a posmodernismo," *Ínsula* 559–60 (July–August 1993): 5–7; and Malcolm Alan Compitello, "Benet and Spanish Postmodernism," *Revista Hispánica Moderna* 44 (1991): 259–73.

101. See Labanyi, *Myth and History in the Contemporary Spanish Novel*, 122.

102. Benet declared his disgust with French experimentalism to Federico Campbell: "I don't believe *at all* in French experiments. . . . That topic doesn't interest me" ("Juan Benet o el azar" 258). Herzberger has mentioned the labyrinth as structural principle shared by both Benet and the *nouveau roman* in "The Emergence of Juan Benet: A New Alternative for the Spanish Novel," *The American Hispanist* 3 (November 1975): 7; see also Corrales Egea, *La novela española actual*, 209–17.

103. Bravo, *Faulkner en España*, 302. For the notion of enigma as a fundamental premise in Benet's conception of the novel, see Herzberger, "Enigma as Narrative Determinant in the Novels of Juan Benet," *Hispanic Review* 47 (1979): 149–57.

104. Constantino Bértolo, for instance, has identified *La verdad sobre el caso Savolta* as the text that inaugurates the commodification of contemporary Spanish literature during the first years of the political transition: "a gratuitous reading that leans toward amusing artifice" ("Introducción a la narrativa española actual," 48).

105. Eduardo Mendoza, *La verdad sobre el caso Savolta* (Barcelona: Seix Barral, 1975), 15; *The Truth about the Savolta Case*, trans. Alfred Mac Adam (New York: Pantheon Books, 1992), 3.

106. "Interrogatorio: Eduardo Mendoza," interview by M. Vidal Santos, *Gimlet* [Barcelona] 8 (October 1981): 20.

107. Julio Ortega, *Poetics of Change: The New Spanish-American Narrative*, trans. Galen D. Greaser (Austin: University of Texas Press, 1984), 9.

108. "Conversación con Manuel Vázquez Montalbán," interview by José Batlló, *Camp de l'Arpa* 4 (November 1972): 20.

109. Linda Hutcheon, *A Poetics of Postmodernism: History, Theory, Fiction* (New York: Routledge, 1988), 34.

110. "This subculture should start from an examination that would identify the conventional linguistic codes of the revolutionary subject . . . and adapt them, by means of technical manipulation, to serve a radically critical culture. It seems to me that this research on the linguistic codes of mass culture is a first, *sine qua non* step. A technical understanding of consumer popular novels, the structure of dance music or love songs, the plastic expression of comic strips, the imaginative and temporal logic of film and television, the invisible semantics of broadcasting, all this is an essential step for obtaining a critical literature that can break the barriers of a language forged by the traditional elitist culture of the bourgeoisie" (Vázquez Montalbán, "Tres notas sobre literatura y dogma," in *Literatura española a treinta años del siglo XXI*, 21).

111. According to the pragmatic approach advanced by Linda Hutcheon, parody is a form of imitation characterized by ironic inversion and recontextualization

which, at the same time, requires a critical distance in relation to the parodied model; see Hutcheon, *A Theory of Parody: The Teachings of Twentieth-Century Art Forms* (New York: Methuen, 1985), 6. It is tempting to categorize the polar models of reading presented in *Volverás a Región* and *La verdad sobre el caso Savolta* according to the two forms of textual pleasure—*jouissance* and *plaisir*—defined and contrasted by Barthes in *The Pleasure of the Text*. It is necessary, however, to question a value system that (despite Barthes's reservations) revitalizes the distinction between elitist and popular art. Arguing against such a dichotomy of pleasure, Andreas Huyssen has analyzed its basic assumptions as an "archeology of modernity": "Barthes's very un-Brechtian distinction between *plaisir* and *jouissance*—which he simultaneously makes and unmakes—reiterates one of the most tired topoi of the modernist aesthetic and of bourgeois culture at large: there are the lower pleasures for the rabble, i.e., mass culture, and then there is the *nouvelle cuisine* of the pleasure of the text, of *jouissance*. . . . Thus his appraisal of *jouissance* depends on the adoption of that traditional view of mass culture that the right and the left, both of which he so emphatically rejects, have shared over the decades" ("Mapping the Postmodern," 139).

112. See Sobejano, "Ante la novela de los años setènta," *Ínsula* 396–97 (November–December 1979): 1, 22, where memory, writing and fantasy are identified as the three dominant features of the Spanish novel during the decade. See also Villanueva, "La novela."

5. Literatures in Revolt

1. It should be pointed out, however, that the international exposure gained by Latin American literature during the turn of the century had remained circumscribed basically to the Spanish-speaking world; it is with the Boom novel that Hispanic literatures gained a more universal audience, and therefore the stakes in the struggle for recognition were higher this time.

2. The first Spanish professor to occupy by *oposición* a chair of Spanish American Literature at the Universidad Complutense in Madrid (at the time the official center of national scholarship) was Francisco Sánchez-Castañer, in 1967. See Sánchez-Castañer, "A manera de prólogo," *Anales de Literatura Hispano-americana* 1 (1972): ix–x.

3. The judgment of some Latin American writers also became significant as sources of critical guidance: early reviewers of *Cien años de soledad* make explicit reference to Vargas Llosa's opinions on the novel as a sort of authority to evaluate the text, and Amorós also quotes Cortázar, "the great master of contemporary novel," in his review of *Cien años de soledad* (60); see also Pascual Maisterra, "*Cien años de soledad*: Un regalo fabuloso de Gabriel García Márquez," *Tele/Exprés* [Barcelona] 28 November 1968: 36.

4. See Manuel Pedro González, "Apostillas a la novela latinoamericana," in *Zona Franca* 48 (August 1967): 4–9; and "Reparos al Premio Rómulo Gallegos," *Zona Franca* 51 (November 1967): 34–38. In the same vein, Ignacio Iglesias argued that young novelists and critics "regard as highly original [what] is no more than mere rehash or vulgar plagiarism" ("Novela y novelistas de hoy," 84), and went on to criticize the "esoteric and formalistic" prose and its lack of authentic

NOTES TO CHAPTER 5

substance. Iglesias's essay was the center of a heated debate on the New Novel that took place in *Mundo Nuevo* between March and June 1969. The novelistic trend was later satirized as a formula for commercial success by René Avilés Fabila in "Cómo escribir una novela y convertirla en *best-seller*," *Mundo Nuevo* 51–52 (September–October 1970): 29–33.

5. Ángel María de Lera, "Bueno está lo bueno . . . ," *ABC* [Madrid], 28 November 1968, sec. "Mirador Literario": 3.

6. Luis Carandell, "Alfonso Grosso: primeros gritos de independencia," *Triunfo* 361 (3 May 1969): 72–73. See "Alfonso Grosso explica algunas cosas," interview by Antonio Bernabéu, *Informaciones* 15 May 1969, sec. "Informaciones de las Artes y las Letras": 1–2; and "Alfonso Grosso contra . . . Antonio Bernabéu," *Informaciones* 29 May 1969, sec. "Informaciones de las Artes y las Letras": 2. See also Cortázar, "Un gran escritor y su soledad."

7. Besides the contributions to *Informaciones*, see Francisco García Pavón, "Escritores al habla," interview by Antonio R. de las Heras, *ABC*, 15 May 1969, sec. "Mirador Literario": 8; Antonio Iglesias Laguna, "El dilema de la novela hispanoamericana," *La Estafeta Literaria* 422 (15 June 1969): 9–10; Joaquín Marco, "Al margen de una polémica," *Destino* 1658 (12 July 1969): 35, and "Al borde de una polémica: 'Realismo,' público, editor y novela en España," *Destino* 1660 (26 July 1969): 33; and Manuel Halcón, "Escritores al habla," interview by Antonio R. de las Heras, *ABC*, 21 August 1969, sec. "Mirador Literario": 6–7.

8. See Quiñonero, "Juan Pedro Quiñonero, contra la polémica," *Informaciones*, 19 June 1969, sec. "Informaciones de las Artes y las Letras": 2. In his "Carta abierta a Alfonso Grosso," Conte warned against the trap of opposing the two sides as if they were completely uniform: "Where's the trap? In the contrast effected between the techniques of these writers and those of Spanish sociological realism. But is that totally clear? Do all these Latin American narrators share identical procedures? Do the Spanish realists? Far from it: technically speaking, *Tiempo de silencio* has nothing to do with *El Jarama*, just as *La casa verde* does not with *Rayuela*, or *Cambio de piel* with *Cien años de soledad*."

9. The labels "generación de la berza" and "generación del sándalo" were first used in 1969 by César Santos Fontenla.

10. See Montero, "Isaac Montero contra algunos y algo," *Informaciones*, 5 June 1969, sec. "Informaciones de las Artes y las Letras": 1, 6.

11. "Martínez-Menchén contra . . . Santos Fontenla," *Informaciones*, 29 May 1969, sec. "Informaciones de las Artes y las Letras": 1.

12. José María Gironella, "Viaje en torno al mundo literario español," *Los domingos de ABC*, 22 February 1970: 8.

13. Baltasar Porcel, "Guerra literaria: españoles contra latinoamericanos," *Destino* 1693 (14 March 1970): 8; and Pere Gimferrer, "De una guerra literaria." Porcel and Gimferrer's theses were disputed by Darío Fernández-Flórez in a letter published in *Destino* 1697 (11 April 1970): 3, 5, and in the editorial note "El 'boom' de la narrativa hispanoamericana: ataques y contrataques," *Ínsula* 282 (May 1970): 2. For information on the Salamanca conference, see Ángel María de Lera, "La novela española en Salamanca," *ABC*, 9 September 1971, sec. "Mirador Literario": 1–2. For the Caracas colloquium, Carlos Barral, "Puntualización de motivos: enfrentamientos novelísticos de continente a continente," *Triunfo* 522 (30 September 1972): 36–37.

14. J. M. Aicardo, *De literatura contemporánea: 1901–1905* (Madrid: Sucesores de Rivadeneyra, 1905), 478–79.

15. Antonio Tovar, *Novela española e hispanoamericana* (Madrid: Alfaguara, 1972), 268.

16. Sánchez-Castañer, "A manera de prólogo," xviii–xix; emphasis added.

17. Ibid., xxvii; emphasis added.

18. Avel·lí Artís-Gener, "Quatre mots del traductor," in *Cent anys de solitud*, by Gabriel García Márquez (Barcelona: Edhasa, 1970), 7. The reviewer of the Catalan version also noted the oddity involved in translating a text readily available in the original: "Though there is no doubt that the novel that has been translated into a great many languages is better read in the original, there it is, selling in Catalan" ("*Cent anys de solitud*, de García Márquez, premio Rómulo Gallegos," *La Vanguardia*, 21 September 1972: 50). The first Catalan edition had a print run of three-thousand copies. García Márquez ranks first among the Latin American writers translated in Spain: two works into Catalan—besides *Cent anys de solitud* (Barcelona: Edhasa, 1970), *Crònica de una mort anunciada* was also translated by Avel·lí Artís-Gener (Barcelona: Grijalbo, 1982)—and three into Basque: *Heriotza iragarritako baten kronika*, trans. Xalbador Garmendia (Donostia: Sendoa Argitaldaria, 1982); *Jenerala bere laberintoan*, trans. Xabier Mendigoren (ELKAR, 1990); and *Koronelai ez dio inork idazten*, trans. Tomás Sarasota (Ibaizabal Edelvides, 1992). Artís-Gener is also the translator of Borges's *L'Aleph* (Barcelona: Gedisa, 1983) and Vargas Llosa's *Els cadells i altres narracions* (Barcelona: Grijalbo, 1984). Cortázar has been translated twice into Basque by Gerardo Markuleta: *Oktaedroa* (Ibaizabal Edelvides, 1992), and *Hegoaldeko aupista* (Erein, 1994).

19. See Miguel Fernández-Braso, *Gabriel García Márquez: Una conversación infinita* (Madrid: Azur, 1969), 51–52.

20. See *Llibres en català*, an annual catalogue of Catalan books in print published for the first time in 1967 by the Instituto Nacional del Libro Español. Four of the translations available in 1972 were editions that dated from before the Civil War: one book of poetry (Manuel de Cabanyes's *Poesies completes*, 1935) and three plays—Emili Gómez de Miguel and Agustí Mundet Álvarez, *El flagell de l'humanitat* (1934); J. López Pinillos, *Esclavitut* (1937); and Ramón J. Sender, *El secret* (1937). The Spanish-language writers of the postwar period available in Catalan translation were: Eduardo Criado (*Los blancos dientes del perro*, in bilingual edition, 1958; *Fang*, 1964), Joaquín Calvo Sotelo (*La visita que no va tocar el timbre*, 1968), Francisco Candel (*Parlem-ne*, 1967; *Trenta mil pessetes per un home i altres narracions*, 1968; *Fruit d'una necessitat*, 1970), Camilo José Cela (*Viatge al Pirineu de Lleida*, 1966; *El rusc*, 1968; *Barcelona*, 1970), Miguel de Cervantes (*Don Quixot de la Mancha*, 1969), José María Gironella (*Els xiprers creuen en Déu*, 1967; *Ha esclatat la pau*, 1968; *Un millió de morts*, 1968), and José Luis Martín Vigil (*Morin els capellans*, 1969; *Un sexe anomenat dèbil*, 1970). As far as the original languages of these literary translations into Catalan are concerned, in 1972 Spanish was the seventh language, preceded by English (with 196 titles), French (110), Italian (40), Latin (36), Greek (28), and German (26).

21. Josep M. Solé i Sabaté and Joan Villarroya, *Cronologia de la repressió de la llengua i la cultura catalanes: 1936–1975* (Barcelona: Curial, 1994), 178 and 204. For a historical analysis of the repression against Catalan culture in Spain, see Josep Benet, *L'intent franquista de genocidi cultural contra Catalunya* (Barcelona: Abadia de Montserrat, 1995).

22. Carles-Jordi Guardiola, *Per la llengua: Llengua i cultura als Països Catalans, 1939–1977* (Barcelona: La Magrana, 1980), 55 and 163.

23. Baltasar Porcel, "Suscinta explicación de Cataluña para castellanos," in *Cataluña vista desde fuera* (Barcelona: Llibres de Sinera, 1970), 84. Gabriel Ferrater, "Gabriel Ferrater o las mujeres," in Campbell, *Infame turba*, 334. The manifesto "El català, llengua de expressió científica" has been reprinted in Guardiola, *Per la llengua*, 231–37.

24. Joan Fuster, *Literatura catalana contemporània* (Barcelona: Curial, 1972), 309.

25. Particularly significant is the Catalan translation in 1961 of Joxeba Andoni Loidi Bizkarrondo's *Amabost egun Urgain'en*, a detective novel published originally in Basque. The publisher proudly announced that *Quinze dies a Urgain* "is possibly . . . the first complete rendering of a Basque literary book in another language. This translation thus places Catalan in an honorable position within a literature that has always deserved the sympathy of Catalan readers" (preface to *Quinze dies a Urgain*, trans. Josep Aguirre [Barcelona: Albertí Editor, 1961]).

26. "Razón de ser," *Cuadernos para el Diálogo* 1 (October 1963): 2.

27. The rules for the Biblioteca Breve quoted here were announced in *Destino* 1834 (25 November 1972): 50. The fifteen initial titles included in the series "Nueva Narrativa Hispánica" were: Gabriel Celaya's *Los buenos negocios*, and Antonio Rabinad's *A veces, a esta hora* (both in 1965); Carlos Martínez Moreno's *Con las primeras luces*, and Claribel Alegría and Darwin J. Flakoll's *Cenizas de Izalco* (in 1966); Marta Traba's *Los laberintos insolados*, Enrique L. Revol's *Los intrusos*, Juan García Hortelano's *Gente de Madrid*, Germán Sánchez Espeso's *Experimento en Génesis*, Jorge Edwards's *Las máscaras* (in 1967); José Alberto Marín Morales's *Carril de un cuerpo*, Jorge Guzmán's *Job-Boj*, J. M. Guelbenzu's *El mercurio*, José Donoso's *Coronación*, Alfonso Grosso's *Ines Just Coming*, and Cortázar's *Ceremonias* (in 1968).

28. "Presentación" to *Situación actual de los estudios de lengua y literatura catalanas*, special issue of *Norte: Revista Hispánica de Amsterdam* 11, 1–2 (January–April 1970): 3.

29. Mario Vargas Llosa, "Carta de batalla por *Tirant lo Blanc*," in *Carta de batalla por Tirant lo Blanc* (Barcelona: Seix Barral, 1991), 9. The first section of Vargas Llosa's text appeared with that same title in *Revista de Occidente* 70 (January 1969): 1–21; and the complete text was published as a prologue to a 1969 paperback Spanish edition of the Catalan classic (Madrid: Alianza, 1969). An English translation of the first two sections by Robert B. Knox was published as "A Challenge on Behalf of *Tirant lo Blanc*," *Research Studies* 37.1 (March 1969): 1–16.

30. See Joaquim Molas, "Pròleg a l'edició catalana," in *Lletra de batalla per Tirant lo Blanc* (Barcelona: Edicions 62, 1969), 15–17. The Catalan text of *Tirant lo Blanc*, edited by Martí de Riquer, appeared in the series "Biblioteca Breve de Bolsillo" (Barcelona: Seix Barral, 1969); the Spanish translation by J. F. Vidal Jové, with prologue by Vargas Llosa, was published in "El libro de bolsillo" (Madrid: Alianza, 1969). Suzanne S. Hintz, in her overview of scholarly criticism on Martorell's book, notes how academic attention increased notably after 1969: "There is only one dissertation recorded prior to 1969 on *Tirant*; this thesis dates from 1917. However, since 1969 [and up to 1990] six dissertations have been writ-

ten on various aspects of the book" ("Scholarship on *Tirant lo Blanc*: On Its Five Hundredth Anniversary," in *Tirant lo Blanc: Text and Context*, ed. Josep M. Solà-Solé [New York: Peter Lang, 1993], 96). The same opinion is voiced by Lourdes Sánchez Rodrigo and Enrique J. Nogueras Valdivieso: "Though in Catalonia several editions had been printed since the beginning of the century, it is only then [1969] that—thanks to Carlos Barral, Mario Vargas Llosa and Martí de Riquer— the first edition targeted for a wider audience appeared" ("Quinientos años de *Tirant lo Blanc*," in *Estudios sobre el Tirant lo Blanc*, ed. Juan Paredes et. al [Granada: Universidad de Granada, 1995], 178). The two English translations of the text, by Ray La Fontaine (1974, published in 1993) and David H. Rosenthal (1984), are preceded by references to Vargas Llosa's authorized opinion as to assure the reader of the modernity of the book; see La Fontaine, "Translator's Introduction," *Tirant lo Blanc: The Complete Translation* (New York: Peter Lang, 1993), 5; and Rosenthal, "Translator's Foreword," *Tirant lo Blanc* (New York: Schocken Books, 1984), vii.

31. Vargas Llosa, "Cabalgando con Tirant," in *Carta de batalla por Tirant lo Blanc* (Barcelona: Seix Barral, 1991), 5. According to Vargas Llosa, the only Spanish writer to share his enthusiasm for *Tirant lo Blanc* was Luis Martín-Santos (ibid., 6).

32. For a commentary on the relations between Vargas Llosa's critical work on *Tirant lo Blanc* and *Cien años de soledad*, and its effect on his own fictional writing, see Kathleen McNerney, *Tirant lo Blanc Revisited: A Critical Study* (Detroit: Medieval and Renaissance Monograph Series, 1983), 66–72; Anton M. Espadaler, "Mario Vargas Llosa i el *Tirant lo Blanc*," in *VI Jornades d'Estudis Catalano-Americans* (Barcelona: Comissió Amèrica i Catalunya, 1992), 219–25; and José Miguel Oviedo, *Mario Vargas Llosa: la invención de una realidad* (Barcelona: Barral, 1970), 47, 58–59, 66–67, 128–29, 136–39, and 154–55. Josep Navarro analyzes *Tirant lo Blanc* as a model for the new Latin American novel in "Una interpretació hispanoamericana del *Tirant lo Blanc*," in *Estudis de llengua i literatura catalanes oferts a R. Aramon i Serra en el seu setantè aniversari* (Barcelona: Curial, 1979), vol. 1: 435–44.

33. Vargas Llosa, "Carta de batalla," 9–10. Indeed, Vargas Llosa has later been very critical of Catalan nationalism, which he perceives as having a negative effect on the cosmopolitan character of Catalan culture. According to Artís-Gener, Vargas Llosa was, as president of the International PEN Club, very reluctant to accept the creation of a Catalan PEN Center independent of the Spanish one; see Avel·lí Artís-Gener, *Viure i veure* (Barcelona: Pòrtic, 1989–1996), vol. 4: 249.

34. Vargas Llosa's assumption about the transparency of the text for the Spanish reader—which, ironically, would have made superfluous the Spanish edition he was presenting—appears to have proved too optimistic: two years later he would quote Martorell in Catalan but provide, in parentheses, a Spanish translation. It was a curious turn, since his "Martorell y el 'elemento añadido' en *Tirant lo Blanc*" appeared as prologue to *El combate imaginario: las cartas de batalla de Joanot Martorell*, edited in collaboration with Martí de Riquer (Barcelona: Barral, 1972), where the letters were published in the Catalan original. This time it was Riquer who argued for the possibility of a direct reading of the text by the "educated" Spanish reader: "In my commentary on the letters, I translate the most interesting passages, and from time to time in the Catalan text there is a note or two

to clarify difficult terminology. I sincerely believe that with this, any non-specialized, educated reader will be perfectly able to understand the texts published here" (introduction to *El combate imaginario*, 31).

35. Vargas Llosa, "Carta de batalla," 26.

36. Ibid., 12 and 32.

37. Ibid., 10.

38. The contrast between dogma and dissent had also been analyzed as an essential component of Spanish heritage in Latin America by Octavio Paz in *El laberinto de la soledad*, where he argued that the influence of Counter-Reformation in America was counterbalanced by a strain of heterodoxy also present in Spain: "If Spain renounced the future and closed herself off from the West at the moment of the Counter Reformation, she did not do so without first adopting almost all the artistic forms of the Renaissance: poetry, the novel, painting and architecture. These forms, along with certain philosophical and political ideas, all permeated with Spanish traditions of a medieval nature, were transplanted to our continent. It is significant that the most vital part of the Spanish heritage in America is made up of those universal elements that Spain assimilated during a period when her history was likewise universal. The absence of [*casticismo*], traditionalism and [*españolismo*] (in the medieval sense that has been given to the word: crust and husk of [chaste Castile]) is a permanent trait of Spanish-American culture, which is always open to the outside world and has a longing for universality. . . . The Spanish tradition that we Spanish-Americans inherited is one that in Spain itself has been looked on with suspicion or contempt: that of heterodoxy, open to French or Italian influences. Our culture, like a certain portion of Spanish culture, is a free election by a few free spirits" (*The Labyrinth of Solitude: Life and Thought in Mexico* [New York: Grove Press, 1961], 98–99; I have modified Lysander Kemp's translation; Spanish original in *El laberinto de la soledad* [Madrid: Cátedra, 1993], 238–39).

39. Domingo F. Sarmiento, *Obras completas de Sarmiento* (Buenos Aires: Editorial Luz del Día, 1949), vol. 5: 186. "Those on Montjuich" were the central government troops stationed in that hill, who carried out the bombardment of Barcelona in 1842 and 1843; for a historical account of the events, see Francesc Curet, *"La Jamància": Les bullangues de 1842 i 1843* (Barcelona: Rafael Dalmau, 1990).

40. Rubén Darío, *España contemporánea* (Paris: Garnier, 1901), 21 and 10. "Oh, if only I could live in this admirable Barcelona!" wrote Darío to Julio Piquet on 5 January 1913 (*Epistolario* [Paris: Biblioteca Latino-Americana, 1920], 42). For the contacts between Darío and Catalan writers, see Andrés R. Quintián, "Rubén Darío y la España catalana," *Cuadernos Hispanoamericanos* 261 (March 1972): 611–22.

41. José Enrique Rodó, "El nacionalismo catalán: Un interesante problema político," in *El camino de Paros: Meditaciones y andanzas* (Valencia: Cervantes, 1918), 109–10.

42. Ricardo Rojas, *Retablo español* (Buenos Aires: Losada, 1938), 321.

43. Gabriel García Márquez, *Cien años de soledad* (Madrid: Cátedra, 1984), 396 and 405; *One Hundred Years of Solitude*, trans. Gregory Rabassa (New York: Harper and Row, 1970), 329 and 473.

44. García Márquez, *Cien años de soledad*, 92. The English translation, however, erases the discrepancy and identifies him from the beginning as her great-great-grandfather; see *One Hundred Years of Solitude* 19–20.

45. García Márquez, *Cien años de soledad*, 275; *One Hundred Years of Solitude*, 203.

46. García Márquez, *Cien años de soledad*, 285; *One Hundred Years of Solitude*, 214. In the words of Lydia D. Hazera, "In Fernanda more than in any other character, García Márquez concentrates his mockery of the false, the hypocritical, the devout, the fanatic, and above all, the reactionary" ("Estudio sinóptico de las personalidades femeninas," in *Explicación de Cien años de soledad*, ed. Francisco E. Porrata and Fausto Avendaño [San José, Costa Rica: Texto, 1976], 157).

47. García Márquez, *Cien años de soledad*, 282; *One Hundred Years of Solitude*, 210–11. According to Carmen Arnau, Fernanda "is a representation of Spanish culture. Her parents' names are themselves already significant: her father is Fernando del Carpio, and her mother, Renata Argote. They are the representatives of a fossilized culture. . . . Fernanda's culture is the Spanish culture of the Golden Age" (*El mundo mítico de Gabriel García Márquez*, 79–80).

48. The first contact between Aureliano and the wise Catalonian, incited by Melquíades, had been effected indirectly through the mediation of Santa Sofía de la Piedad (*Cien años de soledad* 430–31; *One Hundred Years of Solitude*, 362–63).

49. "García Márquez: ahora doscientos años de soledad," interview by Ernesto González Bermejo, in *Gabriel García Márquez*, ed. Peter G. Earle (Madrid: Taurus, 1981), 250. Such biographical reading appears in Arnau, who even excludes the references to the Barranquilla group from the narration itself: "Gabriel and his friends pass by fleetingly. They disappear very quickly from the narration, in which they have never been fully integrated, and we know nothing more of them. There even seems to exist an authorial interest in erasing them once and for all. They had also remained on the edge of the guiding plot in *Cien años*. . . . [García Márquez] wanted to include his friends in the book for entertainment and as a tribute; he wanted to incorporate a real world into his novel" (*El mundo mítico de Gabriel García Márquez*, 106–8). For the relationship between García Márquez and Vinyes, see Miguel Fernández-Braso, *Gabriel García Márquez: Una conversación infinita*, 41–43; and Dasso Saldívar, *García Márquez: El viaje a la semilla* (Madrid: Alfaguara, 1997), 223–51. Vinyes's biography has been studied by Pere Elies i Busqueta, *Un literat de gran volada: Ramon Vinyes i Cluet* (Barcelona: Rafael Dalmau, 1972), and Jacques Gilard, *Entre los Andes y el Caribe: La obra americana de Ramón Vinyes* (Medellín: Universidad de Antioquía, 1989).

50. As Marco Kunz has noted, the bookseller substitutes for Melquíades at the end of the novel: "Before disappearing and going 'peacefully to the meadows of ultimate death,' [Melquíades] refers Aureliano to another initiator. The wise Catalan is a sort of *alter ego* of the immortal prophet in the linear, limited time of humankind, and he is also the author of another mysterious text we can never read. . . . The Catalan bookseller replaces Melquíades" ("Los pergaminos de Melquíades o la muerte anunciada del mundo ficticio," in *Cien años de soledad, 1967–1987*, ed. Julio Peñate Rivero [Neuchâtel: Université de Neuchâtel, 1988], 36).

51. García Márquez, *Cien años de soledad*, 461–62; *One Hundred Years of Solitude*, 394.

52. *Cien años de soledad*, 474; *One Hundred Years of Solitude*, 406. On the significance of translation in the novel, see Aníbal González, "Translation and the Novel: *One Hundred Years of Solitude*," in *Gabriel García Márquez*, ed. Harold Bloom (New York: Chelsea House, 1989), 271–82.

53. *Cien años de soledad*, 475; *One Hundred Years of Solitude*, 406.

54. *Cien años de soledad*, 464–65; *One Hundred Years of Solitude*, 396.

55. *Cien años de soledad*, 475; *One Hundred Years of Solitude*, 406–7. His first words to Aureliano—"Debes estar loco" [You must be crazy]—were also uttered in his native tongue (*Cien años de soledad* 441; *One Hundred Years of Solitude*, 373).

56. As the editors of the special issue on Catalan scholarship published by *Norte* declared in 1970: "Catalan is the linguistic vehicle of one of the most interesting populations of that heterogeneous ethnic group that makes up the Hispanic family. And not only does the Catalan people seems most interesting to us for their proverbial hard-working character, but above all, for having been the most permeable civilizing filter between Spain and Europe, with all that this permeability means historically: a constant and healthy renewal of the cultural scene of the Iberian peninsula, which by itself tends to stagnate and become rarefied in delirious absolutist atavisms. The rest of Spain will never be able to thank Catalonia enough for that purifying influence on its cultural 'ecology' " ("Presentación," *Situación actual de los estudios de lengua y literatura catalanas*, 3).

57. Ferrater, "Gabriel Ferrater o las mujeres," 337.

58. Baltasar Porcel, "Guerra literaria," 8; see also Pere Gimferrer, "De una guerra literaria."

59. "Encuesta," in *Cultura canaria hoy*, special issue of *El Urogallo* (December 1988–January 1989): 83. The labels "narraluces" and "narraguanches" are discussed by Martínez Cachero in *La novela española entre 1936 y 1980*, 309–15.

60. See Jorge Rodríguez Padrón, "Informe objetivo (dentro de lo que cabe) sobre la nueva narrativa canaria," *Camp de l'Arpa* 7 (August–September 1973): 19–24; and Juan Manuel García Ramos, "Narrativa canaria: ocho años de actividad," *Fablas: Arte y Literatura* 74 (April 1979): 5–12. One of the first overviews of contemporary Canarian literature intended for the national audience is given by José Domingo in "El movimiento literario de las Islas Canarias," *Ínsula* 240 (November 1966): 1, 13; and 241 (December 1966): 10, 12. Between 10 July and 21 August 1968 the literary supplement of *Diario de Las Palmas* presented in serial form "Narrativa en Canarias," an anthology of narrative fiction, followed five years later by another anthology edited by Rafael Franquelo, *Aislada órbita* (Las Palmas: Inventarios Provisionales, 1973).

61. Osvaldo Rodríguez, "Aproximaciones externas a la literatura de Canarias," in *Nuevas escrituras canarias: un panorama crítico* (Islas Canarias: Viceconsejería de Cultura y Deportes del Gobierno de Canarias, 1992), 222–23.

62. Sabas Martín, "Insulario de descubrimientos," in *Encuentro de escritores canarios: Isla de La Gomera, noviembre 1992* (Islas Canarias: Viceconsejería de Cultura y Deportes, 1994), 71. Juan Manuel García Ramos, "Presencia de la narrativa hispanoamericana en la novela canaria," in *Canarias y América*, ed. Francisco Morales Padrón and Fernando Fernández Martín (Madrid: Espasa-Calpe, Argantonio, 1988), 266. See also García Ramos, "Caracteres de la nueva narrativa canaria," in *Ensayos del Nuevo Mundo* (Las Palmas: Cabildo Insular de Gran Canaria, 1993), 83–100. For an overview of the state of scholarship on the literary relationships between Latin America and Canary Islands, see Yolanda Arencibia Santana, "Relaciones Canarias-América en literatura: estado de la cuestión," in *X Coloquio de Historia Canario-Americana (1992)*, ed. Manuel Morales Padrón (Las Palmas: Cabildo Insular de Gran Canaria, 1994), vol. 1: 1151–73.

63. Carlos Alberto Morales, *Cuba, Castro, and the Caribbean: The Cuban Revolution and the Crisis in Western Conscience*, trans. Nelson Duran (New Brunswick, N.J., and Oxford: Transaction Books, 1985), 80–81. See also Francisco Morales Padrón, "Las Canarias: Primeras Antillas," in *Canarias y América*, ed. Francisco Morales Padrón and Fernando Fernández Martín (Madrid: Espasa-Calpe, Argantonio, 1988), 59–66.

64. García Márquez, *Cien años de soledad*, 452; *One Hundred Years of Solitude*, 384–85.

65. García Ramos, "Canarias y la Atlanticidad," *Quimera* 153–154 (December 1996–January 1997): 114. See also Jorge Rodríguez Padrón, "Vértices de una escritura atlántica," in *Cultura canaria hoy*, special issue of *El Urogallo* (December 1988–January 1989): 12–18. In his inaugural lecture for the course 1969–70 at the University of La Laguna (Tenerife), Gregorio Salvador noted the successful reception of García Márquez's novel among his students: "I could speak to you of the *Quixote* and I would be speaking of a contemporary novel. . . . But I am not going to play paradox and speak to you of the novel read so many years ago, but of the one you still have on your nightstand or on the most accessible shelf, the one you got as a birthday gift or for last Christmas, that surprising Hispanic bestseller, *Cien años de soledad*, which in the twenty-nine months since its appearance has reached publishing and circulation figures that no other book in Spanish had ever reached so quickly and so dizzyingly" (*Comentarios estructurales a Cien años de soledad* [La Laguna: Universidad de La Laguna, 1970], 10–11).

66. J. J. Armas Marcelo, "Para un archipiélago imaginado," in *Tirios, troyanos y contemporáneos* (Caracas: Academia Nacional de la Historia, 1986), 170–71. See also his *Propuestas para una literatura mestiza* (Islas Canarias: Tauro, 1994), 36.

67. As Emilio Sánchez Ortiz (one of the writers included in the Canarian *boom*) noted, they could even claim to have preceded Peninsular Spaniards in discovering the new Latin American fiction: "While in the Peninsula hardly anyone knew the García Márquezes or Vargas Llosas . . . we already knew all about them. They were smuggled in to us from South America" ("Rebeldía contra infortunio: Del lado de los 'anti-héroes,'" interview by Jean-Michel Fossey, *Informaciones* 12 July 1973, sec. "Informaciones de las Artes y las Letras": 2). The true bestseller of Canarian narrative, Arozarena's *Mararía* (published in 1974 but written in the early fifties), offers at times a sort of magical realism that prompts its association with Latin American fiction. I disagree here with Ventura Doreste's reading of the novel as a text inserted in the aesthetics of testimonial realism, since diegetic elements like the "bay of the drowned," or the mythical symbolism of the island/ woman figure in the title character, seem to depart from the strict objectivism of documentary poetics dominant in 1950s Spain; see Ventura Doreste, "Novelar en Canarias," *Camp de l'Arpa* 7 (August–September 1973): 26.

68. "The Fortunate Islands (fortunate also for having produced a brilliant pleiad of geniuses) could do no more than create a provincial literature, as it is the case with every region in Spain without a language of its own—and even, occasionally, with those that have one. Galdós does not resign himself to being the Pereda of the Canaries; he has too many things to say and leaves for the court" (José F. Montesinos, *Galdós* (Madrid: Castalia, 1968–1972), vol. 1: 10.

Epilogue

1. Rafael M. Mérida, in "La difusión de la literatura hispanoamericana en España: datos para *otra* recepción," has noted that the presence of Latin American literature in the production of the "Círculo de Lectores" book club peaked during the period 1972–1976. As he also points out, however, the peculiarities of the book club as a secondary activity—which deals with products that have already proved their commercial viability in the open market—account for a certain delay in regard to other channels of literary distribution. In fact, the list of Latin American authors published by the club between 1962 and 1991 is led precisely by García Márquez and Vargas Llosa, who retain their appeal beyond the Boom years.

2. Miguel Ángel Asturias (1967), Pablo Neruda (1971), Vicente Aleixandre (1977), Gabriel García Márquez (1982), Camilo José Cela (1989), and Octavio Paz (1990). In contrast, during the first six decades of the prize only four authors writing in Spanish (three Spaniards and one Chilean) won the award: José Echegaray (1904), Jacinto Benavente (1922), Gabriela Mistral (1945), and Juan Ramón Jiménez (1956).

Bibliography

Actas del XXIX Congreso del Instituto Internacional de Literatura Iberoamericana. Edited by Joaquín Marco. Barcelona: PPU, 1994.

Aicardo, J. M. *De literatura contemporánea: 1901–1905*. Madrid: Sucesores de Rivadeneyra, 1905.

Alazraki, Jaime. "España en la obra de Julio Cortázar." In *Actas del XXIX Congreso del Instituto Internacional de Literatura Iberoamericana*, vol. 3: 3–11.

Alemany, Luis. *Una aproximación a la moderna literatura hispanoamericana*. Santa Cruz de Tenerife: Aula de Cultura de Tenerife, 1974.

Alfaya, Javier. "Javier Alfaya contra el confusionismo." *Informaciones* [Madrid] 12 June 1969, sec. "Informaciones de las Artes y las Letras": 1–2.

Alonso, Dámaso. "Con Dámaso Alonso: Hay que respetar el castellano de América." Interview by Francisco Umbral. *Informaciones* [Madrid] 12 December 1968, sec. "Informaciones de las Artes y las Letras": 3.

———. "*Tirant lo Blanc*, novela moderna." In *Primavera temprana de la literatura europea: lírica, épica, novela*, 201–53. Madrid: Guadarrama, 1961.

Álvarez Palacios, Fernando. *Novela y cultura española de postguerra*. Madrid: Edicusa, 1975.

Amell, Samuel. "Los premios literarios y la novela de la postguerra." *Revista del Instituto de Lengua y Cultura Españolas* 1, 2 (1985): 189–98.

Amorós, Andrés. "Carta a José María Guelbenzu y a un posible lector." *Cuadernos Hispanoamericanos* 229 (January 1969): 172–74.

———. "Introducción." In Julio Cortázar, *Rayuela*, 15–93. Madrid: Cátedra, 1988.

———. *Introducción a la novela hispanoamericana actual*. 2nd ed. Salamanca: Anaya, 1973.

———. "Narrativa latinoamericana." *Hispanoamérica: La sangre del espíritu*. Edited by Victorino Polo, 15–38. Murcia: Universidad de Murcia, 1992.

———. "*Rayuela*: nueva lectura." *Anales de Literatura Hispanoamericana* 1 (1972): 281–319.

———. Review of *Cien años de soledad*, by Gabriel García Márquez. *Revista de Occidente* 70 (January 1969): 58–62.

Amorós, Andrés, et al. *Novela española actual*. Madrid: Cátedra/Fundación Juan March, 1977.

Arce, Carlos de. *Grandeza y servidumbre de veinte Premios Planeta*. Barcelona: Picazo, 1972.

Arenal, Celestino del. *Política exterior de España hacia Iberoamérica*. Madrid: Complutense, 1994.

Arencibia Santana, Yolanda. "Relaciones Canarias-América en literatura: estado de la cuestión (Ensayo de aproximación)." In *X Coloquio de Historia Canario-Americana (1992)*. Edited by Manuel Morales Padrón, vol. 1: 1151–73. Las Palmas: Cabildo Insular de Gran Canaria, 1994.

Armas Marcelo, J. J. "Para un archipiélago imaginado." In *Tirios, troyanos y contemporáneos*, 167–94. Caracas: Academia Nacional de la Historia, 1986.

———. *Propuestas para una literatura mestiza*. Islas Canarias: Tauro, 1994.

———. "¿Qué hubo, poeta?" *Letra Internacional* 20 (1990): 21–24.

———. *Vargas Llosa: el vicio de escribir*. Madrid: Temas de Hoy, 1991.

Arnau, Carmen. *El mundo mítico de Gabriel García Márquez*. Barcelona: Península, 1971.

Arozarena, Rafael. *Mararía*. Edited by Manuel Torres Stinga. Santa Cruz de Tenerife: Interinsular Canaria, 1983.

Arte y letras de Venezuela. Special issue of *Ínsula* 272–73 (July-August 1969).

Artís-Gener, Avel·lí. "Quatre mots del traductor." In Gabriel García Márquez, *Cent anys de solitud*, 7–10. Barcelona: Edhasa, 1970.

———. *Viure i veure*. 4 vols. Barcelona: Pòrtic, 1989–1996.

Ashhurst, Anna Wayne. *La literatura hispanoamericana en la crítica española*. Madrid: Gredos, 1980.

Avilés Fabila, René. "Cómo escribir una novela y convertirla en *best-seller*." *Mundo Nuevo* 51–52 (September-October 1970): 29–33.

Azancot, Leopoldo. "Premio de la Crítica 1969: las desventuras de la democracia." *Índice* 246 (1 May 1969): 30–31.

———. "Premios de la Crítica 1970: fin del 'realismo social' español y revisión de la narrativa latinoamericana." *Índice* 267 (15 April 1970): 34–35.

Bakhtin, Mikhail M. *The Dialogic Imagination: Four Essays by M. M. Bakhtin*. Translated by Caryl Emerson and Michael Holquist. Austin: University of Texas Press, 1981.

Bakhtin, Mikhail M., and P. N. Medvedev. *The Formal Method in Literary Scholarship: A Critical Introduction to Sociological Poetics*. Translated by Albert J. Wehrle. Cambridge: Harvard University Press, 1985.

Balestrini, Nanni, ed. *Gruppo 63: Il romanzo sperimentale*. Milano: Feltrinelli, 1966.

Baquero, Gastón. *Escritores hispanoamericanos de hoy*. Madrid: Instituto de Cultura Hispánica, 1961.

Barral, Carlos. *Los años sin excusa*. Madrid: Alianza, 1982.

———. "Carlos Barral, contra el indigenismo." Interview by Baltasar Porcel. *Destino* 1677 (22 November 1969): 26–27.

———. "Carlos Barral o el límite de la heterodoxia." Interview by F. Monegal. *La Vanguardia* [Barcelona] 6 September 1973: 49.

———. *Cuando las horas veloces*. Barcelona: Tusquets, 1988.

———. "Puntualización de motivos: enfrentamientos novelísticos de continente a continente." *Triunfo* 522 (30 September 1972): 36–37.

———. "Reflexiones acerca de las aventuras del estilo en la penúltima literatura española." In *Treinta años de literatura*, 39–42.

Barth, John. "The Literature of Exhaustion." In *The Friday Book: Essays and Other Nonfiction*, 62–76. New York: G.P. Putnam's Sons, 1984.

Barthes, Roland. "An Introduction to the Structural Analysis of Narrative." Translated by Lionel Duisit. *New Literary History* 6 (1975): 237–72.

———. *On Racine*. Translated by Richard Howard. Berkeley: University of California Press, 1992.

———. *The Pleasure of the Text*. Translated by Richard Miller. New York: Hill and Wang, 1975.

Bassel, Naftoli. "National Literature and Interliterary System." Translated by Ilana Gomel. *Poetics Today* 12 (1991): 773–79.

Batlló, José. Review of *La ciudad y los perros*, by Mario Vargas Llosa. *Cuadernos Hispanoamericanos* 178 (October 1964): 199–203.

Benedetti, Mario. "Luis Martín-Santos: nueva invasión del personaje." In *Sobre artes y oficios*, 219–23. Montevideo: Alfa, 1968.

———. "El *nouveau roman* o la nueva retórica." In *Sobre artes y oficios*, 241–47. Montevideo: Alfa, 1968.

Benet, Josep. *L'intent franquista de genocidi cultural contra Catalunya*. Barcelona: Abadia de Montserrat, 1995.

Benet, Juan. "Breve historia de *Volverás a Región*." *Revista de Occidente* 134 (May 1974): 160–65.

———. "La crítica en cuanto antropología." In *En ciernes*, 63–84. Madrid: Taurus, 1976.

———. "De Canudos a Macondo." *Revista de Occidente* 70 (January 1970): 49–57.

———. "Encuentro con Juan Benet." Interview by Antonio Núñez. In *Juan Benet*. Edited by Kathleen M. Vernon, 17–23. Madrid: Taurus, 1986. Originally published in *Ínsula* 269 (April 1969): 4.

———. "Una época troyana." In *En ciernes*, 85–102. Madrid: Taurus, 1976.

———. "La historia editorial y judicial de *Volverás a Región*." In *La moviola de Eurípides y otros ensayos*, 31–44. Madrid: Taurus, 1981.

———. "Juan Benet o el azar." Interview by Federico Campbell. In Campbell, *Infame turba*, 254–67.

———. *Una meditación*. Barcelona: Seix Barral, 1970. *A Meditation*. Translated by Gregory Rabassa (New York: Persea Books, 1982).

———. "Prólogo a la segunda edición." In *Volverás a Región*, 7–11. "Author's Note," in *Return to Región*, v–ix.

———. "Respuesta al señor Montero." In *Literatura española a treinta años del siglo XXI*, 75–76.

———. *Volverás a Región*. Second edition. Madrid: Alianza, 1974. *Return to Región*. Translated by Gregory Rabassa (New York: Columbia University Press, 1985).

Benson, Ken. "Autenticidad y pureza en el discurso de Juan Benet." *Ínsula* 559–60 (July–August 1993): 11–13.

Berenguer Carisomo, Arturo. *Literatura argentina*. Barcelona: Labor, 1970.

Bernstein, Jerome S. "*Rayuela*, Chapter 34: A Structural Reading." *Hispanófila* 52 (September 1974): 61–70.

Bértolo, Constantino. "Introducción a la narrativa española actual." *Revista de Occidente* 98–99 (July–August 1989): 29–60.

Bhabha, Homi, ed. *Nation and Narration*. London: Routledge, 1990.

Biescas, José Antonio, and Manuel Tuñón de Lara. *España bajo la dictadura franquista (1939–1975)*. Vol. 10 of *Historia de España*. Edited by Manuel Tuñón de Lara. Barcelona: Labor, 1983.

Blanco-Fombona, Rufino. "El libro español en América." In Mariano Viada et al., *El libro español: Ciclo de conferencias (15–23 de marzo de 1922)*, 163–82. Barcelona: Cámara Oficial del Libro de Barcelona, 1922.

"El 'boom' de la narrativa hispanoamericana: ataques y contrataques." *Ínsula* 282 (May 1970): 2.

Borges, Jorge Luis. "Autobiographical Essay." In *The Aleph and Other Stories, 1933–1969*. Edited and translated by Norman Thomas di Giovanni, 203–60. New York: E.P. Dutton, 1978.

———. "Kafka and His Precursors." In *Labyrinths: Selected Stories and Other Writings*. Edited by Donald A. Yates and James E. Irby, 199–201. New York: New Directions Books, 1964.

———. "On Exactitude in Science." In *A Universal History of Infamy*. Translated by Norman Thomas di Giovanni, 141. London: Alan Lane, 1973.

Bosch, Andrés, et al. "La nueva novela: coloquio." In *Papeles sobre la "nueva novela" española*. Edited by Manuel García Viñó, 95–109. Pamplona: Universidad de Navarra, 1975. 95–109. Originally published in *Índice* 225 (November 1967): 54–57.

Bourdieu, Pierre. "Le champ littéraire." *Actes de la Recherche en Sciences Sociales* 89 (September 1991): 3–46.

———. "The Market of Symbolic Goods." Translated by Rupert Swyer. *Poetics* 14 (1985): 13–44.

Bozal, Valeriano. "La edición en España: notas para su historia." In *Treinta años de literatura*, 85–93.

———. "Novela hispanoamericana: la estructura narrativa." *Informaciones* [Madrid] 5 December 1968, sec. "Informaciones de las Artes y las Letras": 1–2.

———. Review of *El mercurio*, by José María Guelbenzu. *Cuadernos Hispanoamericanos* 223 (July 1968): 250–55.

Bravo, María Elena. *Faulkner en España: perspectivas de la narrativa de postguerra*. Barcelona: Península, 1985.

———. "Juan Benet: de modernismo a posmodernismo." *Ínsula* 559–60 (July–August 1993): 5–7.

Brody, Robert. *Julio Cortázar: Rayuela*. London: Grant and Cutler, 1976.

Brown, Meg H. *The Reception of Spanish American Fiction in West Germany, 1981–1991: A Study of Best Sellers*. Tübingen, Germany: Max Niemeyer, 1994.

Brushwood, John S. "Two Views of the Boom: North and South." *Latin American Literary Review* 29 (January–June 1987): 13–31.

Butor, Michel. "Michel Butor y sus claves." Interview by Enrique Canito. *Ínsula* 159 (February 1960): 5.

———. "The Novel as Research." In *Inventory*. Edited by Richard Howard, translated by Gerald Fabian, 26–30. New York: Simon and Schuster, 1968.

———. *Sobre literatura: estudios y conferencias 1948–1959*. Translated by Juan Petit. Barcelona: Seix Barral, 1960.

Caballero Bonald, José Manuel, ed. *Narrativa cubana de la revolución*. Madrid: Alianza, 1968.

Cabrera Infante, Guillermo. "Lo que este libro debe al censor." In *Tres tristes tigres*, ix–xii. Caracas: Biblioteca Ayacucho, 1990.

———. "Tres escritores hispanoamericanos en París, I: Con Guillermo Cabrera Infante." Interview by José Corrales Egea. *Ínsula* 195 (February 1963): 7.

———. *Tres tristes tigres*. Barcelona: Seix Barral, 1983. *Three Trapped Tigers*. Translated by Donald Gardner and Suzanne Jill Levine (New York: Harper and Row, 1971).

Campbell, Federico. *Infame turba*. 2nd ed. Barcelona: Lumen, 1994.

Campos, Jorge. "García Márquez: fábula y realidad." *Ínsula* 258 (May 1968): 11.

———. "Otra gran novela: *La ciudad y los perros*." *Ínsula* 209 (April 1964): 11.

———. "*Rayuela*, de Julio Cortázar." *Ínsula* 250 (September 1967): 11.

Canito, Enrique. "Crónica de Formentor: los premios internacionales de novela." *Ínsula* 174 (May 1961): 5.

Cano, Jose Luis. "La Conversaciones Poéticas de Formentor." *Ínsula* 151 (15 June 1959): 10.

Cano Ballesta, Juan. "Décadas de conquista para las letras españolas: poesía y novela (1953–1963)." *Ínsula* 210 (May 1964): 6.

Capdevila Bassols, Josep M. "Algunas consideraciones sobre la industria editorial." *Banca Catalana: Publicación de Información Económica* 3 (December 1966): 18–24.

Carandell, Luis. "Alfono Grosso: primeros gritos de independencia." *Triunfo* 361 (3 May 1969): 72–73.

Carballo, Emmanuel, ed. *Narrativa mexicana de hoy*. Madrid: Alianza, 1969.

Carr, Raymond, and Juan Pablo Fusi. *Spain: Dictatorship to Democracy*. London and New York: Routledge, 1991.

Carrasquer, Francisco. "*Cien años de soledad* y *Volverás a Región*, dos polos." *Norte: Revista Hispánica de Amsterdam* 11, 6 (November–December 1970): 197–201.

Castellano-Girón, Hernán. "Lo galdosiano en Cortázar, lo cortazariano en Galdós: a propósito del capítulo 34 de *Rayuela*." In *Los ochenta mundos de Cortázar: ensayos*. Edited by Antonio Burgos, 129–35. Madrid: EDI-6, 1987.

Castellet, Josep Maria. "La actual literatura latinoamericana vista desde España." In *Panorama actual de la literatura latinoamericana*, 47–61. Madrid: Fundamentos, 1971.

———. "Coloquio Internacional sobre Novela en Formentor." *Cuadernos del Congreso por la Libertad de la Cultura* 38 (September–October 1959): 82–86.

———. "De la objetividad al objeto: a propósito de las novelas de Alain Robbe-Grillet." *Papeles de Son Armadans* 15 (June 1957): 309–32.

———. *Els escenaris de la memòria.* Barcelona: Edicions 62, 1988.

———. *La hora del lector: notas para una iniciación a la literatura narrativa de nuestros días.* Barcelona: Seix Barral, 1957.

———. "El Mestre: Josep Maria Castellet." In Heymann and Mullor-Heimann, *Retratos de escritorio,* 153–68.

———. "El Primer Coloquio Internacional sobre Novela." *Ínsula* 152–53 (July–August 1959): 19, 32.

———. "El Segundo Coloquio Internacional de Novela en Formentor." *Ínsula* 163 (June 1960): 4.

———. "Tiempo de destrucción para la literatura española." In *Literatura, ideología y política,* 135–56. Barcelona: Anagrama, 1976.

Castillo, Debra. "Reading over Her Shoulder: Galdós/Cortázar." *Anales Galdosianos* 21 (1986): 147–60.

Castro y Delgado, Juan de. Review of *La ciudad y los perros,* by Mario Vargas Llosa. *Razón y Fe* 807 (April 1965): 435–36.

Castro-Klarén, Sara, and Héctor Campos. "Traducciones, tirajes, ventas y estrellas: el boom." *Ideologies and Literature* 17 (1983): 319–38.

Catelli, Nora. "Atlántico desdén: la vieja América vista desde la España nueva." In *La crítica literaria española frente a la literatura latinoamericana.* Edited by Leonor Fleming and María Teresa Bosque Latra, 11–18. Mexico: UNAM, 1993.

Cela, Camilo José. "Sobre el concepto de novela." In Ynduráin, *Prosa novelesca actual,* 45–53.

Cendán Pazos, Fernando. *Edición y comercio del libro español: 1900–1972.* Madrid: Editora Nacional, 1972.

"*Cent anys de solitud,* de García Márquez, premio Rómulo Gallegos." *La Vanguardia* [Barcelona] 21 September 1972: 50.

Clausen, Christopher. " 'National Literatures' in English: Toward a New Paradigm." *New Literary History* 25 (1994): 61–72.

Coindreau, Maurice Edgar. "Homenaje a los jóvenes novelistas españoles." *Cuadernos del Congreso por la Libertad de la Cultura* 33 (November–December 1958): 44–47.

"Coloquios sobre el realismo." *Ínsula* 204 (November 1963): 2.

Compitello, Malcolm Alan. "Benet and Spanish Postmodernism." *Revista Hispánica Moderna* 44 (1991): 259–73.

———. *Ordering the Evidence: "Volverás a Región" and Civil War Fiction.* Barcelona: Puvill, 1983.

Conte, Rafael. "Carta abierta a Alfonso Grosso: los avatares del realismo." *Informaciones* [Madrid] 22 May 1969, sec. "Informaciones de las Artes y las Letras": 3.

———. *Lenguaje y violencia: introducción a la nueva novela hispanoamericana.* Madrid: Al-Borak, 1972.

———. "Punto final a una falsa polémica." *Informaciones* [Madrid] 26 June 1969, sec. "Informaciones de las Artes y las Letras": 3.

———. Review of *El día señalado*, by Manuel Mejía Vallejo. *Tele Radio* [Madrid] 11 May 1964.

Corrales Egea, José. *La novela española actual: ensayo de ordenación.* Madrid: Edicusa, 1971.

Cortázar, Julio. "Un gran escritor y su soledad." *Life en español* 33, 7 (7 April 1969): 43–55.

Costa, Luis F. "El lector-viajero en *Volverás a Región.*" *Anales de la Narrativa Española Contemporánea* 4 (1979): 9–18.

Curet, Francesc. *"La Jamància": Les bullangues de 1842 i 1843.* Barcelona: Rafael Dalmau, 1990.

Curutchet, Juan Carlos. "Una lectura de *El mercurio.*" *Cuadernos Hispanoamericanos* 229 (January 1969): 174–77.

Darío, Rubén. *Epistolario.* Paris: Biblioteca Latino-Americana, 1920.

———. *España contemporánea.* Paris: Garnier, 1901.

Delgado Gómez-Escalonilla, Lorenzo. *Diplomacia franquista y política cultural hacia Iberoamérica: 1939–1953.* Madrid: CSIC, 1988.

———. *Imperio de papel: Acción cultural y política exterior durante el primer franquismo.* Madrid: CSIC, 1992.

Díaz, Janet W. "Origins, Aesthetics and the 'Nueva Novela Española.' " *Hispania* 59, 1 (March 1976): 109–17.

Dimić, Milan V. "Space and Boundaries of Literature According to Russian Formalism, The Prague School, and the Polysystem Theory." In *Proceedings of the XIIth Congress of the ICLA.* Edited by Roger Bauer and Douwe Fokkema, vol 5: 30–35. Munich: Iudicium, 1990.

Domingo, José. "Los caminos de la experimentación." *Ínsula* 312 (November 1972): 6.

———. "El movimiento literario de las Islas Canarias." *Ínsula* 240 (November 1966): 1, 13; and 241 (December 1966): 10, 12.

———. Review of *Experimento en Génesis*, by Germán Sánchez Espeso. *Ínsula* 256 (March 1968): 5.

Donoso, José. *Historia personal del boom.* Buenos Aires: Sudamericana/Planeta, 1984.

Doreste, Ventura. "Novelar en Canarias." *Camp de l'Arpa* 7 (August–September 1973): 25–26.

Eco, Umberto. *Postscript to The Name of the Rose.* Translated by William Weaver. New York: Harcourt Brace Jovanovich, 1984.

Edwards, Jorge, et al. "Mesa redonda: la experiencia de los novelistas." *Revista Iberoamericana* 116–17 (1981): 307–21.

Einaudi, Giulio. *Frammenti di memoria.* Milan: Rizzoli, 1988.

Einaudi, Giulio, and Severino Cesari. *Colloquio con Giulio Einaudi.* Rome: Theoria, 1991.

Elies i Busqueta, Pere. *Un literat de gran volada: Ramon Vinyes i Cluet.* Barcelona: Rafael Dalmau, 1972.

"Un episodio literario de 1967: el caso Fuentes." *La Estafeta Literaria* 387 (13 January 1968): 4–7.

Escobar, José. Review of *La ciudad y los perros*, by Mario Vargas Llosa. *Revista de Occidente* 26 (May 1965): 261–67.

Escolar, Hipólito. *Historia del libro*. Madrid: Fundación Germán Sánchez Ruipérez, 1984.

Espadaler, Anton M. "Mario Vargas Llosa i el *Tirant lo Blanc*." In *VI Jornades d'Estudis Catalano-Americans*, 219–25. Barcelona: Comissió Amèrica i Catalunya, 1992.

Espinás, José María. "Cita en Formentor: El II Coloquio Internacional de la Novela." *Destino* 1188 (14 May 1960): 43–44.

———. "El I Coloquio Internacional de Novela, en Formentor." *Destino* 1139 (6 June 1959): 13–15.

———. "Notas al margen de las Conversaciones." *Destino* 1138 (30 May 1959): 38.

Estruch Tobella, Joan. "Un intento de realismo socialista español: La literatura y el PCE en la década de los 50." In *Actas del I Simposio para Profesores de Lengua y Literatura Española: Barcelona, 1–3 mayo 1980*. Edited by Ricardo Velilla Barquero, 133–51. Madrid: Castalia, 1981.

Even-Zohar, Itamar. *Papers in Historical Poetics*. Tel Aviv: The Porter Institute for Poetics and Semiotics, 1978.

———. *Polysystem Studies*. Special issue of *Poetics Today* 11, 1 (spring 1990).

Fernández-Braso, Miguel. *Gabriel García Márquez: Una conversación infinita*. Madrid: Azur, 1969.

Fernández Retamar, Roberto. *Caliban and Other Essays*. Translated by Edward Baker. Minneapolis: University of Minnesota Press, 1989.

Fernández Santos, Francisco. "Desde Cuba: Premios Casa de las Américas 1967." *Índice* 217–18 (1967): 79.

Ferrater, Gabriel. "Gabriel Ferrater o las mujeres." Interview by Federico Campbell. In Campbell, *Infame turba*, 326–38.

Fiedler, Leslie. "Close the Border—Close the Gap." In *A Fiedler Reader*, 270–94. New York: Stein and Day, 1977.

Fletcher, John, and Malcolm Bradbury. "The Introverted Novel." In *Modernism, 1890–1930*. Edited by Malcolm Bradbury and James McFarlane, 394–415. Sussex: Harvester Press; New Jersey: Humanities Press, 1978.

Fogelquist, Donald F. *Españoles de América y americanos de España*. Madrid: Gredos, 1968.

Fortes, José Antonio. "En la historia intelectual de postguerra civil española (Para una lectura del 'Boom' de hispanoamericanos en España: años 60)." *Cuadernos de ALDEEU* 9, 1 (April 1993): 9–24.

———. "Gallimard y la novela española de postguerra: años 1957–1968." *Letras Peninsulares* 1, 2 (fall 1988): 182–99.

———. "La joven novelística del traduccionismo." In *Novelas para la transición política*, 111–19. Madrid: Ediciones Libertarias, 1987.

———. "La novela hispanoamericana en España: apunte bibliográfico, años setenta." In *Novelas para la transición política*, 43–50. Madrid: Ediciones Libertarias, 1987. Originally published in *Insula* 388 (March 1979): 11.

Franquelo, Rafael, ed. *Aislada órbita*. Las Palmas: Inventarios Provisionales, 1973.

"Fuentes y la censura española." *Mundo Nuevo* 17 (November 1967): 90–91.

Fuentes, Carlos. *Cervantes o la crítica de la lectura*. Mexico: Joaquín Mortiz, 1976.

———. "Discurso de recepción del Premio Rómulo Gallegos." In *Premio Internacional de Novela Rómulo Gallegos 1972–1976: Discursos de Carlos Fuentes y Luis García Morales*, 11–32. Caracas: Consejo Nacional de Cultura, 1978.

———. "Mi patria es el idioma español." In *Tres discursos para dos aldeas*, 29–46. Mexico: Fondo de Cultura Económica, 1993.

———. *La nueva novela hispanoamericana*. Mexico: Joaquín Mortiz, 1969.

Fuster, Joan. *Literatura catalana contemporània*. Barcelona: Curial, 1972.

———. "Literatura en lengua catalana." In *Treinta años de literatura*, 19–21.

———. "El I coloquio internacional de novela en Formentor." *Papeles de Son Armadans* 41 (August 1959): 207–12.

Gadamer, Hans Georg. *Truth and Method*. Translated by Garrett Barden and John Cumming. New York: Continuum, 1975.

"Gabriel García Márquez." Dossier. *Índice* 237 (November 1968): 21–37.

Galan, F. W. *Historic Structures: The Prague School Project, 1928–1946*. Austin: University of Texas Press, 1985.

Galán Pérez, José Manuel. *Análisis estructural del sector editorial español*. Madrid: Fundación Germán Sánchez Ruipérez and Ediciones Pirámide, 1986.

García, Salvador. *Las ideas literarias en España entre 1840 y 1850*. Berkeley: University of California Press, 1971.

García Márquez, Gabriel. *Cien años de soledad*. Edited by Jacques Joset. Madrid: Cátedra, 1984. *One Hundred Years of Solitude*. Translated by Gregory Rabassa (New York: Harper and Row, 1970).

———. "Gabriel García Márquez." Interview by José Domingo. *Ínsula* 259 (June 1968): 6, 11.

———. "García Márquez: ahora doscientos años de soledad." Interview by Ernesto González Bermejo. In *Gabriel García Márquez*. Edited by Peter G. Earle, 239–62. Madrid: Taurus, 1981. Originally published in *Triunfo* 441 (14 November 1970): 12–18.

García Márquez, Gabriel, and Mario Vargas Llosa. *La novela en América Latina: diálogo*. Lima: Carlos Milla Batres, [1967].

García Pavón, Francisco. "Escritores al habla: Francisco García Pavón." Interview by Antonio R. de las Heras. *ABC* [Madrid] 15 May 1969, sec. "Mirador Literario": 8.

García Ramos, Juan Manuel. "Canarias y la Atlanticidad." *Quimera* 153–54 (December 1996–January 1997): 114–18.

———. "Caracteres de la nueva narrativa canaria." In *Ensayos del Nuevo Mundo*, 83–100. Las Palmas: Cabildo Insular de Gran Canaria, 1993.

———. "Narrativa canaria: ocho años de actividad." *Fablas: Arte y Literatura* 74 (April 1979): 5–12.

———. "Presencia de la narrativa hispanoamericana en la novela canaria." In *Canarias y América*. Edited by Francisco Morales Padrón and Fernando Fernández Martín, 265–68. Madrid: Espasa-Calpe, Argantonio, 1988.

García Rico, Eduardo. *Literatura y política: en torno al realismo español*. Madrid: Edicusa, 1971.

García Viñó, Manuel. *Novela española actual*. Madrid: Guadarrama, 1967.

———. "Última hora de la novela española." *Nuestro Tiempo* 137 (November 1965): 478–97.

———, ed. *Papeles sobre la "Nueva Novela" española*. Pamplona: Universidad de Navarra, 1975.

Gazarian Gautier, Marie-Lise. *Interviews with Spanish Writers*. Elmwood Park, Ill.: Dalkey Archive Press, 1991.

Genette, Gérard. *Palimpsests: Literature in the Second Degree*. Translated by Channa Newman and Claude Doubinsky. Lincoln and London: University of Nebraska Press, 1997.

———. *Paratexts: Thresholds of Interpretation*. Translated by Jane E. Lewin. Cambridge: Cambridge University Press, 1997.

Gil Casado, Pablo. *La novela deshumanizada española: 1958–1988*. Barcelona: Anthropos, 1990.

———. *La novela social española: 1920–1971*. Barcelona: Seix Barral, 1973.

Gil de Biedma, Jaime. "Las novelas de Alain Robbe-Grillet." *Ínsula* 132 (November 1957): 12.

Gilard, Jacques. *Entre los Andes y el Caribe: La obra americana de Ramón Vinyes*. Medellín: Universidad de Antioquía, 1989.

Giménez Aznar, José. "*El día señalado*, de Manuel Mejía Vallejo." *Por el mundo de los libros y del teatro*. Radio Popular, Zaragoza. Broadcast on 18 March 1964.

Gimferrer, Pere. "De una guerra literaria: ¿combatir en dos frentes?" *Destino* 1697 (11 April 1970): 41.

———. "En torno a *Volverás a Región*, de Juan Benet." *Ínsula* 266 (January 1969): 14.

———. "Notas sobre Juan Benet." In *Juan Benet*. Edited by Kathleen M. Vernon, 45–58. Madrid: Taurus, 1986.

———. "Notas sobre Julio Cortázar." In *Julio Cortázar*. Edited by Pedro Lastra, 253–57. Madrid: Taurus, 1981. Originally published in *Ínsula* 227 (October 1965): 7.

———. "Sobre *Cien años de soledad*." *Destino* 1575 (14 October 1967): 125.

Gironella, José María. "Viaje en torno al mundo literario español." *Los domingos de ABC* [Madrid], 22 February 1970: 8–12.

Godoy Gallardo, Eduardo. "Índice crítico-bibliográfico del Premio Nadal: 1944–1968." *Mapocho* [Santiago de Chile] 22 (1970): 109–36.

Gómez Marín, José Antonio. "Literatura y política: del tremendismo a la nueva narrativa." *Cuadernos Hispanoamericanos* 193 (January 1966): 109–16.

González, Aníbal. "Translation and the Novel: *One Hundred Years of Solitude*." In *Gabriel García Márquez*, edited by Harold Bloom, 271–82. New York: Chelsea House, 1989.

González, Manuel Pedro. "Apostillas a la novela latinoamericana." *Zona Franca* 48 (August 1967): 4–9.

———. "Reparos al Premio Rómulo Gallegos." *Zona Franca* 51 (November 1967): 34–38.

González Echevarría, Roberto. *Myth and Archive: A Theory of Latin American Narrative*. Durham and London: Duke University Press, 1998.

Goytisolo, José Agustín, ed. *Nueva poesía cubana*. Barcelona: Península, 1970.

Goytisolo, Juan. "Destrucción de la España sagrada." Interview by Emir Rodríguez Monegal. *Mundo Nuevo* 12 (June 1967): 44–60.

———. *Disidencias*. Barcelona: Seix Barral, 1977.

———. *En los reinos de taifa*. Barcelona: Seix Barral, 1986. *Realms of Strife: The Memoirs of Juan Goytisolo (1957–1982)*. Translated by Peter Bush (San Francisco: North Point Press, 1990).

———. "Entrevistas a Juan Goytisolo." Interview by Julio Ortega. In *Disidencias*, 289–325.

———. "Examen de conciencia." In *El furgón de cola*, 243–70. Originally published in *Número* [Montevideo] 2nd series, 1, 1 (March–April 1963): 5–16.

———. *El furgón de cola*. Barcelona: Seix Barral, 1976.

———. "Lectura cervantina de *Tres tristes tigres*." In *Disidencias*, 193–219. "A Cervantine Reading of *Three Trapped Tigers*." In *Saracen Chronicles: A Selection of Literary Essays*. Translated by Helen Lane (London: Quartet Books, 1992), 132–53.

———. "Literatura y eutanasia." In *El furgón de cola*, 75–94. Originally published in *Marcha* 1307–8 (June 1966).

———. *Señas de identidad*. Barcelona: Seix Barral, 1979. *Marks of Identity*. Translated by Gregory Rabassa (New York: Grove Press, 1969).

———. "La novela española contemporánea." In *Disidencias*, 153–69. Originally published in *Libre* 2 (December 1971–February 1972): 33–40.

———. "Para una literatura nacional popular." *Ínsula* 146 (January 1959): 6, 11.

———. *Problemas de la novela*. Barcelona: Seix Barral, 1959.

Goytisolo, Luis. "Carta sobre Vargas Llosa." In Mario Vargas Llosa et al., *El autor y su obra: Mario Vargas Llosa*, 139–41. Madrid: Universidad Complutense, 1990.

Grande, Félix. "El 'boom' en España." In *Once artistas y un dios: ensayos sobre literatura hispanoamericana*, 55–73. Madrid: Taurus, 1986.

———. "Con García Márquez en un miércoles de ceniza." *Cuadernos Hispanoamericanos* 222 (June 1968): 632–41.

Grosso, Alfonso. "Alfonso Grosso contra . . . Antonio Bernabéu." *Informaciones* [Madrid], 29 May 1969, sec. "Informaciones de las Artes y las Letras": 2.

———. "Alfonso Grosso explica algunas cosas." Interview by Antonio Bernabéu. *Informaciones* [Madrid], 15 May 1969, sec. "Informaciones de las Artes y las Letras": 1–2.

Guardiola, Carles-Jordi. *Per la llengua: Llengua i cultura als Països Catalans, 1939–1977.* Barcelona: La Magrana, 1980.

Guelbenzu, José María. "Dos libros de Juan Benet." *Cuadernos para el Diálogo* 73 (October 1969): 48.

———. "Literatura, una insoportable soledad." *Cuadernos para el Diálogo* extraordinario 7 (February 1968): 47–50.

———. *El mercurio.* Barcelona: Seix Barral, 1968.

Güell, Antoni M., and Modest Reixach. *La producció editorial a les àrees lingüístiques restringides: el cas català.* Barcelona: Fundació Jaume Bofill, 1978.

Gugelberger, Georg M. "Decolonizing the Canon: Considerations of Third World Literature." *New Literary History* 22 (1991): 505–22.

Guillén, Claudio. *The Challenge of Comparative Literature.* Translated by Cola Franzen. Cambridge: Harvard University Press, 1993.

———. *Literature as System: Essays Toward the Theory of Literary History.* Princeton, N.J.: Princeton University Press, 1971.

Gullón, Germán. *El narrador en la novela del siglo XIX.* Madrid: Taurus, 1976.

Gullón, Ricardo. *García Márquez o el olvidado arte de narrar.* Madrid: Taurus, 1970.

Gutiérrez, Fernando. "Dos novelistas hispanoamericanos." Review of *La ciudad y los perros,* by Mario Vargas Llosa, and *El día señalado,* by Manuel Mejía Vallejo. *La Prensa* [Barcelona], 31 March 1964.

Halcón, Manuel. "Escritores al habla: Manuel Halcón." Interview by Antonio R. de las Heras. *ABC* [Madrid], 21 August 1969, sec. "Mirador Literario": 6–7.

Hawthorne, Julian. "The American Element in Fiction." *The North American Review* 139 (1884): 164–78.

Hazera, Lydia D. "Estudio sinóptico de las personalidades femeninas." In *Explicación de Cien años de soledad.* Edited by Francisco E. Porrata and Fausto Avendaño, 151–69. San José, Costa Rica: Texto, 1976.

Henríquez Ureña, Max. "El intercambio de influencias literarias entre España y América." In *El retorno de los galeones y otros ensayos,* 2nd ed., 7–46. Mexico: Galaxia, 1963.

Herzberger, David K. "The Emergence of Juan Benet: A New Alternative for the Spanish Novel." *The American Hispanist* 3 (November 1975): 6–12.

———. "Enigma as Narrative Determinant in the Novels of Juan Benet." *Hispanic Review* 47 (1979): 149–57.

———. "Experimentation and Alienation in the Novels of José María Guelbenzu." *Hispania* 64 (September 1981): 367–75.

———. "An Overview of Postwar Novel Criticism of the 1970's." *Anales de la Narrativa Española Contemporánea* 5 (1980): 27–38.

———. "Social Realism and the Contingencies of History in the Contemporary Spanish Novel." *Hispanic Review* 59, 2 (spring 1991): 153–73.

Heymann, Jochen, and Montserrat Mullor-Heymann. *Retratos de escritorio: Entrevistas a autores españoles.* Frankfurt am Main: Vervuert, 1991.

Hintz, Suzanne S. "Scholarship on *Tirant lo Blanc*: On Its Five Hundredth Anniversary." In *Tirant lo Blanc: Text and Context*. Edited by Josep M. Solà-Solé, 93–105. New York: Peter Lang, 1993.

Holquist, Michael. *Dialogism: Bakhtin and His World*. London and New York: Routledge, 1990.

Huertas Clavería, Josep M., and Lluís Bassets. "Con el adiós de Vargas Llosa: pequeña historia de los escritores americanos en Barcelona." *Tele/Exprés* [Barcelona], 15 June 1974: 2–3.

Huguet Santos, Montserrat, Antonio Niño Rodríguez, and Pedro Pérez Herrero, eds. *La formación de la imagen de América Latina en España: 1898–1989*. Madrid: Organización de Estados Iberoamericanos, 1992.

Hutcheon, Linda. *A Poetics of Postmodernism: History, Theory, Fiction*. New York: Routledge, 1988.

———. *A Theory of Parody: The Teachings of Twentieth-Century Art Forms*. New York: Methuen, 1985.

Huyssen, Andreas. "Mapping the Postmodern." In *A Postmodern Reader*. Edited by Joseph Natoli and Linda Hutcheon, 105–56. Albany: State University of New York Press, 1993.

Iglesias, Ignacio. "Novelas y novelistas de hoy." *Mundo Nuevo* 28 (October 1968): 84–88.

Iglesias Laguna, Antonio. "El dilema de la novela hispanoamericana." *La Estafeta Literaria* 422 (15 June 1969): 9–10.

———. *¿Por qué no se traduce la literatura española?* Madrid: Editora Nacional, 1964.

Instituto Nacional de Estadística. *Estadística de la producción editorial de libros*. Madrid: INE, 1966–1986.

———. *Estadística de la producción y comercio del libro español: años 1946–1957*. Madrid: INE, 1958.

Instituto Nacional del Libro Español. *Llibres en català*. Madrid: INLE, 1967–.

"José Lezama Lima." Dossier. *Índice* 232 (June 1968): 22–42.

Joset, Jacques. "Introducción." In Gabriel García Márquez, *Cien años de soledad*, 9–44. Madrid: Cátedra, 1984.

"Julio Cortázar." Dossier. *Índice* 221–23 (July–September 1967): 9–24.

Kunz, Marco. "Los pergaminos de Melquíades o la muerte anunciada del mundo ficticio." In *Cien años de soledad, 1967–1987: Actas de las Jornadas Hispánicas de la S.S.E.H., 4–5 diciembre 1987*. Edited by Julio Peñate Rivero, 31–47. Neuchâtel: Université de Neuchâtel, 1988.

La Fontaine, Ray. "Translator's Introduction." In Joanot Martorell and Martí Joan de Galba, *Tirant lo Blanc: The Complete Translation*, 5–34. New York: Peter Lang, 1993.

Labanyi, Jo. *Myth and History in the Contemporary Spanish Novel*. Cambridge: Cambridge University Press, 1989.

Lambert, José. "L'éternelle question des frontières: littératures nationales et systèmes littéraires." In *Langue, dialecte, littérature: Etudes romanes à la mémoire de Hugo Plomteux*. Edited by C. Angelet et al., 355–70. Louvain: Leuven University Press, 1983.

———. "In Quest of Literary World Maps." In *Interculturality and the Historical Study of Literary Translations.* Edited by Harald Kittel and Armin Paul Frank, 133–44. Berlin: Erich Schmidt, 1991.

Larsen, Neil. *Reading North by South: On Latin American Literature, Culture, and Politics.* Minneapolis and London: University of Minnesota Press, 1995.

Lazúrtegui, Julio de. *El libro español en América.* Bilbao: Centro de la Unión Ibero-Americana en Vizcaya, 1919.

Lefevere, André. "Théorie littéraire et littérature traduite." *Canadian Review of Comparative Literature* 9, 2 (June 1982): 137–56.

Lera, Ángel María de. "Bueno está lo bueno . . ." *ABC* [Madrid], 28 November 1968, sec. "Mirador Literario": 3.

———. "La novela española en Salamanca." *ABC* [Madrid], 9 September 1971, sec. "Mirador Literario": 1–2.

———. "Los Premios de la Crítica." *ABC* [Madrid], 29 May 1969, sec. "Mirador Literario": 3.

Letras de América. Special issue of *Ínsula* 303 (February 1972).

Lichtblau, Myron I. "Horacio Oliveira and Pérez Galdós: A Strange Textual Convergence in Cortázar's *Rayuela.*" In *La Chispa '87: Selected Proceedings.* Edited by Gilbert Paolini, 161–67. New Orleans: Tulane University, 1987.

Lie, Nadia. *Transición y transacción: La revista cubana "Casa de las Américas" (1960–1976).* Louvain, Belgium: Leuven University Press and Hispamérica, 1996.

Lieberman, Sima. *Growth and Crisis in the Spanish Economy: 1940–93.* London and New York: Routledge, 1995.

Literatura cubana actual. Special issue of *Ínsula* 260–61 (July–August 1968).

Literatura española a treinta años del siglo XXI. Special issue of *Cuadernos para el Diálogo* extraordinario 23 (December 1970).

London, John. "The Ideology and Practice of Sport." In *Spanish Cultural Studies: An Introduction.* Edited by Helen Graham and Jo Labanyi, 204–7. Oxford: Oxford University Press, 1995.

López Chuchurra, Osvaldo. ". . . Sobre Julio Cortázar." *Cuadernos Hispanoamericanos* 211 (July 1967): 5–30.

Mac Adam, Alfred. *Modern Latin American Narratives: The Dreams of Reason.* Chicago: University of Chicago Press, 1977.

Maisterra, Pascual. "*Cien años de soledad*: Un regalo fabuloso de Gabriel García Márquez." *Tele/Exprés* [Barcelona], 28 November 1968: 36.

Mangini, Shirley. *Rojos y rebeldes: la cultura de la disidencia durante el franquismo.* Barcelona: Anthropos, 1987.

Manteiga, Roberto. "El lector-viajero de Juan Benet." *Ínsula* 559–60 (July–August 1993): 23–24.

Marco, Joaquín. "Al borde de una polémica: 'Realismo,' público, editor y novela en España." *Destino* 1660 (26 July 1969): 33.

———. "Al margen de una polémica." *Destino* 1658 (12 July 1969): 35.

———. "Gabriel García Márquez: Un joven maestro de la literatura colombiana." *Destino* 1575 (14 October 1967): 124–25.

————. *La nueva literatura en España y América*. Barcelona: Lumen, 1972.

Martín, Sabas. "Insulario de descubrimientos." In *Encuentro de escritores canarios: Isla de La Gomera, noviembre 1992*, 67–72. Islas Canarias: Viceconsejería de Cultura y Deportes, 1994.

Martín-Santos, Luis. "Realismo y realidad en la literatura contemporánea." In Juan Luis Suárez Granda, *Tiempo de silencio, de Luis Martín-Santos: Guía de lectura*, 141–42. Madrid: Alhambra, 1986. Originally published in *El mundo en español* [Paris] (December 1963).

Martínez Cachero, José María. *La novela española entre 1936 y 1980: historia de una aventura*. Madrid: Castalia, 1985.

————. "La recepción española de la literatura hispanoamericana posterior al modernismo: primeras notas para su estudio." In *XVII Congreso del Instituto Internacional de Literatura Iberoamericana*, vol. 3: 1499–509. Madrid: Centro Iberoamericano de Cooperación, 1978.

Martínez-Menchén, Antonio. *Del desengaño literario*. Madrid: Helios, 1970.

————. "Martínez-Menchén contra . . . Santos Fontenla." *Informaciones* [Madrid], 29 May 1969, sec. "Informaciones de las Artes y las Letras": 1.

————. "El mismo Martínez-Menchén contra . . . Guelbenzu y Vázquez Montalbán." *Informaciones* [Madrid], 29 May 1969, sec. "Informaciones de las Artes y las Letras": 1–2.

Martínez Ruiz, Florencio. "Pequeña historia de un gran premio." *ABC* [Madrid], 19 April 1980: 25.

Masoliver, Juan Ramón. "Desde el jurado: Mejía, Viguera y compañeros." *La Vanguardia* [Barcelona] 8 January 1964.

————. "Formentor: Por una literatura sin fronteras." *Destino* 1240 (13 May 1961): 41–43.

————. "Poética agitación en la isla de la calma, o las Conversaciones de Formentor." *Destino* 1138 (30 May 1959): 38–39.

————. "Y ahora, el público: *El día señalado*." *La Vanguardia* [Barcelona], 11 March 1964: 13.

McNerney, Kathleen. *Tirant lo Blanc Revisited: A Critical Study*. Detroit: Medieval and Renaissance Monograph Series, 1983.

Mejía Vallejo, Manuel. "Preocupación social y religiosa de *El día señalado*, último Premio Nadal." Interview by Miguel Fernández. *El Diario Vasco* [San Sebastián] 12 April 1964.

Mendoza, Eduardo. "Interrogatorio: Eduardo Mendoza." Interview by M. Vidal Santos. *Gimlet* [Barcelona] 8 (October 1981): 20–21.

————. *La verdad sobre el caso Savolta*. Barcelona: Seix Barral, 1975. *The Truth about the Savolta Case*. Translated by Alfred Mac Adam (New York: Pantheon Books, 1992).

Mérida, Rafael M. "La difusión de la literatura hispanoamericana en España: datos para *otra* recepción." In *Actas del XXIX Congreso del Instituto Internacional de Literatura Iberoamericana*, vol. 3: 429–37.

Molas, Joaquim. "Pròleg a l'edició catalana." In Mario Vargas Llosa, *Lletra de batalla per Tirant lo Blanc.* Translated by Ramon Barnils, 7–17. Barcelona: Edicions 62, 1969.

Molina Campos, Enrique. "Los Premios de la Crítica." *Camp de l'Arpa* 2 (July 1972): 7–11.

Molloy, Sylvia. "El descubrimiento de la literatura hispanoamericana en Francia." *Cuadernos del Congreso por la Libertad de la Cultura* 60 (May 1962): 50–57.

———. *La diffusion de la littérature hispanoaméricaine en France au XXe siècle.* Paris: PUF, 1972.

Montaldo, Graciela. "Destinos y recepción." In Julio Cortázar, *Rayuela.* Edited by Julio Ortega and Saúl Yurkievich, 597–612. Buenos Aires: Fondo de Cultura Económica/Colección Archivos, 1992.

Montero, Isaac. "Acotación a una mesa redonda: respuestas a Juan Benet y defensa apresurada del realismo." In *Literatura española a treinta años del siglo XXI,* 65–74.

———. "Isaac Montero contra algunos y algo." *Informaciones* [Madrid], 5 June 1969, sec. "Informaciones de las Artes y las Letras": 1, 6.

———. "La novela española de 1955 hasta hoy: una crisis entre dos exaltaciones antagónicas." In *La cultura en La España del siglo XX.* Special issue of *Triunfo* 507 (June 1972): 86–95.

Montero, Isaac, et al. "Mesa redonda sobre novela." In *Literatura española a treinta años del siglo XXI,* 45–52.

Montesinos, José F. *Galdós.* 3 vols. Madrid: Castalia, 1968–1972.

Morales, Carlos Alberto. *Cuba, Castro, and the Caribbean: The Cuban Revolution and the Crisis in Western Conscience.* Translated by Nelson Duran. New Brunswick, N.J. and Oxford: Transaction Books, 1985.

Morales Padrón, Francisco. "Las Canarias: Primeras Antillas." In *Canarias y América.* Edited by Francisco Morales Padrón and Fernando Fernández Martín, 59–66. Madrid: Espasa-Calpe, Argantonio, 1988.

Morán, Fernando. *Explicación de una limitación: la novela realista de los años cincuenta en España.* Madrid: Taurus, 1971.

———. *Novela y semidesarrollo: una interpretación de la novela hispanoamericana y española.* Madrid: Taurus, 1971.

Moretti, Franco. "Modern European Literature: A Geographical Sketch." *New Left Review* 206 (1994): 86–109.

Mukařovský, Jan. "Art as Semiotic Fact." In *Semiotics of Art: Prague School Contributions.* Edited by Ladislav Matejka and Irwin R. Titunik, translated by I. R. Titunik, 3–9. Cambridge: MIT Press, 1976.

———. "On Structuralism." In *Structure, Sign, and Function: Selected Essays by Jan Mukařovský.* Edited and translated by John Burbank and Peter Steiner, 3–16. New Haven: Yale University Press, 1978.

Muñoz Molina, Antonio. "Simulacros de realidad: Antonio Muñoz Molina." In Heymann and Mullor-Heymann, *Retratos de escritorio,* 97–115.

Muñoz Suay, Ricardo. "Operación Realismo: precisiones para un debate histórico." *Imprévue* 1–2 (1979): 175–78.

"Narrativa en Canarias." *Diario de Las Palmas* 10 July–21 August 1968, sec. "Cartel de las Letras y las Artes."

Navarro, Josep. "Una interpretació hispanoamericana del *Tirant lo Blanc*." In *Estudis de llengua i literatura catalanes oferts a R. Aramon i Serra en el seu setantè aniversari*, vol. 1: 435–44. Barcelona: Curial, 1979.

Nethersole, Reingard. "From Temporality to Spatiality: Changing Concepts in Literary Criticism." In *Proceedings of the XIIth Congress of the ICLA*. Edited by Roger Bauer and Douwe Fokkema, vol. 5: 59–65. Munich: Iudicium, 1990.

Núñez Ladeveze, Luis. "Polémica sobre la novela española." *Nuestro Tiempo* 200 (February 1971): 33–48.

Oquendo, Abelardo, ed. *Narrativa peruana 1950–1970*. Madrid: Alianza, 1973.

Ortega, Julio. *Poetics of Change: The New Spanish-American Narrative*. Translated by Galen D. Greaser. Austin: University of Texas Press, 1984.

Oviedo, José Miguel. "La cultura española desde América." *Cuadernos para el Diálogo* extraordinario 42 (August 1974): 64–65.

———. *Mario Vargas Llosa: la invención de una realidad*. Barcelona: Barral, 1970.

Panorámica de la edición española de libros. Madrid: Ministerio de Cultura, 1988–1996.

Paoletti, Mario. *El Aguafiestas: La biografía de Mario Benedetti*. Buenos Aires: Seix Barral, 1995.

Paz, Octavio. *El laberinto de la soledad*. Edited by Enrico Mario Santí. Madrid: Cátedra, 1993. *The Labyrinth of Solitude: Life and Thought in Mexico*. Translated by Lysander Kemp (New York: Grove Press, 1961).

Pérez de Mendiola, Marina, ed. *Bridging the Atlantic: Toward a Reassessment of Iberian and Latin American Cultural Ties*. Albany: State University of New York Press, 1996.

Pérez Herrero, Pedro, and Nuria Tabanera, eds. *España/América Latina: un siglo de políticas culturales*. Madrid: AIETI/Síntesis, 1993.

Pérez Minik, Domingo. *La novela extranjera en España*. Madrid: Taller de Ediciones JB, 1973.

Perkins, David. *Is Literary History Possible?* Baltimore: Johns Hopkins University Press, 1992.

Planas Cerdá, Juan. "Prólogo." In Mario Vargas Llosa, *Los jefes*, ix–xi. Barcelona: Rocas, 1959.

Pollman, Leo. *La "nueva novela" en Francia y en Iberoamérica*. Translated by Julio Linares. Madrid: Gredos, 1971.

———. "La Nueva Novela en Francia e Iberoamérica." *New Novel Review* 1, 1 (October 1993): 41–57.

Ponce de León, Luis. Review of *La ciudad y los perros*, by Mario Vargas Llosa. *La Estafeta Literaria* 284 (February 1964): 19.

Pope, Randolph D. "Benet, Faulkner and Bergson's Memory." In *Critical Approaches to the Writings of Juan Benet*. Edited by Roberto C. Manteiga et al., 111–19. Hanover, N.H.: University Press of New England, 1984.

———. "Cgoarltdaozsar: el Galdós intercalado en Cortázar en *Rayuela*." *Anales Galdosianos* 21 (1986): 141–46.

Porcel, Baltasar. "Guerra literaria: españoles contra latinoamericanos." *Destino* 1693 (14 March 1970): 8.

———. "Suscinta explicación de Cataluña para castellanos." In *Cataluña vista desde fuera*, 81–104. Barcelona: Llibres de Sinera, 1970.

Prats i Fons, Nuria. "La narrativa hispanoamericana en el suplemento *Informaciones de las Artes y las Letras*." *Antagonía: Cuadernos de la Fundación Luis Goytisolo* 2 (1997): 75–88.

"Los premios de Crítica 1964." *Destino* 1394 (25 April 1964): 65–66.

"Presentación." Editorial. *Situación actual de los estudios de lengua y literatura catalanas*. Special issue of *Norte: Revista Hispánica de Amsterdam* 11, 1–2 (January–April 1970): 3.

Presentación reunida de escritores argentinos. Special issue of *La Estafeta Literaria* 379–80 (23 September–7 October 1967).

Prisco, Rafael di. *Narrativa venezolana contemporánea*. Madrid: Alianza, 1971.

Puigjaner, Josep Maria. "La producció actual de llibres en català." In J. M. Ainaud, Pere Boigas, and J. M. Puigjaner, *El llibre i la llengua catalana*, 69–73. Barcelona: Curial, 1986.

Quintián, Andrés R. "Rubén Darío y la España catalana." *Cuadernos Hispanoamericanos* 261 (March 1972): 611–22.

Quiñonero, Juan Pedro. "Juan Pedro Quiñonero, contra la polémica." *Informaciones* [Madrid] 19 June 1969, sec. "Informaciones de las Artes y las Letras": 2.

Rama, Ángel. "El 'boom' en perspectiva." In Ángel Rama et al., *Más allá del boom: literatura y mercado*, 51–110. Mexico: Marcha, 1981.

Rama, Carlos M. *Historia de las relaciones culturales entre España y la América Latina: Siglo XIX*. Mexico: Fondo de Cultura Económica, 1982.

"Razón de ser." Editorial. *Cuadernos para el Diálogo* 1 (October 1963): 1–2.

Rees, C. J. van. "Advances in the Empirical Sociology of Literature and the Arts: The Institutional Approach." *Poetics* 12 (1983): 285–310.

Review of *El día señalado*, by Manuel Mejía Vallejo. *La Estafeta Literaria* 288 (28 March 1964): 19.

Review of *El día señalado*, by Manuel Mejía Vallejo. *Mundo* [Madrid] 28 June 1964: 24.

Ridruejo, Dionisio. "Gonzalo Torrente Ballester busca y encuentra: una lectura de *La saga/fuga de J.B.*" In *Sombras y bultos*, 190–200. Barcelona: Destino, 1977. Originally published in *Destino* 1820 (19 August 1972): 8–9.

Riera, Carme. *La Escuela de Barcelona: Barral, Gil de Biedma, Goytisolo*. Barcelona: Anagrama, 1988.

Ripoll, Luis. "Postal de Mallorca: Las Conversaciones Poéticas de Formentor." *Destino* 1137 (23 May 1959): 39–40.

Riquer, Martí de, and Mario Vargas Llosa, eds. *El combate imaginario: las cartas de batalla de Joanot Martorell*. Barcelona: Barral, 1972.

Robbe-Grillet, Alain. "Naturaleza, humanismo, tragedia." Translated by G. A. *Papeles de Son Armadans* 51 (June 1960): 373–402.

———. "Nature, Humanism, Tragedy." In *For a New Novel: Essays on Fiction*. Translated by Richard Howard, 49–75. Freeport, N.Y.: Books for Libraries, 1970.

Rodó, José Enrique. "El nacionalismo catalán: Un interesante problema político." In *El camino de Paros: Meditaciones y andanzas*, 95–112. Valencia: Cervantes, 1918.

Rodríguez, Osvaldo. "Aproximaciones externas a la literatura de Canarias." In *Nuevas escrituras canarias: un panorama crítico*, 211–30. Islas Canarias: Viceconsejería de Cultura y Deportes del Gobierno de Canarias, 1992.

Rodríguez Almodóvar, Antonio. *Lecciones de narrativa hispanoamericana, siglo XX: orientación y crítica*. Sevilla: Universidad de Sevilla, 1972.

Rodríguez Monegal, Emir. *El boom de la novela latinoamericana*. Caracas: Tiempo Nuevo, 1972.

———. "A Literary Myth Exploded." *Review* 72 (1971–72): 56–64.

Rodríguez Padrón, Jorge. "Informe objetivo (dentro de lo que cabe) sobre la nueva narrativa canaria." *Camp de l'Arpa* 7 (August–September 1973): 19–24.

———. "Vértices de una escritura atlántica." In *Cultura canaria hoy*, special issue of *El Urogallo* (December 1988–January 1989): 12–18.

Rodríguez Puértolas, Julio. "Galdós y Cortázar." In *Galdós: burguesía y revolución*, 212–18. Madrid: Turner, 1975.

Rojas, Carlos. "Novela y humanismo." In *Novela y novelistas: Reunión de Málaga 1972*. Edited by Manuel Alvar, 29–43. Málaga: Diputación Provincial, 1973.

———. "Problemas de la nueva novela española." In Paul Conrad Kurz et al., *La nueva novela europea*, 121–35. Madrid: Guadarrama, 1968.

Rojas, Ricardo. *Retablo español*. Buenos Aires: Losada, 1938.

Romea Castro, M. Celia. "Aspectos intertextuales entre *La ciudad y los perros* de M. Vargas Llosa y *Si te dicen que caí* de J. Marsé." In *Actas del XXIX Congreso del Instituto Internacional de Literatura Iberoamericana*, vol. 3: 551–62.

Rosenthal, David H. "Translator's Foreword." In Joanot Martorell and Martí Joan de Galba, *Tirant lo Blanc*, vii–xxiv. New York: Schocken Books, 1984.

Rubio, Rodrigo. *Narrativa española, 1940–1970*. Madrid: EPESA, 1970.

Ruiz-Fornells, Enrique. "La recepción de la literatura hispanoamericana en España (1975–1985)." In *La cultura española en el posfranquismo: diez años de cine, cultura y literatura en España (1975–1985)*. Edited by Samuel Amell and Salvador García Casteñeda, 137–46. Madrid: Playor, 1988.

Sábato, Ernesto. *El escritor y sus fantasmas*. Buenos Aires: Aguilar, 1963.

Saldívar, Dasso. *García Márquez: El viaje a la semilla. La Biografía*. Madrid: Alfaguara, 1997.

Salvador, Gregorio. *Comentarios estructurales a Cien años de soledad*. La Laguna: Universidad de La Laguna, 1970.

———. "Las Islas Afortunadas en *Cien años de soledad*." In *Cuatro conferencias de tema canario*, 43–65. Las Palmas: Cabildo Insular de Gran Canaria, 1977.

Sánchez-Castañer, Francisco. "A manera de prólogo." *Anales de Literatura Hispanoamericana* 1 (1972): ix–xxviii.

Sánchez Espeso, Germán. *Experimento en Génesis*. Barcelona: Seix Barral, 1967.

Sánchez López, Pablo. "La alternativa hispanoamericana: Las primeras novelas del 'boom' en España." *Revista Hispánica Moderna* 51, 1 (June 1998): 102–18.

Sánchez Ortiz, Emilio. "Rebeldía contra infortunio: Del lado de los 'anti-héroes.' " Interview by Jean-Michel Fossey. *Informaciones* [Madrid] 12 July 1973, sec. "Informaciones de las Artes y las Letras": 1–2.

Sánchez Rodrigo, Lourdes, and Enrique J. Nogueras Valdivieso. "Quinientos años de *Tirant lo Blanc*." In *Estudios sobre el Tirant lo Blanc*. Edited by Juan Paredes, Enrique J. Nogueras Valdivieso, and Lourdes Sánchez Rodrigo, 153–79. Granada: Universidad de Granada, 1995.

Sanz Villanueva, Santos. *Historia de la novela social española (1942–1975)*. 2 vols. Madrid: Alhambra, 1980.

———. *Tendencias de la novela española actual (1950–1970)*. Madrid: Edicusa, 1972.

Sarmiento, Domingo F. *Viajes por Europa, África y América: 1845–1847*. Vol. 5 of *Obras completas de Sarmiento*. Buenos Aires: Editorial Luz del Día, 1949.

Sarraute, Nathalie. "Les deux réalités." *Esprit* 329 (July 1964): 72–75.

———. "Nouveau roman et réalité." *Revue de l'Institute de Sociologie* 2 (1963): 431–41.

———. "Novela y realidad." *La Voz de Galicia* [La Coruña] 20 December 1963, sec. "Artes y Letras": 11.

Savater, Fernando. *La infancia recuperada*. Madrid: Taurus, 1976.

Scherber, Peter. " 'Literary Life' as a Topic of Literary History." In *Issues in Slavic Literary and Cultural Theory*. Edited by Karl Eimermacher, Peter Grzybek, and Georg Witte, 571–92. Bochum: Norbert Brockmeyer, 1989.

Schwartz, Jorge, ed. *Las vanguardias latinoamericanas: textos programáticos y críticos*. Madrid: Cátedra, 1991.

Sepúlveda Muñoz, Isidro. *Comunidad cultural e hispano-americanismo, 1885–1936*. Madrid: Universidad Nacional de Educación a Distancia, 1994.

Shaw, Donald L. *Nueva narrativa hispanoamericana*. Madrid: Cátedra, 1981.

Sieburth, Stephanie. *Inventing High and Low: Literature, Mass Culture, and Uneven Modernity in Spain*. Durham, N.C.: Duke University Press, 1994.

Silva Cáceres, Raúl H. Review of *La ciudad y los perros*, by Mario Vargas Llosa. *Cuadernos Hispanoamericanos* 173 (May 1964): 416–22.

Smith, Anthony D. *National Identity*. London: Penguin, 1991.

Sobejano, Gonzalo. "Ante la novela de los años setenta." *Ínsula* 396–97 (November–December 1979): 1, 22.

———. "Cervantes en la novela española contemporánea." *La Torre* 3–4 (July–December 1987): 549–73.

———. "Testimonio y poema en la novela española contemporánea." In *Actas del VIII Congreso de la Asociación Internacional de Hispanistas*. Edited by A. David Kossoft, José Amor y Vázquez, Ruth H. Kossoft, and Geoffrey Ribbans, vol 1: 89–115. Madrid: Istmo, 1986.

Solé i Sabaté, Josep M., and Joan Villarroya. *Cronologia de la repressió de la llengua i la cultura catalanes: 1936–1975*. Barcelona: Curial, 1994.

Sommers, Joseph. "Literatura e ideología: la evaluación novelística del militarismo en Vargas Llosa." In Jean Franco et al., *Cultura y dependencia*, 85–144. Jalisco: Departamento de Bellas Artes, 1976.

Sorel, Andrés. "La nueva novela latinoamericana: Costa Rica y Perú." *Cuadernos Hispanoamericanos* 201 (September 1966): 705–26.

Sötér, István. "L'application de la méthode comparative a l'histoire d'une littérature nationale." In *Proceedings of the VIIIth Congress of the ICLA*. Edited by Béla Köpeczi and György M. Vajda, vol. 2: 449–55. Stuttgart: Erich Bieber, 1980.

"Spécial Espagne: Jugez sur pièces 'le nouveau' roman espagnol." *Les Lettres Françaises* 936 (19–25 July 1962): 1, 4–7.

Spires, Robert C. *Beyond the Metafictional Mode: Directions in the Modern Spanish Novel*. Lexington: University Press of Kentucky, 1984.

———. *La novela española de posguerra*. Madrid: Cupsa, 1978.

Suárez Granda, Juan Luis. "La 'poética' de Luis Martín-Santos de Ribera." In *Luis Martín-Santos*. Edited by Iñaki Beti Sáez, 21–43. San Sebastián: Universidad de Deusto, 1991.

Sueiro, Daniel. "Silencio y crisis de la joven novela española." In Ynduráin, *Prosa novelesca actual: segunda reunión*, 159–78.

Summerhill, Stephen J. "Prohibition and Transgression in *Volverás a Región* and *Una meditación*." In *Critical Approaches to the Writings of Juan Benet*. Edited by Roberto C. Manteiga et al., 51–63. Hanover, N.H.: University Press of New England, 1984.

Swanson, Philip. "Boom or Bust?: Latin America and the Not So New Novel." *New Novel Review* 1 (October 1993): 75–92.

Tamames, Ramón. *La República/La Era de Franco (1931–1970)*. Madrid: Alianza/Alfaguara, 1976.

Tola de Habich, Fernando, and Patricia Grieve. *Los españoles y el boom*. Caracas: Tiempo Nuevo, 1971.

Torbado, Jesús. "La manta a la cabeza: reflexiones urgentes sobre literatura nueva y sociedad española." In Ynduráin, *Prosa novelesca actual*, 83–101.

Torrente Ballester, Gonzalo. "Conversación con Gonzalo Torrente Ballester sobre *La saga/fuga de J.B.*" Interview by Andrés Amorós. *Ínsula* 317 (April 1973): 4, 14–15.

———. *Cuadernos de La Romana*. Barcelona: Destino, 1975.

———. *Panorama de la literatura española contemporánea*. 3rd ed. Madrid: Guadarrama, 1965.

———. *El Quijote como juego*. Madrid: Guadarrama, 1975.

———. *La saga/fuga de J.B.* Barcelona: Destino, 1973.

Tötösy de Zepetnek, Steven. "Systemic Approaches to Literature: An Introduction with Selected Bibliographies." *Canadian Review of Comparative Literature* 19, 1–2 (March–June 1992): 21–93.

Tovar, Antonio. *Novela española e hispanoamericana*. Madrid: Alfaguara, 1972.

Treinta años de literatura: narrativa y poesía española, 1939–1969. Special issue of *Cuadernos para el Diálogo* extraordinario 14 (May 1969).

Valdés, Mario J., and Linda Hutcheon. *Rethinking Literary Theory— Comparatively*. N.p.: American Council of Learned Societies, 1994.

Valéry, Paul. *Introduction a la Poétique*. Paris: Gallimard, 1938.

Valverde, José María. "Carta informativa sobre un prologuillo a *La ciudad y los perros*." In *Asedios a Vargas Llosa*. Edited by Luis A. Díez, 100–06. Santiago de Chile: Editorial Universitaria, 1972.

———. "Un juicio del Dr. José María Valverde." In Mario Vargas Llosa, *La ciudad y los perros*. Barcelona: Seix Barral, 1963.

Vargas Llosa, Mario. "Alain Robbe-Grillet y el simulacro del realismo." *Cinema Universtario* [Salamanca] 19 (January–March 1963): 22–27.

———. "Cabalgando con Tirant." In *Carta de batalla por Tirant lo Blanc*, 5–7.

———. "Carta de batalla por *Tirant lo Blanc*." In *Carta de batalla por Tirant lo Blanc*, 9–58.

———. *Carta de batalla por Tirant lo Blanc*. Barcelona: Seix Barral, 1991.

———. *García Márquez: Historia de un deicidio*. Barcelona: Barral, 1971.

———. "Martorell y el 'elemento añadido' en *Tirant lo Blanc*." In *Carta de batalla por Tirant lo Blanc*, 59–85. Originally published in *El combate imaginario: las cartas de batalla de Joanot Martorell*. Edited by Martí de Riquer and Mario Vargas Llosa. Barcelona: Barral, 1972.

———, et al. "'Realismo' sin límites: Vargas Llosa, diálogo de amistad." *Índice* 224 (October 1967): 21–22.

———, et al. *Semana de autor: Mario Vargas Llosa*. Madrid: Ediciones Cultura Hispánica, 1985.

Vázquez Montalbán, Manuel. "Adiós a Vargas Llosa." *Triunfo* 613 (29 June 1974): 64.

———. "Conversación con Manuel Vázquez Montalbán." Interview by José Batlló. *Camp de l'Arpa* 4 (November 1972): 18–20.

———. "Experimentalismo, vanguardia y neocapitalismo." In Ángel Abad et al., *Reflexiones ante el neocapitalismo*, 103–16. Barcelona: Ediciones de Cultura Popular, 1968.

———. "Literatura y transición." In *Política y literatura*. Edited by Aurora Egido, 125–39. Zaragoza: Caja de Ahorros y Monte de Piedad de Zaragoza, Aragón y Rioja, 1988.

———. "Muere el Premio Barral." *Triunfo* 617 (27 July 1974): 46.

———. "Tres notas sobre literatura y dogma." In *Literatura española a treinta años del siglo XXI*, 17–22.

Vázquez Zamora, Rafael. "El Eugenio Nadal, pionero de los premios novelísticos en la posguerra." *La Estafeta Literaria* 251 (October 1962): 5.

"Veinte escritores argentinos más." Dossier. *La Estafeta Literaria* 381–82 (21 October–4 November 1967): 5–36.

"Venturas y desventuras de un conocido premio literario." *Mundo Nuevo* 38 (August 1969): 93–94.

Vilanova, Antonio. "De la objetividad al subjetivismo en la novela española actual." In Ynduráin, *Prosa novelesca actual*, 133–56.

———. "El Premio Nadal en las letras españolas." In *50 años del Premio Nadal*, 13–32. Barcelona: Destino, 1994.

———. Review of *El día señalado*, by Manuel Mejía Vallejo. *Destino* 1388 (14 March 1964): 56–57.

Villanueva, Darío. "La novela." In *Letras españolas 1976–1986*, 19–64. Madrid: Castalia, 1987.

———. "La novela social: Apostillas a un estado de la cuestón." In *Literatura contemporánea en Castilla y León*, 329–48. Valladolid: Junta de Castilla y León, 1986.

Vilumara, Martín. "El desafío de Torrente Ballester." *Camp de l'Arpa* 6 (March 1973): 22–23.

Vipper, Yuri B. "National Literary History in *History of World Literature*: Theoretical Principles of Treatment." *New Literary History* 16 (1985): 545–58.

Vodička, Felix. "The Concretization of the Literary Work: Problems of the Reception of Neruda's Works." In *The Prague School: Selected Writings, 1929–1946*. Edited by Peter Steiner. Translated by John Burbank, 103–34. Austin: University of Texas Press, 1982.

———. "Response to Verbal Art." In *Semiotics of Art: Prague School Contributions*. Edited by Ladislav Matejka and Irwin R. Titunik. Translated by Ralph Koprince, 197–208. Cambridge: MIT Press, 1976.

West, Rebecca. "L'identità americana di Calvino." *Nuova Corrente* 34 (1987): 363–74.

Yahni, Roberto, ed. *Setenta años de narrativa argentina: 1900–1970*. Madrid: Alianza, 1970.

Yerro Villanueva, Tomás. *Aspectos técnicos y estructurales de la novela española actual*. Pamplona: Universidad de Navarra, 1977.

Ynduráin, Francisco. "Para una estética del *nouveau roman*." *Revista de Ideas Estéticas* 22 (1964): 109–22.

Ynduráin, Francisco, ed. *Prosa novelesca actual*. Madrid: Universidad Internacional Menéndez Pelayo, 1968.

———, ed. *Prosa novelesca actual: segunda reunión*. Madrid: Universidad Internacional Menéndez Pelayo, 1969.

Zalbidea, Víctor. "Víctor Zalbidea contra Cortázar." *Informaciones* [Madrid] 12 June 1969, sec. "Informaciones de las Artes y las Letras": 2.

Zuleta, Emilia de. *Relaciones literarias entre España y la Argentina*. Madrid: Cultura Hispánica, 1983.

———. "Relaciones literarias entre Hispanoamérica y España." In *Relaciones literarias entre España y la Argentina: Seminario 1991*. Edited by E. de Zuleta, 11–28. Buenos Aires: Oficina Cultural de la Embajada de España, 1991.

Index